£20.00

ETHICS
ETHNICITY
AND
EDUCATION

ETHICS
ETHNICITY
AND
EDUCATION

EDITED BY

MAL LEICESTER AND MONICA TAYLOR

KOGAN
PAGE

First published in 1992

Kogan Page Limited
120 Pentonville Road
London N1 9JN

© Mal Leicester and Monica J Taylor, 1992

British Library Cataloguing in Publication Data

A CIP record for this book is available from the British Library.

ISBN 0 7494 0511 2

Typeset by DP Photosetting, Aylesbury, Bucks
Printed and bound in Great Britain by
Biddles Ltd, Guildford and King's Lynn

Contents

Notes on Contributors

Carl A Bagley carried out post-graduate research on social policy and 'race' before joining Aston University as a research assistant to work on a 'race' and housing research project. He qualified as a community worker before being employed as an antiracist strategist in the Department of Continuing Education with Leeds City Council. Recently, he worked as a research assistant on a 'race' and education project at the Open University and obtained his doctorate. He is presently a Research Officer at the National Foundation for Educational Research in England and Wales.

Harbhajan Singh Brar is a Principal Monitoring and Advice Officer working for local government in London. He was formerly a Research Fellow in the Centre for Research in Ethnic Relations at the University of Warwick. He has carried out research and written in the areas of equal opportunities, race and education. He is also the co-author of a number of local government sponsored studies, *Invisible Minorities* (Harlow, 1992), *Implementing Equality* (Brent, 1990) and *Ealing's Dilemma* (Ealing, 1988).

Bruce Carrington is a Senior Lecturer in Education at the University of Newcastle-upon-Tyne. He has a long-standing interest in political education in the primary school and has published widely in the field of multicultural and antiracist education. His most recent book (written with Barry Troyna) is *Education, Racism and Reform* (Routledge, 1990).

Clara Connolly emigrated from Southern Ireland to London in the mid-1970s. Her background is in teaching and youth work, and she currently works in the Education Section of the Commission for Racial Equality. She is a member of Women Against Fundamentalism and of the *Feminist Review* Editorial Collective. She has written a number of articles on race and gender.

Bruce Gill taught in an inner London comprehensive school for eight years and in a range of Birmingham schools after he moved there in 1983 to work as an advisory teacher in the Afro–Caribbean Teaching Unit. He has worked as General Inspector with responsibility for multicultural education in Birmingham and as Inspector for Equal Opportunities in the ILEA Inspectors Based in Schools Team. He is currently Head of the Inspection and Advisory Service in Lambeth. He is a member of the Editorial Board of *Multicultural Teaching*.

J Mark Halstead has worked as a journalist in Lebanon, as a lecturer in Saudi Arabia and as a school teacher in Bradford for twelve years and has recently spent five years in full-time research at Cambridge University. He is currently Senior Lecturer in Religious Education and Multicultural Education at Rolle Faculty of Education, Polytechnic South-West in Devon. He is the author of *Education, Justice and Cultural*

Diversity: an Examination of the Honeyford Affair, 1984–85. (Falmer Press, 1988), several articles and a monograph on the education of Muslim children.

Robert Jackson is Reader in Arts Education at the University of Warwick. He is Director of the Religious Education and Community Project which researches into the transmission of religious culture to children from a variety of religious traditions in Britain. He has published widely in the fields of Religious Education and Religious Studies. His most recent book is *Moral Issues in the Hindu Tradition* (with Dermot Killingley), (Trentham Books, 1991). *Hindu Children in Britain* (with Eleanor Nesbitt) is due for publication by Trentham Books in 1992. He is Chair of the Conference of University Lecturers in Religious Education.

Mal Leicester is a lecturer with the Department of Continuing Education at the University of Warwick. Previously she was Adviser for Multicultural Education in Avon and before that Director of AFFOR (All Faiths for One Race), an antiracist community organisation in Handsworth, Birmingham. Her publications have mainly been in the field of race relations including academic papers, curriculum materials and children's stories. Her recent publications include: *Multicultural Education: From Theory to Practice*, an introduction for teachers (NFER–Nelson, 1989) and *Equal Opportunities in School*, a guide for school governors and their trainers (Longman, 1991). She has a book forthcoming from the Open University Press, *Race For A Change in Continuing and Higher Education*.

Tessa Lovell worked as a community service volunteer after graduation, assisting people with learning disabilities. Currently she is a Research Assistant in Continuing Education at the University of Warwick working on two research projects: adult education and active citizenship; and racism in higher education. A previous research project investigated Southern Asian and Afro-Caribbean women's patterns of leisure. Her publications have been based on her research projects.

T H McLaughlin is University Lecturer in Education and Fellow of St Edmunds College, Cambridge. He specialises in Philosophy of Education, and has published a number of articles on the relationship between a liberal conception of education and religious upbringing and schooling. He has taught English and been Head of Year and Head of Sixth Form in two comprehensive schools. He has recently held a Fellowship at the Centre for Philosophy and Public Affairs, Department of Moral Philosophy, University of St Andrews.

Tariq Modood, having initially taught political theory at a number of British universities, has worked for five years in racial equality policy work, including as Principal Employment Officer at the Commission for Racial Equality. He is currently a visiting research fellow at Nuffield College, Oxford, and is writing a book on the changing nature of the concept of race in contemporary Britain. A collected edition of his writings is being published by the Runnymede Trust. His chapter in this collection is written in a personal capacity.

Richard Pring is Professor of Educational Studies at the University of Oxford. He was formerly Dean of the Faculty of Education at the University of Exeter and prior to that Lecturer in Curriculum Studies at the University of London. He has taught in two London comprehensive schools. He is Editor of the *British Journal of Educational Studies.* He has written widely in philosophy of education, values education and on a range of educational matters. His books include *Personal and Social Education in the Curriculum* (Hodder and Stoughton, 1984).

Robin Richardson is Director of the Runnymede Trust, a charity set up in 1968 to provide information and advice on race relations policies in public services and institutions. In the period 1985–1990 he was Chief Inspector with Brent Education Authority, and before that was Adviser for Multicultural Education in Berkshire. His many publications, mostly in multicultural and values education, include *Daring to be a Teacher; essays, stories and memoranda,* published by Trentham Books in 1990.

Geoffrey Short is Senior Lecturer in Education at Hatfield Polytechnic. He has written extensively on various aspects of 'race' and education and is currently engaged on research into children's understanding of Jewish culture and identity. In 1989 he published (jointly with Bruce Carrington), *Race and the Primary School* (NFER–Nelson).

Monica J Taylor is a Senior Research Officer at the National Foundation for Educational Research. During the early 1980s she was commissioned by the Rampton and Swann Committees to undertake a series of critical reviews of research on the education of ethnic minority pupils (published in four volumes by NFER–Nelson). She has carried out educational research and evaluation for many major sponsors and specialises in personal and social education, religious education and multicultural antiracist education, particularly in secondary education and with a pupil focus. Her most recent publication, of a study for the National Curriculum Council, is *SACREs: Their Formation, Composition, Operation and Role on RE and Worship* (NFER, 1991). Since 1976 she has been Editor of the *Journal of Moral Education,* the only international academic journal in this field.

Editorial

Educating for Pluralism: Ethical Means to Antiracist Ends

Mal Leicester and Monica J Taylor

Conjoin education with ethnicity and ethical issues emerge. Education for pluralism heightens the ethical principles – such as justice, equality, respect for persons – inherent in the concept of education for all. The application of these values in the practice of education gives rise to difficult and often controversial moral judgements.

These ethical issues are so pervasive and important it is surprising that a book such as this has not been available before. Until now there has been no interdisciplinary collection of papers covering the major moral issues in educating for pluralism. The narrower focus on moral education in a multicultural society has been addressed in so far as the *Journal of Moral Education* had a special issue on Race, Culture and Education (vol 15, no 1, January, 1986). The broader subject – moral issues in a multicultural society – would need to include non-educational topics. Some of our contributors do touch on these; for example, the Rushdie affair, being black in Britain, societal myth making. Considering the widespread interest in education for pluralism, we hope that a collection exploring the associated ethical questions will be seen as timely.

We identified key topics connected with antiracist multicultural education and invited contributors to address their ethical dimensions. In so doing, they collectively mapped this complex terrain and have made it possible to draw out recurring themes.

Papers have been contributed by academics drawn from a range of disciplines – philosophy, sociology, psychology and education. They contain a range of perspectives and ideologies. A feminist perspective is provided in one paper, for example, and pupil interests considered in another. Radical, liberal and conservative ideologies are represented. Contributors deal with the education system at all levels – from primary to higher education.

In the overall balance of contributors we wished to take account of ethnicity, gender and the experience of practitioners. In the event, a small number of invited practitioners were not able to find the time to make the contribution they would have liked. This may well indicate both current pressure on educators in translating national policy into practice and their lack of opportunity for reflection. That we lose their school-based experience raises ethical questions about the adequate resourcing of education. Similarly, the expression of direct experience of racism is often muted because institutional discrimination ensures additional barriers to black participation. In the case of this book, this applied to two black female practitioners. Thus we failed to achieve the range of black perspectives we had intended and would have wished.

A related ethical question we posed to ourselves was: Ought two white women to edit such a collection? Is the lack of a black editor justifiable? On the one hand, we believe that white people can and should take antiracist initiatives. On the other hand, given our racist society, that the voice of the direct experience of racism remains unheard in the shaping of this book – though not in the papers themselves – is less than ideal.

Several articles draw on deeply felt professional and personal experience of a kind that is integral to, and may radically change, lives. Such experience often provides the opportunity for profound and painful learning, which these writers have been prepared to share. This degree of involvement, together with the cognitive complexity of the field, tends to make writing difficult.

We have found that sharing the process of editing the collection has been an enjoyable and stimulating collaboration through which our views have been clarified and sharpened. We have also assisted contributors to clarify points in their papers. While we do not agree with all the views expressed, we nevertheless find ourselves in agreement with most.

These views are informed by personal and professional experience of racism in all its diversity. There has already been considerable analysis of the concept of racism, taking account of the range of phenomena to which the term refers. But, however varied the forms that individual, institutional and societal racism take, the interconnecting thread is the inherently unethical quality of the concept and its manifestation in practice.

There has also been much academic debate about the distinction between multicultural and antiracist education (Modgil *et al*, 1986; Grinter, 1985; Leicester, 1986; Modgil *et al*, 1992) which we shall not repeat. Our contributors have moved beyond it, recognising that racism should be opposed in all its forms. All contributors, either explicitly or implicitly, recognise the racism in the society about which they write, and they write from an ethical commitment to oppose it.

Currently, a similar distinction to that between multicultural and antiracist education is being made between moral and political antiracism. Moral antiracism is taken to be an approach to antiracism such that the focus is on *ethical* considerations. The justification for antiracist action is in terms of moral principles and the actions are designed to promote justice for *individuals*. Political antiracism is taken to be an approach to antiracism such that the focus is on *political* considerations. The justification for antiracist action is in terms of political aims and the actions are designed to promote social justice for oppressed *groups*. This is reminiscent of older distinctions between liberal and radical approaches to education for pluralism and between antiracist and multicultural education. No doubt, as with these older distinctions, the more recently posed dichotomy will be taken by some to represent an irreconcilable ideological difference (Troyna, 1987).

The chapters in this collection, with their interweaving of the personal and the political, the individual and the institutional, indicate the oversimplification that such distinctions often mask. Ideologies, political objectives, conceptions of social justice are, of course, value laden. They *are* ethical matters. Political antiracism represents an ethical stance; moral antiracism incorporates social concerns.

Specific chapters in the collection range from fundamental theoretical questions about how we ought to educate – and morally educate – in a democratic pluralist society, to empirical questions that arise at different levels of the educational system and include substantive issues of current concern. A traditional liberal perspective on education for pluralism is set out in the opening chapter by Pring. Following this, Leicester points to some dilemmas in the liberal approach and discusses conflicts of value judgement underpinning pluralism. This links with her exploration of the Swann Report's notion of a common framework of values.

The next two chapters address recent controversial educational events in the UK. Halstead reviews these in relation to cultural diversity, highlighting ethical dimensions such as the nature of racial justice, democratic rights and responsibilities, freedom of choice, freedom of expression and minority rights. Richardson focuses on controversial events with which he was associated in a professional capacity. As a result of these experiences he raises moral questions for antiracism in a racist society and asks: How can we respond ethically to the unethical tactics of the anti-antiracists?

Modood and Gill are both interested in the notion of citizenship. They raise the question of what it is to be a citizen in this society. Could the notion of citizenship that is often used to exclude black people be redefined in relation to shared allegiances and shared values? Modood also analyses notions of racism, recognising cultural racism and the racialisation of Muslims. Gill assesses official stances on multicultural education and provides a rationale for a new 'societal myth', from which a shared notion of citizenship could be generated.

Jackson engages with the claims of theologically conservative Christians for the teaching of religious education and advocates a 'conversational mode of RE' which recognises the integrity of the different religious traditions in British society. McLaughlin and Connolly discuss the issue of separate schooling, focusing on religious schools. Their views are very different. McLaughlin analyses relevant conceptual and ethical distinctions to reveal the philosophical complexity of a practical debate. Connolly is strongly against religious schools; in discussing the role of religions in defining women's place in society, she argues for a more progressive approach to education and community relations.

The final group of papers are influenced by, or report, empirical research. Taylor, in the context of a white secondary school's attempt to provide a democratic antiracist education, examines pupils' experience of racial harassment and curricular strategies to facilitate learning about fairness through empathy in interethnic relations. Bagley addresses teacher experience. He demonstrates the inconsistencies in teacher attitudes by means of a life-history approach and suggests this could be used in changing teacher attitudes to antiracist multicultural education.

The chapters by Brar, and by Carrington and Short, deal directly with the ethical aspects of race-related research in education. Brar discusses four fundamental questions about the conduct of such research and illustrates from his own research experience that academic research has too often simply helped the state to reinforce and reproduce racism. Carrington and Short consider the ethical dimensions of antiracist research in the 'all-white' primary school, particularly in connection with the unwitting reinforcement of stereotypes and the unnecessary infliction of pain. They use three recent studies to illustrate these ethical concerns.

In the final paper Leicester and Lovell highlight ethical issues arising from a survey into antiracist practice in university education. What is 'good' practice in relation to antiracist education? Is there an ethical difference between positive action and positive discrimination? They argue that in relation to access to the universities, positive discrimination may well be good practice.

We turn now to distinguishing some core themes, each of which is common to several chapters. These are: the use of narrative and autobiography; liberal education for active citizenship in a democratic society; cohesion and conflict; negotiation and dialogue; research on race in educational institutions; and whether ethically dubious means can be justified by antiracist ends? There are also many links between pairs and groups of chapters – too many to trace. Since the contributions interconnect, the collection as a whole becomes more than its component parts. Similarly, original insights about each component aspect of the collection (ethics, ethnicity, education) are generated by their juxtaposition.

We were struck by the frequent recurrence of narrative as a linking theme in many of the papers. This is manifested in the use of storytelling, metaphor and myth in the process of constructing shared meaning. The narrative form also occurs as autobiography, as individual authors, some of whom have direct experience of racism, sought to make sense of personal experience and give voice to their learning. Other chapters incorporate teacher and pupil biography. This reflects a current movement in academic thinking and research (see the special issue of the *Journal of Moral Education* on Narrative and the Moral Realm, vol 20, no 3, 1991) but is, perhaps, also to do with the subject of the book as a whole.

Another theme central to several chapters concerns the nature of a liberal education in a democratic society. This is the framework within which the discussion takes place. What kind of society ought we to want and therefore ought we to educate for? An answer to this central moral question would provide a vision to guide educational practice. There is too little public debate of such fundamental questions. The emphasis nowadays is too much on short-term instrumental objectives rather than on education as intrinsically worthwhile. Even the longer-term goals seem directed to developing human 'resources', national vocational qualifications and so on, rather than paying attention to the inherently ethical dimensions of education. Contrast this with the influence, in its time, of the seminal *Ethics and Education* of R S Peters (1966).

A second strand of the theme of a democratic pluralist society, woven through a number of contributions and currently much discussed, is the notion of citizenship. What is it to be a citizen in this society? It is ironic that while the concept of British citizenship is often used to exclude black Britains, citizenship is one of the few aspects of the National Curriculum where antiracist and personal, social and moral education issues can be addressed.

The process of resolving conflict and controversy contributes to creating shared allegiances among active citizens, in order to maintain a cohesive democracy. Is the negotiation of an agreed outcome for value conflicts possible, or is the dialogue itself a sufficient objective? Can we create conditions, occasions or structures conducive to dialogue between different communities? Can such negotiation and dialogue lead to the construction of a common framework of values? Contributors disagreed.

Another set of chapters deals with the common themes discussed above in the context of educational institutions at different levels of the system. These empirically based chapters chiefly draw on projects conducted in mainly white institutions. Most race and education literature has dealt with multiethnic schools yet most institutions are predominantly white. All of these papers raise ethical questions about undertaking research into race and education. Are the ethical issues generated by such research the same issues raised by undertaking educational research in general, or are there additional ethical issues that arise only in situations of unequal power?

The question of whether antiracist ends justify ethically dubious means is posed in different forms in various chapters, particularly in empirically grounded studies. Are ethically dubious means ever justified in conducting the research, such as in gaining access to data, or in breaching confidentiality about reported racism, particulary between teacher and pupil? Several chapters convey a sense of unease about whether certain research or curriculum strategies might reinforce the racism they seek to address. One chapter argues that in some educational situations apparently dubious tactics of discrimination may actually be fair. In another, the issue of whether it is ever right to match the unethical tactics of anti-antiracists with an unethical response is explicitly raised.

Though they are more generally applicable, all our chapters have been written in a particular context – Britain in the 1990s soon after extensive educational legislation bringing great change. The Education Acts (1986 and 1988) tend to move us in an inegalitarian direction from the starting point of a racist society. Antiracist reform will require us to find ways of circumventing racist changes encouraged by this legislation, and to take the opportunities it provides, for example, through its erosion of the power of the local education authority, for antiracist development (such as the chance to obtain more black governors). We need to interpret the Acts as positively as possible.

Thus it is helpful in examining the ethical and ethnic dimensions of educational policy to reconsider the oft-quoted, but invaluable statement on the curriculum set out in the opening lines of ERA.

> The curriculum for a maintained school . . .[should be] a balanced and broadly based curriculum which –
> (a) promotes the spiritual, moral, cultural, mental and physical development of pupils at the school and of society; and
> (b) prepares such pupils for the opportunities, responsibilities and experiences of adult life.
>
> (GB, Statutes, ch 40, part 1; ch 1, section 1 (2))

The importance of this statement is that, for the first time, national educational policy recognises the 'cultural' development of pupils 'and of society' thereby indicating that in this society education should have a wider role and be across the lifespan. Although 'cultural' is not defined, it can be understood, given other national policy statements (e.g. NCC, 1990, p 6) to acknowledge 'Britain as a multicultural, multiethnic, multifaith, multilingual society'.

Indeed, ERA itself recognises a plurality of religions (integrally associated with culture) by requiring that new, locally determined, Agreed Syllabuses for the Religious Education (RE) curriculum:

> shall reflect the fact that the religious traditions in Great Britain are in the main Christian whilst taking account of the principal religions represented in Great Britain. (GB, Statutes, ch 40, part 1; ch 1, section 8 (3))

RE has often been in the vanguard of multicultural curriculum development. This may partly be related to teachers' recognition of the deeply held nature of religious values.

ERA, in line with the Swann Report (GB, P, H of C, 1985), implies the need in society to promote both cultural diversity and cohesion through 'a balanced and broadly based curriculum'.

It puts 'cultural' on a par with other established aspects of education, including the 'moral' and the 'spiritual' which are commonly the curriculum domains in which ethical issues are addressed.

Thus the maintained school, acting as a microcosm of society, is obliged to offer, in its formal and informal curricula, formative experiences ('spiritual, moral, cultural, mental and physical') to develop the whole person. Education, according to ERA, is intended to be an ethical enterprise. Moreover given the overarching value attached to parents' choice in its conception and implementation, such an enterprise should seek to encompass the beliefs and values inherent in their diverse cultural backgrounds.

The Education Acts of 1986 and 1988 have greatly increased the responsibilities of governing bodies. Their demanding new duties, in relation to the local management of schools (LMS), have given them powers previously exercised by the local education authority, which, over the years preceding the Acts, had usually developed some understanding and experience of multicultural antiracist education. In response to community and other pressures, some LEAs had provided specialist advisers and multicultural centres and had encouraged schools to develop multicultural antiracist policies. If governors are to fulfil their new duties in accordance with antiracist aims and objectives, and if they are to continue the antiracist initiatives of the more progressive LEAs they, too, will need to develop an understanding of ethnicity and education.

Over the same period in which ERA brought about these changes, the Home Office revised the criteria for Section 11 grant aid to the LEAs (GB, HO, 1990). Previously Section 11 grants had emphasised English teaching, but had been subverted - dishonestly for good reasons - to include multicultural antiracist education for *all*. The more stringent criteria prevent this (and impede community language provision) whilst grounding the renewed emphasis on English teaching in dishonest antiracist rhetoric.

> The Government's fundamental objective is that Britain should be a fair and just society where everyone, irrespective of ethnic origin, is able to participate freely and fully in the economic, social and public life of the nation while having the freedom to maintain their religious and cultural identity. (GB, 40, 1990, pp 2-3)

Teacher education is likely to be next in line for 'radical reform'. Although multicultural antiracist dimensions of training have to date been inadequate (Eggleston, 1980), the proposed changes are most unlikely to give this a higher profile. Teachers need *more* not less preparation for their moral task as educators. Their training should enable them to develop in their pupils antiracist understanding, values, dispositions and skills. Thus it is critical that teachers increase their own awareness of antiracist issues and their commitment to equality of opportunity. Equality in education is not an alternative to quality in education, but inseparable from it.

Not only is educating a moral task, teachers are also responsible for the moral development of their pupils. Moral education, of which antiracist education is a part, thereby raises the profile of ethnicity and of core values such as justice, equality and respect for persons.

One way forward for educational institutions is explicitly to recognise such basic values by constructing their own values policy statements. Such a policy logically precedes an antiracist policy, which will be grounded in these values. Moreover, just as antiracist policy statements have been triggers for action and have provided guidance for antiracist change, so a statement of values may stimulate and support moral change. The process of constructing a policy, in consultation with parents, pupils and the wider community, will itself be educative. The values agreed will subsequently inform practice – particularly, but not exclusively in the domains of personal, social and moral education and pastoral care.

The need to find new ways of developing antiracist multicultural education is as urgent as ever. At the time of the Swann Report many criticised its conception of education as insufficiently progressive. Since then, the Education Acts could be seen as retreating from Swann, rather than as having advanced beyond it. At this demoralising time of educational uncertainty, education for pluralism may seem superogatory to some, but to keep it on the agenda *and* to give it some priority is actually an ethical imperative.

References

Eggleston, S J, Dunn, D and Anjeli, M (1980) *In Service Teacher Education in a Multiracial Society*, University of Keele, Keele.

Great Britain, Home Office (1990) *Sec 11*. Ethnic Minority Grants. Grant Administration: Policy and Guidelines, HMSO, London.

Great Britain, Parliament, House of Commons (1985) *Education For All*, the report of the Committee of Inquiry into the Education of Children from Ethnic Minority Groups (Swann Report), cmnd 9453, HMSO, London.

Great Britain, Statutes (1986) *Education (No. 2) Act 1986*, HMSO, London.

Great Britain, Statutes (1986) *Education Reform Act 1988*, HMSO, London.

Grinter, R (1985) 'Bridging the gulf: the need for antiracist multicultural education', *Multicultural Teaching*, 3, 2.

Leicester, M (1986) 'Multicultural curriculum or antiracist education: denying the gulf', *Multicultural Teaching*, 4, 2.

Modgil, S, Modgil, C, Mallick, K and Verma, G (1992) *Multicultural Education*, Falmer Press, Lewes.

Modgil, S, Verna, G, Mallick, K, Modgil, C (eds) (1986) *Multicultural Education: The Interminable Debate*, Falmer Press, Lewes.

National Curriculum Council (1990) *Education for Citizenship*, Curriculum Guidance 8, NCC, York.

Peters, R S (1966) *Ethics and Education*, Allen and Unwin Ltd, London.

Troyna, B (1987) 'Beyond multiculturalism: towards the exactment of antiracist education in policy, provision and pedagogy', *Oxford Review of Education*, 13, 3, p 307-20.

Chapter 1
Education for a Pluralist Society

Richard Pring

Abstract

This paper draws attention to the cultural pluralism of society irrespective of the presence of minority ethnic groups and points to the inevitability of this where there is genuine openness of thought and expression. Different traditions develop in morals, the arts, religion, literature and so on. Therefore, the problems associated with pluralism (namely, the need to select from a range of competing cultural traditions and the need also to exclude that which is miseducative) are not, in essence, new as a result of the changing ethnicity of society. They arise equally from class, religious, moral and gender differences that have nothing to do with ethnicity. But ethnicity does, within contemporary society, add the further dimension of occasioning the intergroup hostilities which is referred to as racism. And therefore the most significant aspect of education for a pluralist society today is to promote the value of respecting all persons, whatever the differences, and in doing so to combat racism.

Introduction

The concept of a pluralist society is crucial to an understanding of the Swann Report (GB, P, H of C, 1985) *Education for All* and to what has subsequently happened in the attempts to deal with the racial discrimination identified in that report.

The opening chapter of the Swann Report is called 'The Nature of Society'. The report thereby locates educational and curriculum issues in the wider context of society and an analysis of that – an insight absent from many government reports and from the documents concerned with the National Curriculum in particular. The section on 'pluralism' in 'The Nature of Society' begins as follows:

> We consider that a multi-racial society such as ours would in fact function most effectively and harmoniously on the basis of pluralism which enables, expects and encourages members of all ethnic groups, both minority and majority, to participate fully in shaping the society as a whole within a framework of commonly accepted values, practices and procedures, whilst also allowing and, where necessary, assisting the ethnic minority communities in maintaining their distinct ethnic identities within this common framework. (p 5)

Key ideas are: 'ethnic groups', namely groups having distinct cultural identities based on ethnic origin, and 'common framework', namely a framework of commonly accepted values, practices and procedures which transcend, but are compatible with, those separate cultural groupings. This is expressed elsewhere as 'unity in diversity' and 'socially cohesive and culturally diverse'.

In this chapter I shall, first, draw attention to certain features of a pluralist society which, although accentuated by the presence of various ethnic groups, are not peculiar to that presence; and second, therefore, elaborate the educational task of teaching within a pluralist society which respects this cultural pluralism. That educational task will need to do four things:

- identify those cultural differences which need to be respected;
- show what the educational significance of the difference is;
- show, too, where those cultural differences set up a barrier to educational progress; and
- re-assess the importance of promoting a common framework of values whatever the cultural differences.

The overall aim is, in effect, to put the pluralist debate, particularly as it arises in the context of ethnic differences, in perspective – and also to withstand a tendency in some quarters so to embrace pluralism as to be uncritical of certain cultural differences which affect educational aims. There are two quite opposite errors of which our educational system is too often guilty. First, that of homogenising educational provision, failing to respect differences of value and aspiration of distinct groups within society. Second, that of so respecting cultural differences that any sincerely held values are deemed acceptable irrespective of their miseducative influence. Somehow one needs to steer a middle course.

The idea of a pluralist society

Pluralism requires institutional arrangements and teaching which both strengthen the commonly agreed framework (thereby creating cohesion in society and enabling it to run smoothly) and support the different cultural identities. A stronger version of pluralism in this sense, espoused by the Swann Report, is that the support for the respective cultural identities should be culturally enriching. In other words, pluralism should be seen positively as an enrichment of society rather than negatively as a problem to be tackled. Built into this positive view must be the belief that any specific cultural identity is open to improvement in that it might learn from the values peculiar to other groups, and will need to change where the 'common framework of values, practices and procedures' is incompatible with some of its values.

There is something odd about the concept of 'pluralist society' since it is difficult to conceive of any other kind of society, at least where there is freedom of thought. 'Plural' signifies simply more than one, and society will necessarily be plural – containing many individuals who, together, possess a range of beliefs and values (often incompatible). On almost every topic of human significance there will arise differences and these will be sustained through different cultural traditions. It is a measure of the openness of any society that the growth of such differences will be encouraged and their expression permitted. The relatively recent presence of many minority ethnic groups does not in that respect *create* a pluralist society. It simply provides a fresh dimension to it; it sharpens the issues because of the factor of racism. A pluralist society already existed, containing Catholics, Protestants (of many different kinds), secular Humanists, Marxists, Masons, Fabian as well as Militant Socialists. In that respect the educational challenge of meeting the needs of a pluralist society is not new. There is a new edge to the educational debate, certainly, but nothing theoretically different about the aims of education and the relation of those aims to the aspirations and to the values of culturally distinguishable groups, on the one hand, and to the well-being of society as a whole, on the other.

The educational task

Bearing in mind the pluralism which necessarily exists in any society, one can see that any educational system must find a way of taking on board cultural differences, and not pretending, as so often happens, that they do not exist. In so doing it will have to cope with the following four problems:

1 categorising those differences into types which are relevant to differences in educational provision or treatment;
2 deciding what, in those different types, are factors which *educationally* are worth supporting;
3 identifying what, in those different traditions, are miseducative and should be actively discouraged;
4 identifying those common features shared by the different traditions which need to be fostered for the well-being of society as a whole.

The categorisation of differences

Logically speaking there is an infinite number of ways in which we could represent the pluralism within society. People could be divided according to gender, age, size, colour of skin, measured intelligence, athleticism, political affiliation, geographical location, musical interests, ethnic origin, social class, leisure pursuits, or religious beliefs. Most of these categories, in the not too distant past or in other societies, have been employed implicitly or explicitly in the distinguishing for educational purposes of different groups, thereby recognising and reinforcing the pluralism within society. For example, social class quite clearly has been a criterion for making distinctions in educational provision; an elementary education was deemed suitable for one social group, a public school education for another. Each pursued different aims, aims which, however, were mutually compatible in the provision of an overall hierarchical framework for the efficient organisation of society.

But, there are other, more positive accounts of working-class culture (one thinks, for example, of Richard Hoggart's (1957) *The Uses of Literacy* and of Midwinter's (1975) work among the deprived young people of Liverpool). And there are consequently criticisms of those who, dominated by so-called middle-class tastes, identify educational values with those tastes and ignore the very real interests and values of minority and less dominant groups.

Again, religious belief is the basis of distinctions which affect educational provision (for example, Roman Catholic, Church of England and Jewish schools) and this is acknowledged in the voluntary-aided arrangements for the governance of schools. Special schools are established for potential musicians as these are recognised within some, but not other, musical traditions. Parents send their children to certain private schools or to particular comprehensive schools because of the purported values which they respectively promote (some, for instance, offer a distinctively Christian ethos; others a secular Humanist one). And, until comparatively recently, most secondary boys and girls would be educated separately. Society therefore is and always will be marked by differences, some of cultural importance and acknowledged as relevant to educationally different provision and treatment, others of cultural importance but not acknowledged as relevant. How can one, for instance, acknowledge certain religious differences as relevant for voluntary-aided status, and not others, such as those of the Muslim community?

What is interesting is why some and not other differences are recognised for educational purposes and how far such diversity should affect how the curriculum should be organised or educational provision made. Thus, certain differences in characterising the plural nature of our society might be marginal to some people, but highly relevant to others. Within any society there are different groupings, which are cultural, which are relevant to what they, the young people, see to be significant, and yet which are unacknowledged in our educational provision. Such groupings are neither static (they have within them their own traditions of critical reflection whereby moral, political and aesthetic feelings are refined) nor are they comprehensive in scope. They exist for certain significant purposes, but the members will belong to other groups for other (for example, religious) purposes. Indeed, just as it would be wrong to understand pluralism in terms of a relatively few groups (for there is an infinite number of possible groupings), so it would be wrong to see group membership as quite exclusive and discrete, for there are overlapping interests. Someone may belong to the local Afro–Caribbean Society, be an active member of the Labour Party, attend the local Methodist chapel, support Charlton Athletic and don Air Jordans for his regular visits to hip-hop discos. On the surface, one might, when addressing the issues of pluralism, make an obvious distinction between minority ethnic groups such as Shi-ite Muslims and mainstream white cultural groups. But, there is more in common, for educational purposes, between emerging Protestant and Islamic fundamentalism (the moral and religious certainties, the authoritarianism, the literal interpretation of sacred texts) than there is (within the so-called mainstream culture) between such Protestant culture and that of the secular Humanists or indeed the Catholic Christians. The point is that any analysis of the pluralism in our society must avoid the simplistic categorisation that so often is the case. The world is far too messy for that.

Educational significance of cultural differences

There are two senses in which we use the word culture, and thus cultural differences. There is the purely descriptive sense which picks out those features of a way of life which help to define and make it distinctive. 'Culture' in this sense is not evaluative; its application aims not to indicate something as good or worth pursuing but to pick out and to characterise a set of activities which constitute a form of life. Thus we talk about 'working-class culture', or the 'youth culture', or the culture of the Aztecs, or the culture associated with Tottenham Hotspur.

In this sense, too, one can talk about the cultural differences between one ethnic group and another. And one might also talk of mainstream culture.

There are, however, dangers in this way of speaking. The culture of a particular ethnic group might itself contain significant subcultural differences, different religious traditions which affect participants' conceptions of the good life or of moral obligations or of relations, say, between the sexes. A university educated Muslim may see things very differently from one who, though originating from the same country and superficially sharing the same religious beliefs, has not the wider vision and the different set of understandings that arise from being exposed to academic life.

However, the concept of mainstream culture, as it often appears in books on multicultural education, and as it is contrasted with that of minority ethnic groups, does itself need to be examined critically, for it is a mixture of subcultures, interacting with each other at every point of contact – in music, in religion, in morality, in the arts, in social understanding. And, indeed, this cultural scene with its many intertwining and competing strands (reflected in literature, the arts, architecture, design, philosophy, religion and so on) is itself the focus of critical scrutiny and analysis and is itself interpreted in culturally different ways. Feminists or Marxists or post-modernists or neo-liberals will provide different accounts of the cultural scene – of that which is significant and of that which is peripheral, of the distinctions to be made within it and of differences which can be ignored.

The second sense of the word 'culture' is essentially evaluative – as when one talks about a 'cultured person', or the importance of cultural pursuits. Such pursuits are what 'cultivate' the sensitivities, refine the emotions, sharpen the intellect. In this sense, culture refers to 'the best that has been thought and said' within a literature; it refers to the end product of a critical tradition within which the authentic has been distinguished from the sham, the profound from the trivial, the insightful from the myopic; it refers to a form of life which both reflects and shapes our understanding of human nature and of human motivation; it embraces a moral perspective or at least a set of values which determine our judgements of rights and of responsibilities.

Culture in this evaluative sense is 'a selection' from the many cultural features in the descriptive sense. It picks out some aspects, and not others, as deserving preservation, nurture, and indeed transmission to the next generation. And it is impossible to see education except in those terms, namely, as a highly selective process whereby certain aspects of the many cultural and subcultural traditions, vying for our attention, are picked out as worthy of attention – as an initiation into *some* understandings and feelings and modes of experiencing to the exclusion of others.

To introduce pupils to music requires careful selection from the many different musical traditions; judgements have to be made (even if implicitly) about the traditions which pupils are to be initiated into. No doubt such judgements, if explicit, would be made on many different criteria: the potential for aesthetic satisfaction, the possibilities of further and deeper insight and enjoyment, the opportunities provided for musical participation, technical virtuosity. And the argument over differences of judgement would be largely internal to the world of musicians. Such an argument would, if genuine, be constantly open to new claims for attention as different musical traditions came to be noticed, perhaps because of the presence of particular ethnic groups with their own distinctive musical tastes and understandings. But here, as indeed elsewhere in the 'selection from a culture', there can be no overriding criterion as to what is to count as culture in this evaluuative sense – no simple answer to the question (often asked rhetorically by those who assume a relativist standpoint on matters of value) why certain cultural activities and understandings should be selected for educational transmission rather than others. But the absence of an overriding criterion does not entail that the process of selection is a totally irrational matter or only the exercise of power in a battle between cultures in a pluralist society.

It may be that, but it need not be, for (in an open society) the coming together of different cultural strands stimulates that reflection and deliberation through which any one tradition becomes more self-aware and self-critical. And, indeed, the histories of religion, of the arts, of science and of philosophy are stories of such wide-ranging interaction between different cultural claims. A most important educational objective is to enable students to see that – to see the evolving nature of any one perspective upon human experience, to appreciate the self-critical nature of any tradition that is worthy of attention and to be open to different viewpoints through which one's own might be illuminated or found wanting. Education, in other words, is the initiation into critical modes of thought and feeling and it finds a central place for those distinctive modes of thought and feeling which different cultural traditions provide.

This is not difficult to illustrate – and indeed simply reflects John Stuart Mill's (1859) advocacy of liberty of expression against those who wish to suppress or to ignore different and often contrary opinions:

> If the opinion is right, they are deprived of the opportunity of exchanging error for truth: if wrong, they lose, what is almost as great a benefit, the clearer perception and livelier impression of truth, produced by its collision with error. (p 79)

Thus, religious claims over which bloody wars have been fought, become tempered, more tentative, as contrary religious views are seriously considered or argued with, not supressed; deeper spiritual insights are gained when the 'perennial philosophy', which transcends the distinctive religious manifestations, is perceived; fresh spiritual and moral insight is obtained from acquaintance with forms of social life alien, not so long ago, to our practices and modes of thinking; arrogance in the superiority of our policial institutions is moderated by our awareness of other institutional arrangements which handle affairs more efficiently and human rights more sensitively; music becomes enriched, not simply by the acknowledgement of different musical forms, but also by the internalisation of those within the mainstream tradition.

To sum up, pluralism is the acknowledgement of different traditions of thought and feeling, and the openness to others in the selection of what is to be transmitted to the next generation from the many different cultural strands within our society. Education is thus a conversation not only between the generations of mankind but also between the different cultures within those generations. It is highly selective certainly, but the selection respects the richness of those variations, and their potential enrichment of that conversation.

There are no straightforward rules of selection. Too often 'pluralism' is spoken of in rather superficial terms – a bit of this, that and the other, which is added to a syllabus, incorporated into a programme, ensuring that the pluralistic origins of our differentiated social scene are covered. It is as though one were able to start from scratch, from outside any cultural tradition, and select carefully the components of the new multicultural tradition, so that one gets a balanced and informative picture of the many different cultural differences. But that is foolish for three reasons. First, one simply cannot do this. Schools are located in particular communities and in particular points of time; the teachers have necessarily been brought up and trained within specific cultural traditions; the examination system picks out certain topics and approaches to those topics; the resources available have been built up over time and cannot be instantly replaced. Second, however, and more importantly, such a variegated selection must necessarily lead to superficiality. The religious lesson that covers a range of 'facts' about Catholics (they make the sign of the cross), about Jews (they don't eat pork), about Muslims (they pray on special prayer mats), Hindus (they have a caste system), Orthodox Christians (they venerate icons), Buddhists (they engage in specific modes of meditation), is no education at all. It is to separate the surface aspects of the religion from the religious traditions which give sense to these aspects and which can only be entered into (and thus understood) gradually, with great effort, through a spirit of prayer. Indeed, insight into Islam is no doubt best obtained by one already thoroughly immersed in a religious tradition, albeit a very different one. A person trained in the musical forms of western classical music (and such forms are themselves the evolved product of several musical traditions) may be better able to appreciate the distinctive forms of a different musical tradition than one who is given a pot-pourri of ethnic musical styles. But, third, education is much more than a sampling of different cultures, of collecting lots of information. It is the acquisition of different forms of understanding, of different tools of enquiry, of qualities of openness to argument and to evidence, of the spirit of critical probing of beliefs and values. And therefore it has to select that which most effectively develops those forms and tools and qualities.

We start with educational practices which reflect a range of cultural traditions. These are constantly open to challenge as different viewpoints impinge upon them. The 'purity' of the sciences (itself the product of a particular philosophical culture) is challenged by the critical tradition represented in 'science, technology and society', by a philosophical tradition which stresses the practical and enquiring dimension to science, and by a moral tradition which questions man's dominion over the environment. History, too, now emphasises the skills of enquiry, which, though frequently employed through local histories, are relevant across cultural boundaries; and deals with themes of human significance, which again transcend those boundaries even though they are taught through specific historical events, as indeed they must be (for example, the many struggles from slavery and national dependence).

The point of these examples is: first, for these activities to be *educational*, they must be able to draw upon a specific critical tradition which enables facts to be challenged and informed argument to be engaged in – not any content, in deference to cultural pluralism, will do the task equally as well; but, second, that the particular choice of topics, though in one sense culturally related, is generally immaterial to the broader educational purposes, so long as they are so pursued as to be open to the evidence, to the counter arguments, to the literature, to the beliefs, to the art forms which are available as a result of the range of cultural expressions in a pluralist society. In other words there is a need for the future scientist, historian or artist to be trained in a coherent tradition of enquiry and criticism, but to be so trained that the mind remains open to the richness of other traditions and of other perspectives, where those are relevant.

Cultural barriers to educational progress

Pluralism, therefore, refers to the cultural traditions (arising partly, but not exclusively, from ethnic difference) which affect how we think about and feel towards and shape our separate experiences. Education refers to those activities through which people are introduced to, and get on the inside of, those traditions – through which they enter into a world of ideas that go beyond the common-sense understanding of their immediate experience and unreflective responses. And that world of ideas is itself a self-critical one, conscious of the provisional nature of any one set of understandings. To enter into it requires both mastery of a set of ideas (in history, say, or in aesthetic appreciation of dance or fine arts) together with a care and a respect for those ideas, and, at the same time, an openness to new and different perspectives through which what has been learnt might be constantly challenged, constantly refined.

There are elements, however, of particular cultural traditions which detract from these educational purposes. Such can be the tightness of a tradition, the all-embracing nature of its claims, the inculcation of authoritarianism, the fear of reflection and of criticism, that the mind is closed to further development. Such an attitude may be linked to particular ethnic groups. But one must be careful here. Islamic and Protestant fundamentalists have more in common with each other in this respect than either of them have with mainstream Islam or mainstream Christianity. Both, in the face of the uncertainties arising from increased awareness of cultural differences, or from rational exposition, or from the free circulation of information, or from criticism, seek refuge in literal acceptance of sacred texts, in unquestioned authority of sacred leaders and in the certainties of a historical dogma. It would be wrong, in recognising the plural nature of our society, and in thereby finding a place for the beliefs and values of various cultural, including ethnic, traditions, to grant equal educational status to all traditions, for some can only be described as anti-educational, closing the mind to reflection and to further enquiry, creating an authoritarianism which is truly illiberal. I need to be persuaded for example that the respect for cultural differences in Northern Ireland, leading to separate educational provision, leads to a system of learning which is educationally defensible.

Fostering a common framework

There are some, who, confronted with the pluralism arising particularly from various ethnic communities, say that there is a need to show equal respect for those different values inherent within them (for there is no meta-ethical theory which enables one to judge between different ethical systems), and, it is therefore necessary to negotiate a common framework which, despite differences, enables these cultural units to work harmoniously together to common social purpose. And the word 'negotiate' is chosen as a contrasting verb to that of 'reason', for (so it is argued) there are no rational grounds for reconciling differences, 'rationally' being defined *within* particular systems of thought.

From what I have so far argued, both these positions are mistaken.

1   It is not the case that, for educational purposes, each distinct cultural group is of equal worth. Apart from the difficulties I referred to in identifying distinct cultural groups, there are some that attempt to put an impenetrable fence around a way of life such that people can neither enter nor get out. Such is the authoritarianism built in to some forms of life, no doubt arising from a fear of intellectual adventure and of the uncertainties that go with it, that they simply cannot be defended in educational terms, for education is the introduction to traditions of thought and of feeling which attempt (inadequately perhaps, falteringly, humbly, openly in the light of argument and evidence) to make sense of experience. And the moral grounds that make us welcome the pluralist nature of society (a pluralism that is constantly changing as new interests, new ethnic groupings make their presence known) are the same grounds for requiring each unit in that rich pluralism to be open to each other, learning from each other, making available their respective insights.

2   There is, therefore, only limited room for 'negotiation'. Negotiation would suggest a kind of bargaining or trading of rights or commodities between rival parties ('I'll give this up if you . . .'). One negotiates wage settlements or the secession of land or a marriage dowry. But a jury does not negotiate its decisions of guilty or not guilty, or the judge the sentence to be imposed. The parent may negotiate some arrangements with the child ('If you help with the cleaning, I'll increase your pocket money'), but there must be severe limits to the negotiation if the parent is to act responsibly in the upbringing of the child. Similarly with schooling, it is possible for certain practices to be negotiated because they may be, in a sense, educationally neutral – where the precise content of the curriculum does not affect profoundly the cognitive aim or educational purpose. Examples in art, design and technology can be drawn from many ethnic traditions. And this could be 'negotiated'. Moreover, there could be negotiation of the amount of time that might be given to religious interests.

However, there are limits to such negotiation because education should not be seen primarily as a kind of bargaining between teachers (or curriculum planners) on the one hand, and 'customers' on the other. 'Negotiation' is a metaphor borrowed from a different context, although a context that seems increasingly less inappropriate as other aspects of the market-place enter into the educational vocabulary. For negotiation is invoked as a substitute for reason, where reasoning is ruled out as a logically impossible solution to the problems raised. It is as though reason cannot resolve the difficulties as education becomes the stage on which ethnic and other cultural differences seek recognition.

That, however, is due to an impoverished notion of rationality. To be rational is indeed to give reasons; it is to respect basic rules of logic; it is to ensure consistency in argument. But it is also to be open to others' reasons; it is to speculate and to deliberate when new perspectives are suggested; it is to reflect on experience and others' interpretation of it; it is to be always less than certain about one's own view of things and thus to be ready to learn from other, culturally different perspectives.

A pluralist society, if it is to mean more than the acknowledgement of different sets of values and beliefs in society (for all societies must be pluralists in that sense), is one where such openness becomes a major educational aim, where one comes to see the values of others' understandings and where one welcomes these as points of illumination. Hinduism makes us think differently about the relation of man to nature; Islam is a challenge to the materialism of so much 'Western' religious life; Marxism questions the cosy explanations of national history; black self-consciousness, and its manifestations in art and music, poses questions about the adequacy of our political institutions. And so we could go on. The point is, not that one should sit down with representatives of these groups to negotiate the content and processes of education (Which groups? There is an infinite number of possible groups), but rather so to organise our educational system and so to conduct our teaching that schools are open to these different voices – to what people from other cultural and ethnic backgrounds have to say – in dealing with those matters of deeply human significance which literature, history, the arts, religious and social studies explore in the classroom. An example would be the much greater use in English of the growing literature from Commonwealth countries.

Implicit within such rational deliberation will be a concern for the central educational aims: the sharpening of the intellect through the different forms of understanding and mental capacities, the awareness of the variety of perspectives which impinge upon our understanding of the social and economic world, the intellectual and moral virtues crucial to intellectual growth, personal qualities such as empathy, and attachment to aesthetic forms of expression. These aims, and the valuing of them, are not to be negotiated. They are what teachers, operating within an educational tradition (not within a tradition of vocational training or of indoctrination), will fight for. These values are intrinsic to their educational task. They will, therefore, form the essential framework which all should share. Within such a framework there will be a non-negotiable curriculum content since it is the educator's task to determine, from within a tradition of rational criticism and enquiry, what are the ideas to be learnt and the activities to be undertaken.

The relevance of ethnic difference

My argument about the significance of pluralism to educational practice and to the educational system relies on several things:

- the necessary pluralism of an open society;
- the overlapping nature of these pluralist traditions, belying the assumption that we are dealing with ring-fenced cultural units;
- the necessity for any educational programme to select from this richly pluralist scene whatever extends the power of the mind;
- the crucial importance in such an education of encouraging that openness to different perspectives.

These however are general arguments and do not apply specifically to the ethnic differences which were the basis of the deliberations of the Swann Report. Is there not something very special about that pluralism which arises out of ethnic differences such that there are considerations over and above those which arise from the pluralism of a society that contains different social classes, different youth cultures, and so on?

There are two respects in which the ethnic aspect of the pluralist society in which we live affects the general points I have made:

1   The significance of ethnic identity to the self-respect which the learner is seeking. A central moral principle is respect for persons, and a central motivation in any educational activity is the support for that moral principle. The son or daughter of a secular Humanist will be less affronted by the school's disregard for secular Humanism than will be the son or daughter of a devout Muslim, where the symbols of a deep-felt set of values are either ignored or treated with contempt – where that which shapes a significant part of his or her identity finds no place in the educational provision. For children within minority ethnic groups there must be a place for *their* history, *their* language, *their* religions and *their* art – where their participation in those studies and activities (supported by the school) is encouraged and flows into mainstream schooling (as in drama, the arts and the humanities).

2   Ethnic identity, unlike the other cultural identities I have referred to raises particular questions about discrimination, where individuals are shown disrespect or are unfairly treated. Education for pluralism is, as I explained at the beginning, in one sense no different for minority ethnic groups that it is for others – they are but one kind of 'unit' in a plural society, and education, as I have argued, must constantly be welcoming the diversity in society as an enriching process. But the peculiar significance of ethnicity lies in the reactions of others towards the members of those ethnic groups, reactions very often of hatred and contempt. And thus there comes the further educational task of shifting attitudes from those of arrogance and hostility to ones of openness to distinctive ethnic traditions, and to seeing the good that is in them. Indeed, multiculturalism in this sense (which includes quite explicit programmes of antiracism) is part of that common framework of values that cannot be negotiated.

Conclusion

My argument has been that advocacy of pluralism, because so often identified with ethnic pluralism, misses an essential point about society and thus about the education of people for that society. That point is that, quite apart from the ethnic issue, society is plural in a range of educationally significant ways and that teaching and the curriculum should always be striving to accommodate this pluralism. Ethnicity adds an important dimension to this. It does not affect the basic educational task.

That task is to steer a course between, on the one hand, a neglect of cultural, particularly ethnic, differences on the one hand and an uncritical openness to them on the other – between neglecting differences which, despite their educational significance, are too often submerged beneath an insensitive 'mainstream' tradition (and this neglect extends to women's experience or to aspects of regional and working-class culture as well as to that of the Islamic or Hindu or Judaic communities) and being uncritically open to all cultural differences as vociferous lobbies negotiate for a place on the curriculum. There are educational values which should be promoted for all and which shape the joint selection from the many cultures.

References

Great Britain, Parliament, House of Commons (1985) *Education for All*, Report of the Committee of Inquiry into the Education of Children from Ethnic Minority Groups (Swann Report), cmnd 9453, HMSO, London

Hoggart, R (1957) *The Uses of Literacy*, Chatto and Windus, London.

Midwinter, E (1975) *Education and Community*, Allen and Unwin, London.

Mill, J S (1859) 'On liberty', in: Acton, H B (ed), *J S Mill – Utilitarianism, Liberty and Representative Government*, Dent and Son, London.

Chapter 2
Values, Cultural Conflict and Education

Mal Leicester

Abstract

In our culturally plural society there occur, from time to time, serious social and educational conflicts, such as the Rushdie and Honeyford affairs, involving different ethnic groups. Such conflicts arise from a clash of those fundamental values by which we justify our arguments and behaviour and which are deeply rooted in a cultural tradition. This paper describes liberal and epistemological dilemmas connected with making a democratic resolution of such conflicts and considers, given competing values, the question of which values should underpin moral education.

Central to the Swann Report's ideal of multicultural education for all is the notion of a framework of commonly accepted values shared across the various cultural groups which constitute our multicultural society (GB, P, H of C, 1985, pp 316–17). Such a shared framework could be distinguished from a commonly imposed one. 'Shared values' are those with which all groups freely agree. 'Imposed values' implies that adherence to them is backed by sanctions – as with those embedded in the legal system, for example. With these one may or may not agree, though one must comply or be punished. An imposed framework is required, particularly in the absence of an agreed one, for social cohesion and control. That the latter is indeed absent from our society is evident in its serious social conflicts and in the existence of various, and competing, conceptions of multicultural education. In this paper I explore dilemmas connected with seeking to resolve such cultural conflicts and ask what, given that we do not have a shared framework of values, moral education in a pluralist society should be like. Conflicts about values certainly suggest that we need to ask about what and whose values 'should' be taught.

Social conflicts

In our culturally plural society there occur, from time to time, serious conflicts involving different ethnic groups.[1] By serious I mean that harm or distress is caused to members of one or more groups, both through the events leading to the conflict and through the conflict itself. Whatever the content of the conflict, whether it occurs in the wider society, as in the Rushdie affair, or in the form of educational controversies such as those discussed in Halstead's chapter (pp 39–56), particularly entrenched social conflicts always involve a clash of fundamental values. (Try to imagine one that does not.) For example, in the Rushdie affair the value many attach to freedom of expression is in conflict with the value others attach to the protection of the sacred from blasphemous critique. Fundamental values are those by which we justify our arguments and behaviour, but which are themselves not justified. 'At the end of reason comes persuasion' (Wittgenstein, 1974). They are deeply rooted in a web of attitudes, beliefs and practices. It is not surprising then, that it is in the values domain that differences between socio-cultural groups are likely to be particularly problematic, leading to conflicts which are emotionally charged and difficult to resolve.

These conflicts occur in a deeply racist society, in which power relationships between the disputants is far from equal. Racism is often a factor in the progress of the dispute. Both its presentation in the media and the ways with which it is dealt reflect the interests of the white, indigenous, dominant ethnic group. This is so even when the dispute is between the minority ethnic groups. For example, both would be presented as trouble makers unless one side's interests coincided with white interests. The racism of our society thus multiplies the practical and ethical complexities around social conflicts because, in practice, the achievement of a fair resolution of conflict is problematic.

Educational conflicts

Not only do some social conflicts occur in the sphere of education (eg the Honeyford affair); the issue of cultural conflict affects the very concept of education. Since education is value laden, cultural differences in fundamental values are reflected in different ideas about what education in our multicultural society should be like. Thus, when the Swann Report (GB, P, H of C, 1985) advocates an education for all based on shared values, one Muslim response (Islamic Academy, 1985) advocated separate education so that all children could be offered an education based on their own community's culture and values. Each model of education could be seen as fair and appropriate for a multicultural society. The former, which could be called *integrational pluralism* is appropriate in that all are educated together, and the latter, which could be called *dynamic pluralism*, is appropriate precisely because it allows for the preservation of several cultural traditions, with the different groups sharing in social development from positions of religious identity and strength (Skinner, 1990). Similarly, as we see in the chapter by Jackson (pp 100–113) some Christians advocate Religious Education only in terms of their own religious traditions – though some would impose this on children from non-Christian backgrounds.

Political and philosophical dilemmas

I have suggested that we do not have a common framework of values and that social and educational conflicts occur when incompatible values that are fundamental for different cultural traditions clash with each other. For each dispute there is a practical question (or questions) about what should be done to resolve the dispute – a question that surely arises in situations such that continuation of the dispute is seriously damaging in some way. For example, with reference to the Rushdie affair again, the questions arise of whether *The Satanic Verses* (Rushdie, 1988) should be withdrawn, whether it should have been issued in paperback or not and whether the blasphemy laws should be retained, extended to protect Islam and other faiths or abolished altogether. For a person committed to democratic solutions, these practical questions are complicated by both a political and a philosophical dilemma.

The political dilemma is this. The open democratic society, indeed the very ideals of social and educational pluralism, rest on 'liberal' values of open procedures for critical debate and tolerance of diverse points of view and so on. In recognising the right of other views to be respected the liberal confronts the problem of views which deny these pluralist ideals. What is the liberal response, for example, to those Muslims who wish to promote dynamic pluralism, and, therefore, for their own children mono-cultural Islamic schools?

One possible response is a kind of militant liberalism: that is tolerance short of tolerance for that which would endanger liberalism itself. (Are liberal values endangered by a number of Islamic or Jewish or Christian denominational schools? On the other hand, if one values pluralism, is one not committed to seeking to ensure that each child benefits from a liberal education?)

The philosophical problem is that of the philosopher or sociologist who accepts a constructivist epistemology: accepts, that is, that knowledge is socially constructed and is, at least in some respects, relative to a cultural tradition. This epistemological thesis is not equivalent to an 'anything is equal to anything else' form of relativism. The thesis allows that within a cultural tradition there are standards of right and wrong and criteria for truth and falsehood, but denies that there are culture-transcendent criteria for making judgements between incompatible or *conflicting* cultural views.

It is worth noting that a liberal (in values) could be (though most, perhaps, are not) a non-constructivist, epistemologically. Such a liberal, while accepting another's right to different value judgements, nevertheless believes that some accepted as valid in a particular tradition are simply mistaken. Such a liberal is likely to believe that we are fallible in relation to the absolute (tradition-independent) values which he or she believes do nevertheless exist. A non-liberal (authoritarian) in values, is, however, unlikely to be an epistemological constructivist, since his or her authoritarianism rests on the belief in one 'infallible' authority or ideology, which thus provides absolute, tradition-transcendent value judgements.

The political problem is exacerbated by the philosophical one. The liberal cannot justify the overriding of value systems which would endanger liberal values with an argument based on culture-transcendent principles or values – if these do not exist. This form of a rational solution to conflict is therefore denied. Dwight Boyd (1992), in his paper, 'The moral part of pluralism as the plural part of moral education', is motivated by his liberal values to find a solution to these dilemmas. Consonant with his pluralist ideals he seeks for a universally defensible framework of procedural values.

His answer is to see moral education as teaching children to maintain the common human condition of dialogue as the foundation of dealing with value differences and giving them the concepts, knowledge, skills and dispositions necessry to their being equal participants and responsible partners in the ongoing debate about how the pluralist society and education should be. (That this is close to my own position can be seen in what I say later about moral education.)

Ian Vine (1990), like Boyd, has also recognised that values education within pluralist societies is problematic, since there are diverging subcultural conceptions of its goals. The Western notion of multiculturalism embodies the (liberal) ideal of equality between cultural groups. But this, Vine points out, fails to confront the challenge of values systems radically at variance with it. In his reply to Boyd's paper Vine points out that attempts such as Boyd's presuppose liberal values already. Vine's implicit acceptance of liberalism and epistemological constructivism leads him to an honest acknowledgement that his (and any) stance is 'partisan'; his stances being (partly in the interest of emancipating future generations of disadvantaged minorities) that: 'For democrats, the majority's fundamental moral ideology takes precedence – although ideally in as flexible and minimally oppressive way as can be devised. It has to set limits on the collective rights of minorities' (ibid). Incidentally, if democracies are not to turn into 'elected dictatorships' – dictating the majority, or even just the dominant view – then there must be limits on the collective rights of the majority too.

Given a constructive epistemology there is no *philosophical* solution to cultural conflicts of value. There simply is no 'absolute' (ie cultural-transcendent) value system.

Most writers working in the 'liberal education' tradition do not confront problems about resolving such conflicts. They base their prescriptions on liberal values and argue in (unproblematised) liberal terms for their own preferred solution to any practical problem that may arise when cultural perspectives conflict.

In Pring's chapter, (pp 19–30) we have a clear description of the liberal's response to education in pluralist societies. In other words, *given* a liberal conception of education, this is what education in pluralist societies should indeed be like. However, those with different values, with, therefore, a differing conception of education, may not want their children to be educated in this way.

Practical decisions arising from this must be made. This is so even if one rejects, as Pring does, that what counts on 'rational grounds' for one's chosen educational agenda is meaningful only *within* particular systems of thought. The point of the liberal dilemma is that it raises the issue, when such decisions are made, of how fair it is for a society based on democratic liberal values to dismiss sincerely held competing views. Additionally once one does accept what I called 'constructivism', which entails that what count as 'rational grounds' are at least, to a significant extent, meaningful only within a particular system of thought, then one recognises the partisan nature of one's position and the dismissal of other educational agenda as 'anti-educational' is more (philosophically) problematic, even though, in liberal terms, they are.

Incidentally, as Pring indicates in linking Christian and Islamic fundamentalism, it is not so much cultural traditions as such which are liberal or illiberal as differentiable strands within them. There are different epistemological approaches to each tradition – constituting these different strands. Thus

- some take their tradition, and only their tradition (whichever that is) to be based on true foundations which provide the only guiding (rational) principles even for modern development and dilemmas. Other traditions would be held to be not based on these true foundations (a fundamentalist approach);

- others would not claim such foundations, but nevertheless believe that the wisdom (incorrigible truth and rational principles) established over time should be conserved and re-applied (a conservative approach);
- yet others see traditions as ongoing, dynamic structures which, through a rational process of critical debate, continue to evolve to meet new situations (a liberal approach).

For the fundamentalist, knowledge (including moral judgement) arises from the application of given foundation principles. For the conservative and liberal (epistemologically speaking) knowledge is socially constructed, and for the liberal continues to develop and change, in his or her own tradition and in others.

Towards resolution

I have argued that practical questions about resolving social and educational conflicts of value in pluralist societies are complicated by what could be called liberal and epistemological dilemmas. We cannot avoid the practical questions, since they inescapably arise in a pluralist situation. For example, should we educate all children in common schools, or allow separate Muslim, Jewish and Christian denominational state-funded institutions? Because values are at stake, the separate schools debate is strongly argued from competing perspectives (see papers by McLaughlin and Connolly, pp 114–136 and pp 137–145).

The democratic society should, logically and morally, seek to answer such questions in line with its own inherent liberal values. Thus it would seem to me incompatible with those values (and probably an example of cultural racism) to allow Jewish and Christian, but not Muslim, schools. However, there would be a case, *perhaps*, for disallowing schools of whichever religious tradition which adopted a fundamentalist approach to that tradition and thus failed to offer a liberal education (see chapter by McLaughlin, pp 114–136). On the other hand, *if* children do learn to be less ethnocentric, more open to other perspectives, less racist and so on, through a shared liberal education in common schools, these are, *prima facie*, considerations in favour of abolishing *all* separate provision.

Some groups have values that, for them, override the liberal values in this abolition argument and it seems to me that awareness of the liberal and epistemological problems outlined will at least lead to a greater sensitivity to these non-liberal views. (This is a good reason to raise problems, even if they are ultimately insoluble.) This greater sensitivity might, for example, produce greater efforts to ensure that the (compulsory and contested) common schools offer an antiracist and genuinely *pluralist* education (Leicester, 1989). Moreover, I would claim that, if taken into account, the political and philosophical dilemmas may at least encourage a process of negotiation which is sensitive to 'non-liberal' value systems. Pring's chapter supports this claim in that it illustrates how non-recognition of the dilemmas discussed in this paper can lead to a view that such negotiation is inappropriate. Rather, for Pring, culture-transcendent rational debate will establish the superiority of the liberal-based value stance over the non-liberal. 'Negotiation' becomes an inappropriate term for it is asserted as a substitute for reason where reasoning is ruled out as logically possible.

Yet negotiations can sometimes lead to a compromise which is mutually acceptable. On a small scale for example, I was involved with a school where many Muslim fathers were unhappy about their daughters having swimming lessons as part of physical education. After sensitive discussion (that is with openness and goodwill on each side) it was agreed that swimming was acceptable to the parents provided that the girls were separated from the boys and were taught by female staff. On a larger scale it might be, for example, that a genuinely open separate schools debate, with goodwill on all sides, would lead to a compromise such that integrational and dynamic pluralism were combined: that is for each child whose parents and 'community' so wished, some shared and some separate state-funded educational provision contributed to their schooling. Some existing schools already seek to provide 'community language' teaching and school worship in faiths other than Christianity and so on. However, the synthesis of integrational and dynamic pluralism would involve more than this. The child's school week would be partly controlled and offered by the common school and partly controlled and offered by a culturally distinct providing body.

Such negotiation is not a case of finding the culture-transcendent rational solution, as though competing *rational* solutions could not exist, but it does involve exchange of reasons. As each group comes to understand what counts for the other group as a reason, with goodwill, each side seeks to find a new solution which is acceptable to both.[2] Liberal values themselves endorse ongoing open debate and the accommodation of plurality – at least short of endangering democracy itself. (And to the democrat, pluralism is presumably worth paying the price of the conflicts, even damaging and irresolvable conflicts, that it brings in its wake.)

The absence of a shared framework of values (as distinct from the imposed framework of liberal values) need not deter us from seeking to establish *agreed* procedures for resolving conflicts (Haydon, 1987). The liberal and epistemological dilemmas I've outlined seem to me to support Haydon's suggestion that we should engage in such a task. (Those SACREs (Standing Advisory Councils for Religious Education) and Agreed Syllabus Conferences which work well perhaps provide an example of a structure through which distinct *faith* groups may reach agreement about educational matters (Taylor, 1991).)

It is in the light of having described these dilemmas and with the recognition through so doing of the *partisan* nature of what I will say, that I finally consider education, and moral education, in and for a multicultural society.

Education, moral education and pluralism

I have questioned the existence of a shared framework of fundamental values. 'Framework' suggests something approaching a structure and system. The onus is on one who disagrees to set out (as the Swann Report did not) of what this framework consists. However, it does seem possible, even likely, that the various cultural traditions have *some* values in common. Human beings share the human condition. Because within cultural traditions ethnic groups have separately constructed their evolving value systems, it does not follow that we have necessarily done so in totally different ways. It is surely an urgent task of those in higher education to undertake further empirical and philosophical work in relation to the existence of shared values.

Moreover, should not education provide a forum for debate about resolving conflicts of value – both general debate (can we construct an agreed procedure?) and debate about particular disputes? Obviously all cultural groups should be part of this process. A less-closed system of higher education would contribute to (and be indicative of) a more open and democratic society. And an emphasis on equality as a social value should encourage recognition of the rights of minority groups to have a real voice in the social and educational debates and decisions to which I have referred.

At the school level it will be useful for older pupils to develop some understanding of moral theory. An introduction to meta-ethics may help pupils to appreciate that diversity at the first order level of moral judgements is not due to moral blindness or perversity on the part of members of other cultural traditions but to differences in fundamental values and justificatory beliefs. Similarly, an introduction to epistemology will help pupils to appreciate that there may not be, or always be, or always be known to be, one exclusively right answer. No single cultural tradition has a monopoly on truth, the establishment of which, in all domains, is complex and error prone.

Specifically *moral* education in pluralist societies could be based on developing those qualities and values in pupils which will contribute to a just and harmonious pluralism. Thus an essential requirement is for an antiracist dimension to moral education (Leicester, 1982). The pupils, as developing moral agents, should develop a commitment to eliminate racism and to acquire knowledge and skills relevant to this.

Pluralism will also require the development of qualities and values that discourage the use of power to settle conflicts and will encourage, rather, a willingness to negotiate and compromise. This in turn highlights the importance of the development of goodwill, and of a moral education appropriate to this end. Moreover, if the pluralist society must, paradoxically, also impose liberal values, let its education at least seek to ensure that pupils do learn to respect the various cultural traditions and the equal rights of all citizens. It is my belief that a multicultural education for all children in common schools will encourage further convergence of values.

Those values required for the effective functioning of a just and harmonious pluralist society should be exhibited in the micro society of the school itself. This 'should' is both a moral ought, deriving from liberal values, and a pragmatic must for *effective* moral education. Thus my final picture is of a just community school, serving the whole community and teaching antiracist pluralist values through its very functioning. Such an institution would recognise the right of all cultural groups to have a voice in negotiating what, in practice, just and pluralist provision will be like.

Notes

1 In this paper I am primarily concerned with conflicts in the public domain, though much of what I say is also relevant to culture-related conflicts between individuals.

2 This process of negotiation could not be extended to groups, such as the National Front, for example, who did not bring goodwill to resolving the conflict. Where the ideology or value judgements in question *presuppose* antipathy and illwill to other social groups, negotiation is ruled out.

References

Boyd, D (1992) 'The moral part of pluralism as the plural part of moral education', in Power, F C and Lapsley, D K (eds) *The Challenge of Pluralism, Education, Politics and Values*, University of Notre Dame Press, Notre Dame.

Great Britain, Parliament, House of Commons (1985) *Education For All*, report of the Committee of Inquiry into the Education of Children from Ethnic Minority Groups (Swann Report), cmnd 9453, HMSO, London.

Haydon, G (ed) (1987) *Education For a Pluralist Society*, Bedford Way Papers, Institute of Education, University of London, London.

Islamic Academy (1985) *Swann Committee Report – An Evaluation from the Muslim Point of View*, Islamic Academy, Cambridge.

Leicester, M (1982) 'Morals, emotions and race: educational links', *Journal of Moral Education*, 11, 3, pp 186–93.

Leicester, M (1989) *Multicultural Education From Theory to Practice*, NFER–Nelson, Windsor.

Rushdie, S (1988) *The Satanic Verses*, Viking, London.

Skinner, G (1990) 'Religion, culture and education' in Pumfrey, P D and Verma, G K (eds) *Race Relations And Urban Education*, Falmer Press, Lewes.

Taylor, M J (1991) *SACREs: Their Formation, Composition, Operation and Role on RE and Worship*, NFER, Slough.

Vine, I (1990) Unpublished paper to MOSAIC Annual Conference, Hungary.

Wittgenstein, L (1974) *On Certainty*, trans Anscombe, E M and Paul, D, edited by Anscombe, G H and Wright, Von, Basil Blackwell, Oxford.

Chapter 3

Ethical Dimensions of Controversial Events in Multicultural Education

Mark Halstead

Abstract

The various controversial events which feature significantly in the history of multicultural education in England in the last 20 years are important for many reasons, not least because the debates to which they have given rise have helped to clarify thinking and shape attitudes and opinions. This article focuses on some of the ethical debates which have surfaced as a result of these controversial events. They are analysed and discussed under three headings:

- *situations where there is agreement over the existence of a particular moral imperative, but disagreement over how to interpret it;*
- *situations where there are conflicting moral imperatives and uncertainty over which should take priority;*
- *situations where disagreement arises because groups do not share the same fundamental moral principles.*

The discussion is concerned mainly with the nature of racial injustice; democratic rights and responsibilities; freedom of choice and freedom of expression; and minority rights and conflicting values with particular reference to the Muslim community in England.

A controversial event is one which is capable of being understood and interpreted in different ways, and one on which different individuals or groups are likely, in practice, to have conflicting views. Though individuals may maintain that there is only one appropriate attitude to hold or morally acceptable approach to adopt, a controversial event is by definition one on which universal or near universal agreement cannot be reached. Any interpretation or response that is proposed will prove objectionable to some individuals or groups and is likely to arouse disagreement, hostility or protest.

The history of multicultural education in England in the last 20 years is full of such events, which have aroused both passionate feelings and significant academic debate. Some have been long-running stories which the media have kept in the public eye for months or even years. Prominent among these are:

- the Honeyford affair, in which a protracted campaign was carried out in 1984–5 calling for the dismissal of a headteacher in Bradford whose articles opposing multicultural education had caused offence to significant numbers of ethnic minority parents and others;

- the McGoldrick affair, in which a Brent headteacher was suspended in 1986 after allegedly stating that she did not want any more black teachers at her school;
- the Dewsbury affair, involving 26 white parents who refused in 1987 to send their children to a school which was 85 per cent Asian; and
- the Burnage affair, in which the tragic killing of an Asian boy in a Manchester school gave rise to claims, particularly after the completion of a report on the incident in 1988, that the school's antiracist policies were somehow to blame.

Other events have had a lower profile or have lasted for a shorter duration, but nonetheless have raised important issues. As early as 1973, a Muslim parent, Abdullah Patel, objected on religious grounds to the placement of his daughter in a co-educational upper school in Bradford, and pursued an ultimately unsuccessful campaign for over two years to have her transferred to a girls only school. In 1985, a Bristol teacher, Jonathan Savery, was accused of racism in an incident which was almost a carbon copy of the Honeyford affair. In 1990, two Muslim pupils were sent home by a Trafford headteacher when they refused to remove their headscarves in school. In 1991, the issue of a parent's right to choose a school on racial or cultural grounds was raised again in the Cleveland case, which concerned the transfer of a five year-old girl from a 60 per cent Asian school to a 98 per cent white school. In 1991 eight Christian families in Hampshire decided to withdraw their children from a Christmas production of a Hindu play. In 1992 a serious clash between the head of the grant-maintained Stratford School in East London and some of the school's Asian governors received much media coverage. Longer-running controversial events include the introduction and eventual abandonment of the policy adopted by several local authorities of dispersing ethnic minority pupils throughout their schools by means of 'bussing'; and also the provision of *halal* meat for school dinners for Muslim pupils, introduced by some local authorities in the 1980s but strongly opposed by animal rights activists and others. Furthermore, there is a group of events which, while only indirectly related to education, have in fact had a significant impact on the educational experiences of ethnic minority children. In this category may be included the so-called 'race riots' of 1981, the Rushdie affair and the Gulf War.

What makes these events so important is that they have highlighted disagreements between people, and the consequent debates and exchanges of ideas have helped to clarify concepts, define boundaries and shape attitudes and opinions in the area of multicultural education. They have also drawn attention to the complexity of many of the issues involved. What all these events have in common is their controversiality. Many are *politically* controversial and have led to extended debates in both local and national government, with all political parties putting forward strongly argued responses. It would be a mistake, however, to assume that in each case there was a straightforward disagreement between the antiracist left and the traditionalist right. Opposition to 'bussing', for example, developed simultaneously from the far left and the far right, and in fact it was a complaint by a member of the National Front to the Race Relations Board which led to the investigation and eventual demise of Bradford's policy of dispersal (Kirp, 1979, p 96). Still in Bradford, when the Honeyford affair burst onto public attention, one of his most outspoken critics was the

Conservative chairman of the Educational Services Committee, Peter Gilmour (who had, incidentally, been a major architect of Bradford's innovative multicultural policies), while his supporters included the Labour Lord Mayor, Norman Free (who had, incidentally, opposed the provision of *halal* meat in schools). Even at the political level, therefore, the controversial events under discussion played havoc with normal party political divisions (Halstead, 1988, p 75).

The role of the media in fuelling the controversies must not be underestimated and is itself highly controversial. It may take many forms, including: the biased reporting or interpretation of events; the attribution of words or ideas to key figures in the events which they did not actually say; the use of emotive language, as in the description of the specialist teachers recruited by Brent as 'race spies' (*Today*, 20 October, 1986) and 'thought police' (*Daily Express*, 30 March, 1985); and the invention of stories with little or no foundation in fact, such as the 'Brides for Sale' story in the *Daily Mail* (5 August, 1985) and the *Mail on Sunday*'s report that Haringey Council had banned the use of black bin liners because they were 'racially offensive'. The failings of the right-wing press have been well documented (cf Gordon and Rosenberg, 1989), but, as I have pointed out elsewhere (Halstead, 1988, pp 75–83), it would be a mistake to assume that distortions and misleading innuendoes in the media are exclusively a right-wing phenomenon.

Some of the events currently under consideration are extremely complicated because they contain a number of different but intertwined controversies which must be unraveled before the principles that lie behind them can be discussed. The Rushdie affair, for example, involves separate debates about the nature of blasphemy; the principle of freedom of expression; the rights of minority groups such as the Muslims in the UK; possible justifications for the interference of one state in the internal affairs of another; the use of death threats; and literary issues including ways of responding to contemporary fiction (cf Akhtar, 1989; Appignanesi and Maitland, 1989; CRE, 1990; Modood, 1990; Nielsen, 1989; Qureshi and Khan, 1989; Ruthven, 1990; Webster, 1990; Ahsan and Kidwai, 1991).

The remainder of the present chapter will be concerned solely with the *ethical* dimensions of these controversial events. It is impossible to take each event in turn, but it is intended to separate out certain key ethical issues which occur with some regularity, to explore these issues with reference to several events at the same time, and to highlight some of the directions which further discussion might take.

From an ethical point of view, what makes an event controversial is one of three sets of circumstances.

- There may be situations where individuals or groups agree over a particular moral imperative but interpret that imperative differently. By a moral imperative, I mean what others have called a 'second-order moral principle'. Among the many lists of such principles, Biggs and Blocher (1987, p 110), for example, include: telling the truth; respecting other people and their property; respecting people's rights to determine their fates; keeping promises; safeguarding the rights of those who cannot do so themselves; improving ourselves; doing no wilful harm to others; generally treating everyone equally; and believing all living things are intrinsically valuable.
- There may be situations where conflicting moral imperatives are recognised as

relevant to a given event, and individuals or groups disagree over which should take priority. This and the previous category both imply that the individuals or groups concerned share the same framework of fundamental values.

- Disagreement between individuals or groups may arise because they start from different premises and do not share the same framework of values.

This categorisation provides the structure for the remainder of the chapter. For each category, one main example of an ethical controversy will be taken and examined with reference to one or more of the events already listed.

Different interpretations of an agreed moral imperative

Racism, most people agree, is something which merits strong moral censure. Honeyford, for example, has called racism 'a failure of the human spirit' (1985, p 17) and has argued that to judge people by the colour of their skin

is an outrage, and any society that permits this stands condemned by all those with any claim to decent moral instincts. (1988, p ix)

Yet the question of racism lies at the very heart of many of the controversial events mentioned above. This is because, while there is general agreement that racism is wrong, there is less agreement over how to conceptualise or identify racism, and over precisely what is wrong with it. Ray Honeyford, Maureen McGoldrick, Jonathan Savery and the Dewsbury parents were all accused of being racists, and they all vehemently denied the charge. This suggests that perhaps different understandings of the term 'racism' are in use. This impression is reinforced by the large number of activities or situations which are or have been described as racist. Not too long ago, to collect racial statistics would have been considered racist, but now to refuse to collect them lays an organisation open to the same charge, and in 1991 the British census included a question on racial or ethnic origin for the first time. This decision in turn, however, has been condemned as discriminatory by some British Muslims, because they would like to see their ethnic identity defined in terms of religion rather than by racial or national origin (cf *The Muslim News*, 19 April, 1991, p 1). In Britain, the policy of 'bussing' involved intentional racial *mixing* by dispersing black children throughout the schools of a district, whereas in the USA, 'bussing' involved intentional racial *segregation*; both policies, however, were condemned and eventually abandoned as racially discriminatory. Not surprisingly, even well-intentioned white people have sometimes become confused by such apparent contradictions and discouraged in their attempts to avoid racism (cf Wellman, 1977, p 118). Clearly, some conceptual clarification is required before any adequate attempt can be made either to identify instances of racism or to evaluate an appropriate level of moral disapprobation.

I have elsewhere identified six distinct types of racism which may be found within contemporary writing on the topic (Halstead, 1988, ch 6), but for present purposes it is perhaps sufficient merely to distinguish between 'strong' and 'weak' racism. Strong racism implies racial hatred, which may find expression in hostile behaviour and in attempts to reject or dominate groups which are identified by specific physical and/or cultural characteristics. It includes positive acts of overt racism such as bullying and abuse, as well as scapegoating and the avoidance of social contacts. These practices are sometimes rationalised in some way, as the verbal and physical abuse directed towards Muslim children was during the time of the Gulf War (Peeran, 1991; NUT, 1991). In its most extreme form, 'strong' racism may lead to murder; Darren Coulburn was convicted in 1987 of the murder of Ahmed Ullah at Burnage High School, and the inquiry panel concluded that the murder was racist (though they also acknowledged that the issue was complicated by the fact that Coulburn was an unhappy child with a long history of antisocial behaviour: cf Hall, 1988, p 22). 'Weak' racism does not involve hatred or hostile behaviour, but simply the reinforcement of white privilege, whether or not this is conscious or intended. It may be exemplified by the policy of 'bussing' black children (but not white) to ensure a racial mix in local authority schools. What made this an example of racism was not that it necessarily had a harmful outcome, nor that it was consciously used by white people to reinforce their own privilege, but simply that it denied racial minorities the freedom to determine for themselves the pattern of their own future lives and implied, perhaps in a rather subtle way, the superiority of the white people who made the decisions.

It is here, however, that the controversy begins. Honeyford and other writers of the New Right are prepared to identify racism only in terms of what I here call 'strong' racism; they tend to dismiss what I call 'weak' racism as largely a figment of the antiracist imagination. I shall argue shortly, however, that racism is best understood as racial injustice, and that this injustice can take a wide variety of forms. One of the problems in agreeing what should be included within the concept of racism has been the inadequacy of some of the methods traditionally used to identify it. The commonly used formula that racism equals power plus prejudice and discrimination does not stand up to close analysis, for if power is necessarily involved, this implies that lower working-class whites cannot be guilty of racism (which the Burnage story clearly negates), and if prejudice and discrimination are necessarily involved, this sees no fault in a 'colour-blind' approach which insists on treating everyone the same and fails to take account of relevant differences. Neither can racism be identified merely in terms of outcome, for this ignores the attitudes behind the actions and suggests that racial hatred does not matter so long as it is repressed; the report on the Burnage affair (MacDonald *et al*, 1989) emphasises the dangers of encouraging people to 'bury their racism without changing their attitude'. To identify racism in terms of inequality, whether of treatment, of respect or of opportunity, may also be unhelpful, for equality of opportunity guarantees future inequalities, equality of respect is impossible to quantify and equality of treatment (at least when it is taken to mean identity of treatment) is likely to lead to the injustices associated with a 'colour-blind' approach. Inequality of various sorts is in any case intrinsic to the structure of British society, and antiracists appear to be divided over whether they are seeking some sort of reshuffling of social goods and power so that these are shared more evenly between blacks and whites, or whether they are seeking a more radical political reform involving the abandonment of hierarchical power structures and competitive individualism in favour of a system based on need, not merit (cf Gaine, 1987, pp 32–8).

To define racism as racial injustice suggests a way out of all of these problems. It relates the problem of racism to a fundamental value of our society, indeed, a fundamental human value. It identifies racism as one particular manifestation of a broader moral issue (justice), and shows how it shares the same overarching theoretical framework with the search for justice in other areas. It thus avoids the danger, highlighted in the report on the Burnage affair, of placing racism in 'some kind of a moral vacuum, ... totally divorced from the more complex reality of human relations' (MacDonald *et al*, 1989). If campaigning against racism involves campaigning against certain types of injustice, then it cannot involve taking the side of black people against white irrespective of circumstances – though of course it is clear that in our present society it would be the lot of blacks, not whites, that would be improved by the elimination of racial injustice. Racial injustice may occur both in isolated instances on the part of an individual and in a systematic way that permeates a whole society. It may be intentional or unintentional, conscious or unconcscious. It may emanate from insecurity, from ignorance, from the belief that certain races are genetically superior to others, from institutional practices and procedures which were established long before Britain became a multiracial society, from well-intentioned but misguided responses to the perceived needs and problems of racial minorities, or from the denial that such special needs and problems exist.

To define racism as racial injustice ensures that our understanding of the term is not tied to a particular political theory or ideology. This is of course not to deny that injustice may have far-reaching political implications and may be politically mediated and understood. But if opposition to racial injustice were dependent on a specifically politicised form of antiracism (such as the explicit anti-Tory approach recommended by Hatcher, 1985), then there is the danger that those who reject that particular form of antiracism may come to deny the existence of racial injustice altogether, except in its most extreme manifestations. This seems to be a trap into which Honeyford and other members of the New Right are at times in danger of falling. To define racism as injustice, on the other hand, implies that what is wrong with it is ultimately a matter of moral, not political, concern, though of course the moral shortcoming may be seen in a political and economic context just as much as in a social, cultural or individual one. And if one particular group is always on the receiving end of the injustice, this may have grave social and political consequences, as the so-called 'race riots' of 1981 testify. Nevertheless, if we accept that racism is at root a moral issue, then this suggests that any attempt to eradicate it through education belongs to the domain of moral education rather than political education as recommended by some recent writers (Carrington and Troyna, 1988; Troyna and Carrington, 1990).

The identification of racism with racial injustice enables us to begin to answer two crucial questions relating to the degree of moral disapproval which racism should engender. The first is how far individuals may be censured as racists for the practices and procedures involved in institutional racism, or for the ideologies, beliefs or assumptions which underlie those practices. Sarup (1986, p 23) ends up rejecting moral explanations of institutional racism entirely, in favour of economic and political ones, but elsewhere in the antiracist movement there is an emphasis on individual responsibility (as seen in the posters which proclaim, 'If you are not part of the solution, you are part of the problem'). Spears (1978) claims that merely going about business as usual may make one an 'accomplice in racism'. This is rather an odd phrase, however, because institutional racism is not a crime (though of course *some* forms of racism are illegal). What is needed in this case is not the encouragement of individual guilt (a point emphasised by MacDonald *et al*, 1989), but careful reflection on the justice or otherwise of the institution under consideration, followed by the appropriate social and political action. Indeed, if 'racist' becomes a slogan which is applied indiscriminately to all white people on the grounds that they are all implicated to a greater or lesser extent in institutional racism, this may have two adverse results. First, the moral force of the term will be diminished (for 'if all whites were racist, it can't be so bad as all that'), and second, it is likely to drive a wedge between whites and blacks, increase prejudice on both sides and make racial conflict more probable. There would seem to be much sense in applying the term 'racist' to individuals only if they are personally racist, and applying the term to practices and procedures rather than to people when institutional racism is under consideration.

The second question is whether all forms of racism are equally worthy of censure. In an absolute sense, perhaps an affirmative answer is required. Rawls (1972, p 3) calls justice 'the first virtue of social institutions' and as such not a matter for compromise. But in this present imperfect world we generally recognise degrees of injustice. The eradication of certains forms of injustice may be worth dying for, but that of others most certainly is not. Racism similarly covers a wide range of injustice, from the outrageous and obscene, to the rather trivial, and appropriate responses will vary accordingly. The crude distinction between 'strong' and 'weak' racism with which this section began does not convey a sense of the wide range that is possible, but it does draw attention to one important point, that at one end of the continuum of injustice encompassed by the term 'racism' there is widespread agreement over its moral unacceptability, while at the other end of the continuum there is much that is open to debate. At the strong end is the overt disadvantaging of individuals simply because of the racial group to which they belong; at the 'weak' end is the benevolent paternalism which leads the (white) government to act 'in the best interests of' its black citizens without consulting them, or the 'colour-blind' approach which ignores a potentially important aspect of a person's identity (cf GB, P, H of C, 1985, pp 26f). There is near unanimity in the condemnation of 'strong racism' as morally outrageous because it is in conflict with the most fundamental moral principles of our society. What I have called 'weak' racism, on the other hand, may be viewed as controversial because while some people consider it just as unacceptable as 'strong' racism, others deny that it is racism at all, yet others argue that many instances of 'weak' racism are comparatively trivial and do not merit severe moral censure, while others again maintain that though 'weak' racism may involve serious injustice there is no absolute obligation to oppose it but it must be weighed against other values relevant to the situation under consideration. In situations where conflicting moral imperatives are operating, it seems unlikely that the obligation to combat 'strong' racism would ever give way to a higher imperative, but it is possible that combatting 'weak' racism might. It is to situations where conflicting moral imperatives are seen to be in operation to which we must now turn.

Disagreement over priorities in the case of conflicting moral imperatives

Honeyford undoubtedly believed that it was more important to tell the truth as he saw it about multicultural education than to avoid the danger of offending his pupils' parents by keeping quiet. In a situation like this, two different moral imperatives can be detected, each suggesting a quite different course of action; a morally autonomous individual is in the position to weigh up the two imperatives and decide which to give priority to in the particular circumstances prevailing. In the event under consideration, Honeyford's opponents were convinced that he made the wrong decision. They argued that his professional accountability to his parents and pupils, to his employers and to the local community should have led him to keep quiet. His criticisms of multicultural education included criticisms of, and injudicious statements about, ethnic minorities, and this, it is argued, caused him to lose the confidence of many parents who no longer wished to entrust their children to him. Council officers also queried whether he could carry out his responsibilities as a Local Education Authority (LEA) employee when he was so implacably opposed to crucial LEA policies.

Honeyford's response was to claim the democratic right as a citizen to criticise LEA policies. This claim was based on the liberal belief that the freedoms of speech, expression and the press are fundamental to any free, open and democratic society. However, in Honeyford's case, the situation was complicated by two factors:

- the policies which he criticised had been agreed by the democratic processes of local government, and
- Honeyford was a public employee responsible for putting those policies into effect.

It is clear that once the Council had agreed on specific policies, it was morally and politically authorised to ensure that they were carried out. Faced with an employee whose views were diametrically opposed to those underlying official policies, the least an LEA could do would be to check that the employee's views were not adversely affecting his capacity or willingness to carry out the policies. The LEA might also question the appropriateness of leaving responsibility for carrying out the policies in the hands of someone who had publicly expressed opposition to them. Neither of these responses, however, necessarily involved the denial of free speech to the individual.

To sum up, Honeyford justifiably claimed the right as an individual to express his opinions freely within the law, whether he was engaged in political debate or in criticising public policies, individuals or cultures. He was also justified in claiming that any attempt to suppress his right to free speech as an individual on the grounds that the opinions he expressed were offensive would be an intrusion on his personal liberty. For toleration is not limited to what is inoffensive, and to tolerate the expression of an opinion does not in any way imply endorsement of that opinion. However, there is an equally strong argument that as a public employee in a position of authority and responsibility, he was operating within tighter moral constraints than he would be as merely a private individual, and these constraints could be defined in terms of his accountability to his employer and his clients. On this view, it would be these constraints, not a more sinister attempt to suppress free speech, that would create the strong moral pressure on him to remain silent. What is interesting to note about this debate is that although it is ultimately irresolvable – and this is what makes it a controversial issue – there is a framework of agreed fundamental values, such as democracy, within which the debate is conducted. Several years later, Nizami and Browning (1989) wrote in similar terms about the Rushdie affair:

The debate surrounding *The Satanic Verses* should be as much about the responsible use of the freedom of expression as about that freedom itself.

I shall argue shortly, however, that behind the Rushdie affair are two value systems that are fundamentally in conflict, and this makes it not only more difficult to resolve, but also ultimately more dangerous.

Most events where conflicting moral imperatives are in evidence involve a clash between personal freedom on the one hand and some kind of social obligation on the other. Such a clash can be seen in the various controversial events in which the main issue is parents' freedom of choice regarding the school which their children are to attend. In 1973, Abdullah Patel requested the transfer of his daughter from a co-educational to a girls' school, for religious reasons. Bradford LEA refused, with DES connivance, on the grounds that its policy of maintaining a racial balance in its schools might be affected if too many Muslim girls were transferred to the city's only remaining girls' school. There were other reasons for the refusal as well. If there were sound educational arguments for a policy such as co-education in the first place, and if the policy were agreed by the democratic decision of the Council, then it was considered justifiable to compel parents to conform. Indeed, the Council could defend such compulsion in terms of protecting the rights of individual children to equality of treatment, as well as in terms of the promotion of the public interest. To make an exception of parents such as Patel would undermine the Council's policy of treating all children the same (Halstead, 1988, pp 47-8). Of course, policy has changed dramatically over the last 15 years; Muslims in Bradford may now send their daughters to the school of their choice, and the city's one girls' school is now overwhelmingly Muslim. But the clash between the principle of parents' freedom of choice and the various principles advanced by Bradford Council in 1973 still remain very much a matter for debate.

Parents' freedom of choice was again a central issue in the debate about 'bussing'. Few parents agreed with the principle. Indigenous parents objected strongly if they found their own children refused a place at a local school to make room for ethnic minority children coming from a distance, and minority group parents objected to being deprived of the benefits of a neighbourhood school. Nevertheless, the policy persisted in Bradford for more than 15 years (it was phased out much sooner in other parts of the country), because councillors believed that there were strong practical and moral reasons for retaining it: they believed that minority group children would be integrated more quickly if they were dispersed throughout the city's schools, and they believed that it was important for all white children to have some contact with the ethnic minorities so that they could learn to live in harmony (Halstead, 1988, pp 37-9). Though the policy of 'bussing' has now been abandoned, debate about the principles involved continues, and support for the policy itself has never completely died out.

The question of parents' freedom of choice re-emerged in September 1987 when the parents of 26 children in Dewsbury refused to send their children to the school to which they had been allocated. The schools they wanted were nearer their homes, and had places available. On this occasion, however, the protesting parents were white, and the school to which their children had been allocated was 85 per cent Asian. Racist motives were widely attributed to the parents, though they insisted throughout that they were motivated simply by the desire 'that their children should be educated in a traditional English and Christian environment' (Naylor, 1989, p 154). As the parents saw it, the question of racism was simply a distraction; the real issue, on their view, was whether they could send their children to the school of their choice, or whether they could legitimately be denied that right so that the LEA could retain some degree of racial mixing in its schools. The parents received support from various quarters, including the Muslim Parents Association, who saw parallels with their own calls for separate Muslim voluntary-aided schools. The case was watched with considerable interest, not least because it coincided with public discussion of the proposals put forward in the 1987 Education Bill for increased parental choice in schooling. Concern was expressed that racially or culturally segregated schools might be the price the government had to pay for increasing parental choice. In the event, after an extended legal battle Kirklees LEA backed down and allowed all the children involved to go to the schools of their parents' choice. And with the introduction of open enrolment in the 1988 Education Act, the principle of parental choice now seems to be legally established as taking priority over other considerations even if it encourages 'white flight' and contributes to the further development of racially segregated schools (Troyna and Carrington, 1990, p 94).

Though the legal pendulum has swung from one extreme to the other, the moral debate remains. In the words of one champion of the parents' cause,

> Should we, as the egalitarians and comprehensivists urge, override parental wishes in order to achieve racially balanced schools, or should we, as the defenders of freedom counsel, resist such social engineering? (Naylor, 1989, p 126)

The debate requires a consideration of who has the best right to make fundamental decisions about the education and upbringing of children. It is clear that children are physically, psychologically and morally immature and that at least young children lack the rational capacity to exercise the responsibilities of citizenship. This is taken to justify paternalism, and the question then arises whether the parents or the state should be the primary paternalistic agent in respect of the child. Though the extension of the state's control over the child at the expense of the family in the last century has been viewed with concern in some quarters (eg Geach and Szwed, 1983, pp 1–2), such control is generally limited to the public development of the child (ie as a future citizen). The state recognises that the child can only learn what it is to be a person and develop communal feelings and social attitudes from other individuals, and this task is likely to be best carried out by those who have the strongest sense of duty and commitment to the child, who know the child and its needs most intimately and who are attached to it most closely by bonds of affection. This relationship between child, parent and state can perhaps be expressed most clearly in terms of a hypothetical social contract made between parents and the state on the birth of the child. The biological parents are recognised as trustees of the child; the terms of the trusteeship require them to make decisions that are in the best interests of the child and not against the public interest; in return, they are allowed to determine the course of their family life without undue interference from the state. The state remains the final arbiter when the terms of the trusteeship are abused by the natural parents, and thus has the right to find substitute parents or to take over the trusteeship itself if the natural parents are clearly either not acting in the interests of the child (eg by engaging in child abuse) or acting in conflict with the public interest (eg by encouraging the child to commit crimes). Otherwise, state involvement in the upbringing of children is limited to situations where the state has an interest in what happens (for example, to increase industrial performance, develop social competencies or prepare children for democratic citizenship). Thus parents are not barred in principle from making fundamental decisions about the education of their children – unless those decisions conflict with either the public interest or their children's own interests.

What sort of parental decisions *could* clash with the public interest? In fact, the general public has both a positive and a negative interest in education. First, there is the concern that children should develop competencies which will help to create a stable and democratic society. Since all citizens share the same laws, the same political rights and the same economic system, it is important that they should be able to 'interact harmoniously and communicate intelligibly' and 'function properly in a just society' (Strike, 1982, p 159). Secondly, there is the concern to protect the public interest from harm. If parents sought to bring up their children, for example, in a way which was seen to 'fuel intolerance and undermine social co-operation' (Coons and Sugarman, 1978, p 91), the state would have the right to overrule the parents to prevent the public interest from being harmed. But in asking whether these considerations give the state the right to insist on racial integration in all its schools, irrespective of parental wishes, we have returned to the question with which the present discussion started.

Again, the debate has gone a full circle without reaching an uncontestable conclusion, though it has become apparent that there is at least a framework of shared fundamental values within which the debate can be carried out. In the final section, situations will be examined where two quite different value systems are involved and disagreement arises because of the absence of a sufficient degree of overlap between the two systems, with the result that the moral imperatives to which they give rise are not infrequently in conflict. Islam provides the clearest example of a value system within the UK which is at odds in several crucial respects with the dominant Western liberal democratic framework of values, and this will provide the focus of attention in the final section.

Disagreement based on conflicting value systems

The case of the two Trafford schoolgirls who were sent home in 1990 because they refused to remove the headscarves which they claimed their Islamic faith required them to wear exemplifies the clash between two conflicting sets of values. There have been similar events in a number of other European countries. As far as the headmistress was concerned, school rules should apply equally to all, and in this case there was only one relevant consideration: the need to ensure safety in laboratories and the gym. The fact that only two out of a much larger group of Muslim girls at the school insisted on wearing headscarves merely confirmed her in her view that it would be a mistake to treat them differently from anyone else in the school. For the two girls concerned, however, the obligations which they believed they were under as a result of their Islamic faith far outweighed any merely secular rules imposed by the school.

Although in one sense a trivial event, at least compared to the Rushdie affair, this case raises a number of crucial ethical questions for Western educators:

- To what extent and in what circumstances can religious belief be allowed to override educational considerations in decisions relating to the education of children with strong religious beliefs?
- Who is to make such decisions?
- What right do they have to do so?
- By what criteria should the decisions be made?
- What rights and obligations do individual children have?
- What rights and obligations do minority religious groups have?
- Does the school ever have the right to put children in a position where they are expected to act against their consciences or their deeply held beliefs?
- Is meeting the needs of children more important than respecting their or their parents' beliefs, and if so, how are these needs to be defined, and by whom?

Each of these questions raises important philosophical issues which I have considered in some detail elsewhere (Halstead, 1989). Before any can be discussed adequately, however, it is important to examine the value system which lies behind the continuing demands made by many Muslims for concessions to their beliefs.

Religion lies at the very heart of the Islamic system. It is the focal point of every aspect of human life, whether legal, political, economic, educational or ethical. It ties the world-wide community of believers together with strong bands of loyalty and gives them a sense of belonging to something vaster and more permanent than themselves. Islamic values are based on divine revelation, which is not itself open to challenge. They are enshrined in Islamic law (*shari'a*), which sets out not only universal moral principles but also detailed instructions for many aspects of human life, and neither the individual believer nor the Islamic community may legitimately deviate from them. The ultimate goal of human existence is the worship of God, which involves accepting God's will as revealed in the Qur'an as supreme and seeking the realisation on earth of divinely ordained moral imperatives. Individual freedom in Islam thus barely extends beyond the capacity to choose to accept or reject the guidance contained in the *shari'a*. Equality, on the other hand, is a fundamental value in Islam, though it is understood primarily in spiritual rather than economic terms: all are equal in God's eyes, except in their degree of piety, but equality in this sense is not considered incompatible with differentiated social roles (cf Halstead, 1991). Of all the basic Islamic values, perhaps it is justice which comes closest to its Western counterpart, though even this is based more on the Qur'anic revelation of God's nature (to which humans are to aspire) than on rationally constructed moral principles. In the political domain, Islam does not countenance any separation of religion and state (Al Faruqi, 1982, p 165). Religious leaders expect the laws of the state to be in line with the Qur'an, and the religious beliefs of its citizens are a matter of concern to the state. Consequently, there is little difference between treason and apostasy in Muslim eyes. Western talk of the politicising of religion makes little sense to Muslims, for politics in their view is just one branch growing out of the trunk of religion.

Not surprisingly, this system produces an approach to education which is at odds at several crucial points with the Western system. In Islam, the ultimate goal of education is to nurture children in the faith, to make them good Muslims. Children are not encouraged to question the fundamentals of the faith but are expected to accept them on the authority of their elders. Religious teaching is the most important part of the curriculum, and all other subjects must be taught in a way which is consistent with religious belief. Although, of course, there are minor disagreements among Muslims about their faith and although the degree of commitment shown by individual Muslims will vary, the principles set out above are fairly rigid and are not open to individual interpretation in the way that might be expected in the West. Indeed, it may be said that they explain what it is to be a Muslim (Ashraf, 1988; Halstead, 1989).

The differences between the Islamic system of values set out above and the liberal democratic framework of values which is dominant in Western societies are plain to see, and do not need to be elaborated here. Each system has a coherence when taken in isolation, but problems are bound to arise when a minority group with a primary commitment to the Islamic system is living alongside a majority group committed to a quite different framework of values. Most of the controversial events involving Muslims which were listed at the start of this paper have come about as a result of situations where the two different value systems have given rise to conflicting moral imperatives. There would appear to be four courses of action open to the majority group in such situations, two of them extreme and two more moderate. Each of these will now be briefly examined.

1   The whole Islamic framework of values may be dismissed by the majority group as intolerable. There is a paradox, as Mendus (1989, p 18f) reminds us, between the view of toleration as a virtue and the recognition that where toleration involves moral disapproval, this implies that the thing tolerated is wrong and ought not to exist. After the Rushdie affair and the Gulf War, toleration of Islamic values has dwindled in some quarters and it has become almost intellectually respectable in the UK to speak disparagingly of Islam and 'the moral inferiority of Muslim values' (Selbourne, 1991). The one positive thing that can be said about this wholesale rejection of Islamic values is that it respects the Islamic doctrine of *tauhid* (unity), which emphasises the interdependence of all Islamic beliefs and values: if one is rejected, the whole edifice crumbles. For many people, however, the wholesale dismissal of the values of a major world religion is arrogant, unjust and unwise.

2   At the other extreme, Muslims may be permitted to form a largely autonomous subgroup within British society, in which the Islamic framework of values would be the norm. At a conference organised by the Muslim Institute in London in 1990, a 'Muslim manifesto' was launched which included a 'unilateral declaration of autonomy' for the Muslim community in Britain. Dr Kalim Siddiqui argued that the only way for the Muslim community to survive in Britain was 'to create in Britain institutions normally associated with a sovereign territorial state' (Ibrahim, 1990) and the 'Muslim Parliament' has now been established. It is not clear how much support there is for Siddiqui's ideas within the Muslim community, but there has been almost universal condemnation elsewhere. The chairman of the Commission for Racial Equality (CRE) has dismissed them as separatist and extremist.

3 A possible course of action would be to make no concessions to the Islamic framework of values in the public domain though private individuals would be left free to live their lives according to Islamic principles so long as these did not impinge on the public interest in any way. This was by and large the policy adopted in Britain in the 1960s and 1970s and is well illustrated by the case of Abdullah Patel to which reference has already been made. This approach is also broadly in line with Honeyford's views. In one article he provides an account of the visit of a Muslim father to his school to request the withdrawal of his daughter from swimming lessons (Honeyford, 1987). Honeyford came out with arguments that would be very acceptable to many Western educationalists: the welfare and safety of the child were paramount considerations; no one had the right to restrict her human possibilities; it was important to provide equal opportunities for girls; and anyway she enjoyed learning to swim. Then he tried a different tack, and mentioned the ways in which the school, under LEA guidance, sought to accommodate Muslim views about segregation of the sexes: no males were present in the swimming baths, there was a female instructor, and changing took place in private cubicles. In each case, however, he met with the brick wall response, 'It is against my religion'. For Honeyford himself, the dispute did not really comprise a controversial event. All the sound educational arguments were on his side, and the challenge to his educational judgement came from unacceptable religious bigotry; he saw no need for concessions in this case. The parent's perspective on the event, however, was quite different: what, in his belief, was required of him and his daughter by his religion was paramount, not even open to question or debate, and any other considerations were unimportant in comparison. In the event, Honeyford temporarily forsook his liberal instincts and took refuge in his authority as headteacher. He insisted that school rules should be obeyed and that the girl should learn swimming, and the parent acquiesced. Opponents of this approach argue that it is based on a lack of respect for other cultures and that in any case it is not justifiable to force children into a position where they are required to act in a way which is contrary to their deeply held beliefs.

4 The final approach involves making a limited number of concessions in the public domain to the demands of Muslim parents and leaders, as a way of showing respect for their beliefs, so long as these demands are not seen to be fundamentally in conflict with Western values. This approach is currently in favour in the UK, and many LEAs are now halting any further moves towards co-education, allowing Muslim pupils to dress in accordance with Islamic rules on modesty and decency, not insisting on school attendance during Muslim religious festivals, and making other concessions in schools to Muslim sensitivities. The demand for the provision of *halal* meat for Muslims in state schools and hospitals has been more controversial, however, because the Muslim method of slaughter (which takes place without pre-stunning) has been judged by some non-Muslims to be barbaric and in conflict with the moral imperative to respect the intrinsic value of all living things. The issue has been debated extensively in some local authorities and several are now providing *halal* meat in public institutions in spite of fierce protests from animal rights activists (Halstead, 1988, pp 45f, 247). Even where educational principles or legal requirements are at stake (as in the wish of some Muslim parents to withdraw their children from compulsory elements of the curriculum such as sex education), a blind

eye may be turned by the authorities on the grounds that the alternative may involve a breakdown of good will on the part of the Muslims.

From a non-Muslim perspective, one problem about this fourth approach is the increasing number of demands emanating from the Muslim community. Currently, there are demands for the extension of the blasphemy laws to include Islam and permission for the establishment of Muslim voluntary-aided schools, and even more educational demands (relating, perhaps, to art, music and science teaching) are looming on the horizon. There is a growing feeling in some quarters that to make further concessions to Islamic beliefs and values may in fact be counterproductive, since far from contributing to the growth of a genuinely pluralist society, it may simply encourage the disintegration of society and the growth of a divisive, ghetto mentality.

From a Muslim perspective, although there is something initially seductive about being on the receiving end of a number of concessions made to one's own beliefs and values, there are two major problems with this policy. The first is that the terms in which the concessions are defined are based on Western values, not Islamic ones. Thus the whole debate is expressed in terms of equal rights: if Christians are not required to attend school on their major festivals, then equality of respect demands that Muslims should be given the same right; if Christians and Jews have the right to set up voluntary-aided schools, then it seems unjust to deny Muslims the right to do the same. This is not really an Islamic perspective, however. Muslims merely wish to be allowed to carry out their Muslim duties without restriction or interference by the state, and they are happy for other religious groups to have the same privilege, but they will not argue their case in terms of equal rights. What they object to is not the discrimination *per se* but anything which gets in the way of their religious duty. Hence the calls which have been made recently by groups like the National Secular Society and Women Against Fundamentalism and individuals like Ruthven (1990) and Lee (1990) for the abolition of the blasphemy laws do not begin to address the Muslim perspective, even though they are based on the principle of setting all religious groups on an equal footing. The same applies to calls for the abolition of the voluntary-aided school system. The principle of equal rights for all religious groups might be satisfied by such a move, but it would still discriminate against those people who wanted their children to be educated in line with their own religious beliefs.

The second major problem from the Muslim perspective is that the policy of making a limited number of concessions to their beliefs conceals a subtle form of cultural domination. The problem is that they are piecemeal concessions selected by non-Muslims on the basis of a quite different set of values and that they relate to the external manifestations of Islam without paying any attention to the priorities of Muslims themselves or to the underlying spiritual beliefs and values which give them coherence. This failure to take account of the underlying, unifying Islamic beliefs and values makes the concessions tokenistic, reinforces the impression of Islamic beliefs as arbitrary, eccentric, even devoid of meaning, and papers over the most significant differences between the Western and Islamic world views. The rhetoric in which the concessions are wrapped, which emphasises the 'celebration of diversity', appears hollow and trivial: few non-Muslims are likely to 'celebrate' the sacrifice of a goat on the street or in the backyard during the Muslim festival of Eid al-Adha, any more than Muslims are likely to celebrate values like free love which may bring shame and dishonour to their family. The notion of 'celebration of diversity' is based on the selection of bits of different cultures, and again the selection is based on a framework of values which is alien to Muslims. However well intentioned multicultural education may be, it is likely to reinforce the cultural domination of the majority group over minorities like the Muslims unless they are empowered to make decisions themselves when these affect their own community. I have elsewhere called this kind of cultural domination 'paternalistic racism', and have suggested that multicultural education may be seen as a way of maintaining social stability, increasing the mutual understanding of different groups and defusing racial conflict without at the same time bringing to light and firmly rejecting the underlying injustices experienced by minority groups like the Muslims (Halstead, 1988, pp 152-3). On this analysis, although multicultural education may bring considerable advantages to minority groups, its hidden agenda involves the maintenance and reinforcement of a Western system of values. Even the proposal by White (1987) and Haydon (1987) for a forum in which the framework of shared values may be discussed and hammered out by all the groups that make up our society presupposes a Western system of values; values cannot be agreed in this way in Islam.

This argument seems to be leading to the suggestion that if Western liberals are unable to persuade Muslims to adopt a liberal democratic framework of values, then it may be the lesser of two evils to tolerate the coexistence of an alternative framework of values and the version of education to which it gives rise, rather than to impose an alien set of values on an unwilling minority and force children to conform to patterns of behaviour in school that are in conflict with their deeply held beliefs. Such an approach would leave Muslims free to give religion a central place in the education of their own children, whatever was going on in the wider society; no doubt in practical terms this would involve the establishment of at least some Muslim voluntary-aided schools.

However, events of the last four years, and particularly the Rushdie affair, have led an increasing number of people in the UK to question Islamic values and to express doubts about whether it would be appropriate to allow Muslims unrestricted freedom to live fully in accordance with their religion. By responding in the way they did to what they considered to be the blasphemy of *The Satanic Verses*, Muslims succeeded in reinforcing the popular prejudiced view of Islam as oppressive, fanatical, irrational and murderous, and serious damage was done to race relations. And by pausing to ponder over which of the two sides in the Gulf War was closer to Islamic principles, British Muslims laid themselves open to accusations of disloyalty. With the decline of the perceived threat to the West from the Soviet block, it is not surprising that Islam has begun to emerge in the Western consciousness as the foremost challenger to Western values (Webster, 1990, p 145), or that the Western press has consequently turned on Muslims, as in this recent piece by Peregrine Worsthorne:

> Islam, once a great civilisation worthy of being argued with, has degenerated into a primitive enemy fit only to be sensibly subjugated. (*Sunday Telegraph*, 3 February, 1991)

On the other hand, Parekh (1990) has argued that such a response to Islam is a denial of the values of tolerance and respect which are central to the Western liberal tradition. He criticises journalists who attacked

> the entire Muslim community as barbarians unfit to be citizens of a civilised society. The widely used and never clearly defined term 'fundamentalism' became a popularly accepted disguise under which racism masqueraded itself... The term became a devious device for blackmailing Muslims into rejecting their values.

And so the debate goes on. Among so many intertwining controversies, about freedom and rights, equality and oppression, domination and paternalism, toleration and prejudice, and religious and secular world views, I have not been able in this final section to do more than untangle some of the central issues. But let me end on a sombre note. I have treated the controversial events throughout this paper as matters for intellectual debate. For other people, however, they may be matters of life and death. All the main figures in the Honeyford affair were the targets of death threats. Ahmed Ullah tragically lost his life at the age of 13. Several people have been killed in anti-Rushdie riots in Bombay and Kashmir, and Rushdie himself has been in hiding for many months as a result of death threats. We fail at our peril to recognise the seriousness of some of these issues.

References

Ahsan, M M and Kidwai, A R (1991) *Sacrilege Versus Civility: Muslim Perspectives on the* Satanic Verses *Affair*, Islamic Foundation, Leicester.

Akhtar, S (1989) *Be Careful with Muhammad: the Salman Rushdie Affair*, Bellew, London.

Al Faruqi, I (1982) Islam as culture and civilisation, in Azzam, S (ed) *Islam and Contemporary Society*, Longman, London.

Appignanesi, L and Maitland, S (eds) (1989) *The Rushdie File*, Fourth Estate, London.

Ashraf, S A (1988) *Islam: Teacher's Manual*, Mary Glasgow, London.

Biggs, D A and Blocher, D H (1987) *Foundations of Ethical Counselling*, Springer, New York.

Carrington, B and Troyna, B (eds) (1988) *Children and Controversial Issues: Strategies for the Early and Middle Years of Schooling*, Falmer Press, Lewes.

Commission for Racial Equality (1990) *Law, Blasphemy and the Multi-Faith Society*, CRE, London.

Coons, J E and Sugarman, S D (1978) *Education by Choice: the Case for Family Control*, University of California Press, Berkeley.

Gaine, C (1987) *No Problem Here: a Practical Approach to Education and Race in White Schools*, Hutchinson, London.

Geach, H and Szwed, E (eds) (1983) *Providing Civil Justice for Children*, Arnold, London.

Gordon, P and Rosenberg, D (1989) *Daily Racism: the Press and Black People in Britain*, Runnymede Trust, London.

Great Britain, Parliament, House of Commons (1985) *Education for All*, (Swann Report), cmnd 9453, HMSO, London.

Hall, M M (1988) 'The terrible lesson of Ahmed's murder', *Telegraph Weekend Magazine*, 19 November, pp 16–25.

Halstead, J M (1988) *Education, Justice and Cultural Diversity: an Examination of the Honeyford Affair, 1984–85*. Falmer Press, Lewes.

Halstead, J M (1989) 'Education for Muslim Children in the UK: Liberal and Islamic Approaches', unpublished PhD thesis, University of Cambridge.

Halstead, J M (1991) 'Radical feminism, Islam and the single-sex schools debate', *Gender and Education*, 4, 13, 3, 263–78.

Hatcher, R (1985) On 'Education for Racial Equality', *Multiracial Education*, 13, 1, 30–46.

Haydon, G (1987) 'Towards a framework of commonly accepted values', in Haydon, G (ed) *Education for a Pluralist Society: Philosophical Perspectives on the Swann Report*, Bedford Way Paper 30, Institute of Education, University of London.

Honeyford, R (1985) 'The hounding of Honeyford – the head's own story', *Daily Mail*, 17–19 December.

Honeyford, R (1987) 'Muslims in the swim', *The Spectator*, 3 January.

Honeyford, R (1988) *Integration or Disintegration? Towards a Non-Racist Society*, Claridge Press, London.

Ibrahim, N (1990) 'Kalim Siddiqui declares UDA', *The Muslim News*, 27 July.

Kirp, D L (1979) *Doing Good by Doing Little: Race and Schooling in Britain*, University of California Press, Berkeley.

Lee, S (1990) *The Cost of Free Speech*, Faber and Faber, London.

MacDonald, T, Bhavnani, R, Khan, L and John, G (1989) *Murder in the Playground*, Longsight Press, London.

Mendus, S (1989) *Toleration and the Limits of Liberalism*, Humanities Press International, Atlantic Highlands.

Modood, T (1990) 'British Asian Muslims and the Rushdie affair', *The Political Quarterly*, 61, 2, pp 143–60.

Naylor, F (1989) *Dewsbury: The School above the Pub: a Case-Study in Multicultural Education*, Claridge Press, London.

Nielsen, J (ed) (1989) *The Rushdie Affair: A Documentation*, research papers: Muslims in Europe, no 42. Centre for the Study of Islam and Christian–Muslim Relations, Birmingham.

Nizami, F A and Browning, D G (1989) letter to *The Times*, 22 February.

NUT (1991) *Gulf War: the Impact on Schools. Union Advice*, NUT, London.

Parekh, B (1990) 'The Rushdie affair and the British Press', in: CRE *Free Speech*, Commission for Racial Equality, London.

Peeran, A (1991) 'Saddam taunts follow pupils to school', *The Muslim News*, 15 February.

Qureshi, S and Khan, J (1989) *The Politics of Satanic Verses: Unmasking Western Attitudes*, Muslim Community Studies Institute, Leicester.

Rawls, J (1972) *A Theory of Justice*, University Press, Oxford.

Ruthven, M (1990) *A Satanic Affair: Salman Rushdie and the Rage of Islam*, Chatto and Windus, London.

Sarup, M (1986) *The Politics of Multiracial Education*, Routledge and Kegan Paul, London.

Selbourne, D (1991) 'The intellectual battle', *The Sunday Times*, 27 January.

Spears, A K (1978) 'Institutional Racism and the Education of Blacks', *Anthropology and Education Quarterly*, 9, 2, 127–136.

Strike, K A (1982) *Liberty and Learning*, Martin Robertson, Oxford.

Troyna, B and Carrington, B (1990) *Education, Racism and Reform*, Routledge, London.

Webster, R (1990) *A Brief History of Blasphemy: Liberalism, Censorship and 'The Satanic Verses'*, Orwell Press, Southwold.

Wellman, D T (1977) *Portraits of White Racism*, University Press, Cambridge.

White, J (1987) 'The quest for common values', in Haydon, G (ed) *Education for a Pluralist Society: Philosophical Perspectives on the Swann Report*, Bedford Way Paper 30, Institute of Education, University of London.

Chapter 4

Rottweilers and Racism – Notes and Stories Towards Ethical Resistance

Robin Richardson

Abstract

How to act ethically when one's opponents and critics appear to have no such scruples, and when moral principles may then be defeated by brute force, or by manipulation and deceit? This is a recurring dilemma in all social contexts and at all times, but is particularly pertinent in the British education system at the present time: for the opponents and enemies of race equality initiatives frequently seem to use tactics which involve disinformation and dishonesty, and disdain for established procedures of fairness and rational debate. This chapter describes three sets of events where this dilemma was present: an attack on a primary school in East London; an attack on an LEA race equality initiative; and an attack by politicians on one individual LEA officer. It concludes by briefly setting out six principles to guide ethical resistance to such attacks: the avoidance of demonising; the value of social fabric; the concept of the just community; the principle of holism; the importance of narrative; personal risk taking.

Introduction

A cat and her kittens were walking along a city street, miaowing and purring softly and gently to each other as cats are wont to do. Arriving at a street corner, they found themselves face to face with a rottweiler dog. He looked to be a particularly savage and psychopathic specimen of his breed, and had every appearance of being about to massacre and devour the whole cat family in one single fell snap of his jaws. 'Woof!' said the mother cat to the rottweiller. 'Woof! Woof! Woof!' The rottweiler stared at her in amazement, then turned on his heels, and fled in terrified panic as fast as his paws would take him. 'You see, my children,' said the mother cat, turning to her kittens, 'it's very valuable to be able to speak a second language.'

The story introduces some of the main themes of this chapter. The pattern of the chapter is as follows. First, there will be brief recollection in abstract terms of what 'rottweiler' behaviour involves when the metaphor is used to refer to unprincipled and unethical behaviour by politicians and officials. Second, and mainly, there will be three narratives. These will be about, respectively, an attack made by politicians and the media on child-centred education at a multiracial school in East London; an attack made by politicians and the press on a race equality programme in the London Borough of Brent; and an attack made by politicians on myself. In all three instances the attacks by politicians were supported and assisted by officials in local or national government who colluded with the politicians' disdain for customary conventions of courtesy and propriety. Third and finally, there will be some reflections on how such behaviour by politicians and officials may appropriately – that is, ethically as well as effectively – be opposed and resisted: for clearly it is important to devise ways of resisting, opposing and defeating such behaviour without being merely deceitful and manipulative oneself.

Dangerous dogs gripped the popular imagination in Britain at much the same time in cultural history that the 'evil empire' of Eastern Europe was collapsing, and they were perhaps pressed into service by the popular media as alternative devils or demons, all the more insidious for being an enemy within. They also provided, for many people working in or with local education authorities, a powerful metaphor to describe certain kinds of unprincipled behaviour by politicians and senior officers.

This unprincipled behaviour was marked by, in particular, the use of brute force to implement decisions, with little or no respect paid to the need for reasoned debate, due process, professional ethics and integrity, and careful consultation. The effect of such behaviour was often to undermine and weaken, and perhaps indeed to destroy, a whole range of activities, projects and practices which had been designed and brought into being to combat institutional racism and to promote race equality. Certain politicians made no secret of the fact that their conscious motivation was indeed the destruction of antiracism and of initiatives to create and maintain greater race equality. Officials, however, as distinct from politicians, have shown their opposition to antiracism not through their explicit statements but through their silences, collusions and non-actions. Their operations have been characterised by, in a word, carelessness.

The moral life, Maxine Greene (1990) has argued, is marked by attentiveness and concern, and by mindfulness and care. She quotes John Dewey: 'Mind is care, in the sense of solicitude, anxiety, as well as of active looking after things that need to be tended: we mind our step, our course of action, emotionally as well as thoughtfully.' Also, it might be added, we mind the shop: which is to say in the present context that we have had entrusted to us certain procedures of rational debate, decision making and courtesy, and our first task is to maintain these in good repair for the sake of those who will in due course replace us. Maxine Greene recalls some words by the narrator of *The Great Gatsby* about two of the novel's main characters, Tom and Daisy Buchanan:

> It was all very careless and confused. They were careless people, Tom and Daisy – they smashed up things and creatures and then retreated back into their money or their vast carelessness, or whatever it was that kept them together and let other people clean up the mess they had made. (Fitzgerald, 1926)

Greene adds that it is not accidental that Tom Buchanan is fascinated by crude racialist ideas, and that from time to time in the novel he warmly, but casually, commends beliefs about white supremacy. It was white people, he says at one point, who 'produced all the things that go to make civilisation – oh, science and art and all that'. Carelessness is not the same as racism, nor is the use of brute, unreflecting force, but often these three go together. In the narratives which follow we shall see these three in a variety of combinations. In the first narrative, relating to Culloden Primary School in East London, we shall see how a savage and politically motivated attack on child-centred education was carelessly assisted by members of Her Majesty's Inspectorate.

Attacks on child-centred education

In 1990 Culloden School welcomed television cameras into its daily life, to capture on film the realities of its work. Six programmes were then shown at peak viewing times in the spring of 1991. These were praised by critics across the whole spectrum of the press, and the school received many supportive messages from all over the country from teachers expressing relief that, at last, some of the realities of their professional lives had been made visible to a wider audience. The *Daily Telegraph* (15.1.91) observed that 'numbers of our state schools could do with a vast dose of many of the ideals observed at multi-racial Culloden Primary', and *The Times* commended the school's approach to discipline: 'Traditionalists may blench at small children calling teachers by first names, but not at Culloden's commitment to discipline. (The headteacher) is no libertarian trendy . . .'. An article in *The Teacher* (January 1991) commented that

> Culloden works because the staff work hard. Despite the fact that the children come to school with a variety of problems and difficulties, the vast majority thrive in its warm, secure atmosphere. Reading levels are high and discipline problems relatively few . . . Culloden's success is the result of treating the children as responsible equals while making it clear that certain behaviour – such as racism, sexism and bullying – will not be tolerated.

Culloden is a multiracial, multicultural, multilingual school, which takes very seriously its commitment to building and maintaining race equality, and to confronting and challenging all kinds of racism, including the East End racism which children sometimes enact and encounter in the playground. Its commitment to equality is part and parcel of its overall child-centred philosophy of education, and is therefore also integrally related to many other basic values and commitments. For example, it adopts the 'real books' approach to the teaching of reading, as distinct from a 'reading scheme' approach, as indeed do very many inner-city schools throughout the country, not only because real books are a better basis for real and abiding literacy but because virtually all commercial reading schemes fail to reflect adequately Britain's multiracial, multicultural nature, and therefore present false or misleading images and messages to the pupils. It follows that attacks on Culloden's overall philosophy are in effect attacks on, among other things, its commitment to equality. More generally, critiques of 'progressive', 'caring' primary education in Britain as a whole may also be attacks, in intention or in practical effect, or both, on multicultural education and education for race equality.

The attack specifically on Culloden culminated in a full inspection of the school by

Her Majesty's Inspectorate.[1] With regard to the overall inspection process, there were five main areas of concern. The first was to do with the reasons which were given to the school for the inspection being mounted: the formal letter from the Inspectorate which the school received began with the words 'In view of the much publicised concern about reading standards at Culloden School . . .' This was a reference to a single newspaper article, and to its recycling in one other paper. The article had been based on a procedure which the vast majority of headteachers, teachers and governors throughout the country would surely consider to be totally unacceptable: the paper had arranged, without the slightest consultation with the head and governors, for an unrepresentative sample of pupils to take a reading test, and had then run a story claiming to have 'discovered the real truth' about the school. It is extraordinary that a full HMI inspection was arranged on such a very flimsy basis, and that no reference was made to the much larger amount of favourable press publicity which the school had received, from the full spectrum of educational and political opinion, in connection with the TV documentary series in which it had featured earlier in the year.

A second area of concern related to the way in which the school heard that it was to be inspected: it received the news by seeing mentions in the press, not by receiving a letter or a telephone call from the DES. One interpretation is that this episode was simply due to human fallibility: such lapses of courtesy and consideration can happen in almost any organisation, and can be forgiven. Another interpretation, however, inevitably more plausible and persuasive in view of what subsequently happened, is that this lapse of good manners implied a massive lack of straightforward professional respect and care for the governors, head and staff of the school, and disrespect bordering on contempt for the inner-city community which the school serves.

A third area of concern was similarly perhaps only to do with a forgivable lapse in good manners: but a more sinister interpretation is not only possible in the light of what later occurred but also more plausible. A friend of the school, the Bishop of Stepney, wrote to the DES before the inspection began to request a formal reassurance that the eventual report would not be issued to the press before it had first been presented to, and discussed with, the school governors, as is the usual practice. His letter was acknowledged, but not answered until after the report had been leaked to the press.

Fourth, there was the manner in which the report was published. A booklet issued by the DES in April, 1991, entitled *HMI: its Work and Publications 1991*, stated categorically and without qualification that HMI reports 'are first issued by the Secretary of State to those who are most directly involved, such as the governing body or the LEA. Two weeks later, the report is published and becomes available to the general public.'

This procedure was not followed in the case of Culloden. On the contrary, the report was leaked in advance of publication to the very same newspaper whose testing of an unrepresentative sample of pupils had been cited as the official reason for the inspection being mounted in the first place. Further, the report was issued to the rest of the press two days *before* it was due to be discussed orally with the school governors. In consequence, the vast majority of the governors read about the report in their newspaper before they actually received their own personal copy. All the press reporting was based considerably more, proportionately, on a DES press release than on the report itself, and it was thus through the filter of this press release, which contained various emphases and additional references not present in the actual report, that governors first received the HMI evaluation of their school. This procedure on the part of the DES, coming after everything which had gone before, inevitably implied disdain and contempt for the governors and staff of the school, and for the East End community which the school serves. In these circumstances it was all but impossible for friends, admirers and supporters of Culloden to perceive the HMI report as genuinely independent and professional.

The attacks on Culloden were part and parcel of attacks on primary education more generally. These involved maintaining a false dichotomy between 'real books' and 'phonics', and providing extraordinary disinformation about the nature of so-called real books. In the context of reporting on a statement by the Secretary of State about Culloden, journalists explained that the real books approach involves absolutely no more than 'surrounding children with books and hoping they will read them' (*Daily Mail*, 17 April, 1991); that it merely and only 'encourages children to read by hearing stories and exchanging books' (ibid); and that the sole requirement is that 'children should be left to teach themselves by selecting their own attractive books' (*Evening Standard*, 16 April, 1991). This disinformation was combined with attacks on the professional judgement of teachers and on intellectual research and theorising, with 'trendy' becoming in this regard a widespread term of abuse. Further, there were attacks on any attempt in education to engage with the real world beyond the school gates, or to reflect and affirm the personal and emotional experience of pupils, and of their parents and communities; and on integration and holism, and all kinds of linking and combining, with any attempt to make connections and wholes in education being compared to disgusting and foreign food: merely a 'hotch-potch', or a 'mish-mash'. These attacks on holism and connections within schools derived added strength from being combined with attacks on any attempt to contextualise education within its social surroundings, for example any attempt to make links between education, the labour market and the housing system. In particular, in this regard, there was derision for any claim that 'standards' are related to the wider social context. 'Excuses, excuses, excuses', sneered one journalist when Culloden staff insisted that schools are situated in society, and that schools can do only a little to compensate for poverty, disadvantage, unemployment, homelessness and inequality in wider society. Lastly, of particular concern to practitioners and theorists of moral education, there were attacks on 'caring': the task of schools, it was said, is to teach, and this takes total precedence over concerns for pupils as individuals, and – for example – over projects to combat racism and sexism, or to engage with issues of child sexual abuse.

The attacks were separate from each other, but also they were interwoven, and they gave strength and texture to each other. Certainly their cumulative consequence – and quite possibly their specific motivation – was to question and undermine commitments and ideals relating to race equality and cultural pluralism. The attack on race equality was indirect and coded, however, not explicit. The second narrative to be presented in this chapter is about an attack on antiracism which was entirely frontal.

Attacks on a race equality programme

In summer and autumn 1986, immediately after the local elections in May at which the Labour Party had been voted into power with a large majority, we designed in the London Borough of Brent an initiative which we called the Development Programme for Race Equality (DPRE). It was based on entirely sound and conventional theories about how to promote change in education, but also on the belief that a very major obstacle to raising educational achievement, in a place such as Brent, can be summarised with the shorthand term 'institutionalised racism'. With regard to the management of change, there were eight main principles.

1   The Programme was based on the assumption that the responsibility for raising attainment, and for introducing and managing change aimed at raising attainment, lies with headteachers. The role of DPRE staff was to assist headteachers, and other senior staff. Headteachers for their part are accountable for raising attainment to their governing bodies, and there was explicit reference in DPRE job descriptions to regular reports on progress to governing bodies. We considered it essential that the Programme should be embedded in existing management and accountability structures, and in already well-established procedures and practices for the management of organisational and curricular change.

2   Most DPRE staff were members of the senior management structure of the schools where they were based. This enabled them to have an overview of the schools as wholes, and to contribute to decision making on important cross-curricular and organisational matters. In this respect they were different from Section 11 staff in most other local authorities, who typically are on low salary scales and can make very little impact on whole-school policies and decision making. In order that they could assist headteachers with management and coordination tasks DPRE staff did not at the outset of the Programme have direct contact with pupils for more than about 40 per cent of their time. This proportion was similar to that of other staff of comparable seniority and responsibility. Later, they had considerably more contact time.

3   The DPRE reflected the conclusions of international 'school effectiveness research', which has shown that raising educational attainment requires, simultaneously, three main kinds of development: curriculum development, teacher development and organisational development. These three separate but overlapping and interacting dimensions of change were expressed formally, as follows, in various early documents:

- *Curriculum development* – The development of new subject-matter, topics and materials, and of new practical classroom methods and approaches.
- *Staff development* – The development of new perspectives, skills and expectations amongst teachers, both as individuals and also as teams, groups, departments and whole staffs.
- *Organisational development* – The development of new practices, procedures and customs, for example in decision-making, and in relationships between schools and the wider community.

4   The DPRE staff worked in practice mainly through participation in team planning, and through collaborative or tandem teaching. These processes have been shown throughout Britain in recent years, and indeed in many other countries also,

to be extremely effective ways of promoting and supporting change in schools aimed at raising attainment. For example, these are the two main ways in which DES educational support grants for raising attainment in primary mathematics and science have been used. In addition, DPRE staff taught on their own as well as collaboratively. Their role in this respect was not only to have an immediate impact on pupils' learning but also to develop modules, materials and examples which could be adopted by other staff.

5   There was a focus on classroom pedagogy. One of the main conclusions to be drawn from the last 30 years of curriculum development and improvement is that we do not change what pupils learn merely by changing what teachers teach. For what really makes a difference is not the 'what' of teaching, the content, but the 'how', the pedagogy and process. The key practical tasks are to do with enabling each individual pupil to engage successfully and perseveringly with the concepts and principles which are to be learnt. This means paying close attention to the relationships between teachers and pupils, and the quality of the interaction between them. Also, and just as importantly, it involves attending to the quality of relationships between pupils.

6   A distinctive feature of the DPRE was the close relationships which it was expected to develop with advisers (later known in Brent as inspectors), advisory teachers and other support services. The overarching policy framework for all work by these groupings, as for all Brent schools and colleges, was outlined in a major document entitled *Equality and Excellence*, first published in summer 1987. The fundamental intention was that the Programme should not be marginalised within the LEA as whole, as so often happens with Section 11-funded services in other parts of the country, but on the contrary that it should be strongly integrated with all other services and agencies working from outside schools to promote and support change.

7   Particular care was taken to support the learning and professional development of DPRE staff. An assistant head of the programme had responsibility for overseeing this aspect of DPRE activities, and there were three in-service tutors. The immediate purpose was to provide moral and professional support, and in this way to benefit the schools where DPRE staff were working. The longer-term purpose was to help staff return, in due course, to mainstream posts. In this latter respect, incidentally, the Programme was extremely successful: more than 9 in 10 of the DPRE staff subsequently gained promotion to more senior and responsible posts, virtually all in the mainstream of education (as distinct, that is, from Section 11 posts), and are now working as headteachers, deputy heads, inspectors, advisers, senior lecturers and so on.

8   There was the matter of dual accountability. DPRE staff were to be catalysts and agents of change, but also were, of course, expected to respect, and to adapt to, the specific circumstances, history, traditions and personalities of the schools where they worked. In order that they could take on successfully these two complementary, but at times perhaps contradictory, sets of tasks, it was essential that they should be able to receive guidance and support from outside the school where they were based. Among other things, such external support and guidance enabled there to be certain consistency between projects and initiatives in different schools. Thus staff had a dual accountability – both to headteachers for their day-to-day work and also to the head of the programme for overall policy issues. Such dual accountability in the case of the

DPRE was precisely analogous, incidentally, to that which exists in all other support services.

DPRE's formal statement of aims was as follows:

To enable schools to develop methodologies, structures and curricula which will improve the attainment and life-chances of black pupils, and thereby create greater race equality.

A few days after the main body of staff had been interviewed and appointed in October 1986, the media descended on us with a hysterical campaign about 'race spies'.[2] The attack was led by the *Mail* newspapers, with headlines such as 'Cashier these Commissars', 'The Force that Drives the Trots' and 'This Most Evil Force in Britain'. But also prominent in the hysteria were *The Sun*, which parodied itself with the rhythmic and alliterative headline 'Spies in Class to Snoop on Sir', the *Express*, which pleaded 'Save us From this Epidemic of Nitwits', and the *London Standard*, which ran a headline 'Race Spies Like the Days of Hitler'. These and several other papers referred to Orwellian 'thought-police', and most used the term 'evil'. The recurrent subliminal imagery was of East European authoritarianism, an evil and alien empire taking form in Britain only a taxi ride from Fleet Street. What was particularly evil and sinister about Brent, the papers implied, was that the borough was run as much by black people as by white.

A cartoon in the *Daily Mirror*, for example, showed clearly some of the real battle lines. Brent has more black people living within its borders than any other local authority in Europe, and more black people involved in the political leadership. The *Daily Mirror* portrayed Brent Town Hall as a Native American tepee, and showed Brent councillors as half-naked savages brandishing tomahawks, and dancing in heathen ecstasy round a white sacrificial victim. Some of us received obscene anonymous letters and death threats, and these, too, showed totally clearly that one of the forces expressed and released by the media scare was a most virulent and primitive kind of racism. Brent was demonised by right-wing politicians and the press, to the point of becoming a kind of Bonaparte figure. 'Eat up your greens', said a parent to a child in a cartoon in *The Guardian*, 'or Brent Council will get you'. The eventual outcome was that the DPRE never recovered from its savaging by the media, and that it dwindled in due course to an ignominious close, its last remaining members of staff being made redundant by a Conservative-led Education Committee.

Attacks on an individual

At the same meeting of the Education Committee on 7 August, 1990 the post of chief inspector was deleted, and the postholder was made redundant. There was no public debate or discussion, and no formal vote was taken. No reasons for the decision were given. On 1 October the case was reopened. At the meeting of the Education Committee on that day there was a debate as to whether the post should be reinstated. The Liberal Democrats voted with the Tories, and by a majority of 19 votes to 15 the original decision made on 7 August was confirmed. It was again the case, however, that no reasons were given as to why this post, as distinct from any other post, should be deleted. I shall describe the events as dispassionately as possible, and as if I was not personally involved. However, the person who held the post of chief inspector was myself, and the neutrality in the account which follows may appear, or may indeed be, merely disingenuous.

Very considerable concern was expressed by headteachers about the Education Committee's decision. Formal letters were written to the Committee on behalf of all 13 secondary heads, and of all 69 primary heads. The secondary heads wrote as follows:

> We are deeply concerned that the post of Chief Inspector has been deleted. We believe that a strong inspectorate is vital to the development of national initiatives and the maintenance of educational standards. Proper leadership of the inspectorate is essential to this process and we are firmly of the view that the post of Chief Inspector should be retained.

The letter from primary heads included the following points:

> We as primary school headteachers are disturbed and concerned by the proposed decision of the Education Committee on 7th August to declare the post of Chief Inspector redundant. We view this cut as a direct cut to schools, as the Chief Inspector's role involves direct support to schools. We perceive the thrust of the Chief Inspector's responsibilities to be teacher and school orientated, to be continually involved with headteachers and their staffs in the professional management of the service rather than administration. A clear management structure in the inspectorate service is essential for adequate representation of the Authority at DES, national and local level . . . The absence of a clearly defined leader within the structure is not conducive to sound management and support.

Neither of these letters received an answer.

The Brent Head Teachers Association (BHTA) passed a unanimous resolution at its Annual General Meeting calling for the reinstatement of the post:

> The BHTA firmly believes that there is a continuing need for the post in its present form. It is one of critical importance to the efficient service in Brent and will continue to be so. . . . The BHTA was also critical of the complete lack of consultation with Heads in the process that led to such a decision being taken. Head Teachers are managers of the education service and should be consulted on any aspect of the administration of the service that will have bearing in the schools.

Similarly this letter was never answered.

The general secretary of the National Association of Inspectors and Educational Advisers (NAIEA) criticised the Education Committee's decision on the grounds that every LEA needs a chief inspector or adviser, and wrote also as follows:

> The procedure adopted by the Authority has not been, in my opinion, in accordance with normal industrial relations legislation, nor has it been in accordance with the principles of natural justice. There was no prior discussion with either the individual most affected or the Association about the potential

redundancy, and it would be surprising if the decision reached were not deemed to be unfair.

The arguments in the Association's letter were never answered.

Under the provisions of the Employment Protection Act 1975 and the Employment Protection Consolidation Act 1978, the normal and proper procedure, before posts are deleted and before postholders are made redundant, is for objective and reasonable criteria to be established. Further, the procedures for the application of these criteria have to be published, and trade unions have to be formally consulted both about the proposed criteria and about the proposed procedures. In this instance Brent Council did not state publicly any objective criteria according to which the post of chief inspector might be considered to be unnecessary and redundant, nor any procedures for the application of such criteria. Nor did it engage in even the slightest kind of consultation with the trade union to which the chief inspector belonged, in the sense in which the concept of consultation is defined by good industrial relations practice. The Council, was, however, formally reminded by its Director of Personnel and Industrial Relations, at its meeting on 6 August 1990, what the normal and proper procedures of good industrial relations practice are. Here are some brief extracts from official documentation, and brief notes on the ways in which the procedures were flouted in the case under consideration:

> Consultation means jointly examining and discussing problems of concern to both management and employees. It involves seeking mutually acceptable solutions through a genuine exchange of views and information (Paragraph 65 of the Code of Practice issued under section 6 of the Employment Protection Act 1975).

Absolutely no consultation, in this sense, was at any stage attempted either with the chief inspector or with his professional association.

> In considering the reasonableness of a redundancy dismissal where a selection has to be made between those who are to be retained and those who are to be dismissed, the most important matter on which the employer has to satisfy the tribunal is that he acted reasonably in respect of the selection of the particular employee. That normally involves two questions, namely whether the employer adopted reasonable criteria for selection, and whether those reasonable criteria were reasonably and fairly applied in respect of the individual. (Employment Appeal Tribunal 1982, *Williams and Others* v. *Compair Maxam Ltd*, p 163)

No attempt was at any stage made to consult the chief inspector or his professional association about (a) the criteria for selection or (b) the procedures for applying the criteria; further, the criteria used by the employer were not communicated to him or to his association, nor was any information provided about how they were applied.

> When . . . a basis of selection is to be used which is open to the possibility of being influenced by over-subjective assessments, or even sheer prejudice, on the part of the person making the choice, it is important that management be able to show that they took sufficient steps to make their decision as objective and unbiased as possible. . . . In any selection for redundancy elements of personal judgement are bound to be required thereby involving the risk of judgement

being clouded by personal animosity. Unless some objective criteria are included, it is impossible to demonstrate to an employee . . . that the choice was not determined by personal likes and dislikes alone. (ibid, p 166).

Since no pre-ordained and objective criteria were ever provided, there were indeed suspicions that the decision to cut the post was influenced or clouded by 'over-subjective assessments', 'prejudice', 'personal animosity', and 'personal likes and dislikes'. In particular there was widespread speculation that the post had been cut as retribution for the postholder's association over the years with projects and publications promoting antiracist education. For example, he had a few years previously published a satirical article criticising the Education Reform Act as likely to increase inequality in society and the education system (reprinted in Richardson, 1990), and had played an active part in a successful campaign to maintain in existence the Berkshire policy papers on education for racial equality.[3] Further, he had been very involved, along with the Education Department's race relations adviser, in designing and trying to defend thh DPRE. Perhaps most seriously of all, from the point of view of leading politicians, he was the figurehead of a radical and extremely committed and skilful Inspection and Advice Service, and this was very considerably more concerned with issues of equality in education, particularly race equality, than leading politicians deemed appropriate.

Principles of ethical resistance

The attacks on Culloden School, Brent's DPRE and the post of Brent's chief inspector were characterised, to repeat and summarise, by various kinds of irregularity and lack of care. How should such attacks be resisted? First, in answer to this question, it is vital to emphasise that if at all possible we do indeed have to find ways of resisting which are not similarly, in their own turn, unprincipled and unethical. Otherwise, there is no real gain; the likelihood is merely, as Yeats (1934) said in a famous brief reflection, that beggars will change places while the lash goes on:

Hurrah for revolution and more cannon-shot!
A beggar upon horseback lashes a beggar on foot.
Hurrah for revolution and cannon come again!
The beggars have changed places, but the lash goes on.

This is a pragmatic point in the first instance rather than a principled one: the wrong means actually prevent you from reaching the right ends.

I shall close with six main suggestions about the features of a resistance movement which tries to embody within itself the principles for which it is fighting.

1   There is a need to avoid demonising the enemy. Certainly the right-wing press has demonised Asian and Black politicians and leaders, together also with a number of individual officers; and the onslaught on 'trendy', 'progressive' teachers has similarly been characterised by a demonising tendency. But that is no excuse for the rest of us to demonise the Right. The avoidance of demonising has two aspects: the acknowledgement of faults and findings within one's own ranks, and the parallel acknowledgement of sincerity and insight among one's opponents. The journal *Marxism Today* provided, through the late 1980s, many examples of these two

acknowledgements: without losing its commitment to equality and social justice, it pointed out glaring weaknesses in the practical applications of municipal socialism, and acknowledged that many of the institutional reforms advocated by, for example, right-wing libertarians, are not intrinsically and necessarily antisocialist in their effects.

2   It is important to attend not only to social justice as a value but also to social fabric. The distinction has been outlined as follows:

> There might be a danger in trying to make a fetish of social justice, in the belief that a good society must conform to some logical criterion of distributive fairness. The more serious problem, it might be argued, is the creation of a social fabric which allows an abundance of moral space; a fabric which is based on a trust between persons who recognise, despite all their outward differences, the value of each other's personhood, and carry this through with skill and insight. Pervasive forms of domination, or grossly inequitable distributions of the burdens and benefits of social existence, make the existence of such a social fabric impossible because of the deformation of persons that is entailed. Social justice, then, . . . is not to be regarded as an ultimate end; rather, the lack of it is to be avoided, because otherwise moral space is impossible to sustain. (Kitwood, 1990)

The author of these words, Tom Kitwood, explains the concept of moral space as being to do with two or more individuals giving each other free attention. 'To give free attention is an art, demanding honesty and awareness', he writes, and involves cultivating the 'skill of seeing, meeting and respecting the being of each unique other, in treating his or her subjectivity as of equal value with one's own.' Three points emerge from these recollections of social fabric and moral space: our opposition to 'rottweilers and racism' (to use an admittedly demonising and simplifying shorthand phrase) has to be based on a desire to protect and maintain social fabric as well to redress any particular injustice; at the very least we have to find ways of protecting and maintaining social fabric in our relationships and dealings with each other; and at best we have to find ways, as for example Gandhi did, of giving free attention to our opponents even while resisting critiquing and confronting them.

3   It is important that certain principles should be embodied within our own spheres of action and responsibility, such that the base, so to speak, for our resistance is as strong and as inwardly coherent as possible. It is important, for example, that schools and other institutions (including local education authority bureaucracies) should have the characteristics of a just community:

> The new questions are:
> How do you get individuals to commit themselves to a group and to have a sense of their own identity as part of a group?
> How do you promote values that are shared by the group?
> How do you establish group norms and the expectation that the individuals will support and enforce these norms?
> How do you build a sense of identity with the group?
> How do you establish behaviour that will contribute to group goals and give support to individuals? (Rest, 1989)

4   There is the moral imperative of holism. Curricula which we design, promote, deliver or evaluate should be holistic, and in this way should resist the reductionist requirement of right-wing politicians and journalists that curricular subjects should on the contrary be kept pure and uncontaminated from each other. It follows also that our concepts of moral education need to be enriched by the ethics of caring as well as the ethics of justice. Our discourse (both text and talk) about education should seldom, if ever, be conducted without awareness and acknowledgement of inequalities in wider society – in income, access to and occupancy of decent housing, access to employment and training, health and medical services, and – not least – widespread racial prejudice and discrimination in the labour market, particularly in access to posts in senior management, in the media (through making Asian and Black people invisible unless as problems and threats), and in immigration policies and procedures.

5   We need to recognise the crucial importance of story and narrative. It is relevant in this respect to analyse in some detail the story of the cat family and the rottweiler. It recalls that there is a power imbalance in Britain between those who speak English as their first language and those who are speakers of other languages, and that therefore the teaching and learning of English is a sociolinguistic, not merely a linguistic, activity. (*Mutatis mutandis*, this is, of course, true in other countries also. Frantz Fanon (1952) observed that 'the Negro of the Antilles will be proportionately whiter – that is, he will come closer to being a real human being – in direct ratio to his mastery of the French language.') It follows that communicative competence cannot be pursued independently of attention to surrounding contexts, and that there may well be times when it is more urgent to modify or change the contexts than to respond to the 'special or specific needs' (to quote the Section 11 documentation) of individual learners. The story recalls, too, that the moral skills required in situations of unequal power are very similar to, or in practice sometimes indistinguishable from, those which are known as assertiveness. This latter concept was developed for educational work with those who are lacking in power, both personal and positional, but has clear implications for others also, for example senior managers in industry and commerce.

But was the cat in our opening story merely being assertive? Was she not also sly and deceitful, trying to communicate to the rottweiler something which was not actually true, that is, that she was physically dangerous? And do not many similar stories featuring a power differential – for example, particularly obviously, West African Anansi stories – similarly commend subterfuge, trickery and deceit? Can such stories really be valuable in moral education, other than as cautionary tales about unethical strategies?

There are two key questions here in relation to the story of the cats and the rottweiler; the one is about events in the narrative, and the other is about our feelings. Analogous questions can be asked about, for example, Anansi stories. Why, runs the first question, did the rottweiler run away? Why, runs the second, do we find the story satisfying? The answer to the first question is that the dog was frightened by incongruity, and that this incongruity had two separate aspects: (a) the spectacle of a cat speaking like a dog; and (b) the spectacle of a creature standing up to him – someone being assertive. The answer to the second is that our pleasure lies in the cat's inventiveness and ingenuity, but also, and mainly, in the way in which an incongruity is posed and resolved. At first split-second hearing, the cat's explanation to her kittens at the end is incongruous; but almost immediately we realise that there is a deep insight here, into the link between language learning and power.

So actually it is not the case that the cat's resistance is unethical: its qualities are inventiveness; linguistic skill; assertiveness and insight. The story's deep message is that cats are as good as rottweilers, that indeed 'cats are beautiful', that cat pride is a value. It has the qualities which Walter Benjamin found in fairy tales: 'The wisest thing, so the fairy tale taught mankind in olden times, and teaches children to this day, is to meet the forces of the mythical world with cunning and high spirits' (1968).

The story is satisfying not only because it introduces and resolves an incongruity but because, quite simply, it is a story. The genre itself is significant: it derives its power from the brevity and succinctness with which a complex sociolinguistic body of theory and experience is recalled. The pleasure we feel includes admiration for the skill of the storyteller, and reassurance that such skill may be consonant with, and the basis of, the capacity to beat off rottweilers. Thus the sharing of stories – stories about 'real life' as well as fables and parables – is an essential part of the battle against careless bureaucracy and institutionalised racism. (Similarly racism itself is constructed and perpetuated in the media and in daily informal conversations through a series of stylised stories: the immigrants living at the taxpayers' expense; the muggers; the loony left borough; the crazy political leader; the hordes of illegal immigrants battering against Britain's defences; 'swamping'; 'snoopers'; mobs rampaging and rioting; fundamentalists and fanatics; and so on.) It is only if we construct and narrate stories about the operations and strategies of our opponents that we shall be able adequately to resist them, and only if we have accounts and histories of our own endeavours, including our defeats and failures, that we shall have sufficient inner strength and resilience within ourselves, both individually and collectively.

6   Finally, we need, both as individuals and also culturally in our interactions with each other, an awareness and acknowledgement that there will be many setbacks and disappointments, and that many of our successes and victories will be no more than provisional. In Albert Camus's novel *La Peste* the main characters know that their battle against the plague, itself a symbol in the book of injustice and careless collusion with injustice, will be in the last resort 'une interminable defaite', an unending defeat (1947). But 'ce n'est pas une raison de cesser de lutter', that's not a reason to cease struggling. It follows that a capacity to take risks is required of all of us, and of our learners and students. 'It is only,' says Maxine Greene (1990), 'when persons experience themselves as taking risks, embarking on new beginnings, that the predictable gives way to the possible.'

Such risk-taking requires, in its turn, humility and restraint. Scott Fitzgerald's *The Great Gatsby* ends with a recollection of boundless possibilities, but also with an awareness of unending defeat. The recurring dream of humankind, symbolised in European culture for several centuries by the continent of North America, is to be, says Fitzgerald (1926), 'face to face in history with something commensurate to our capacity for wonder'. The novel names and emphasises at the end also, however, and rather, 'the orgastic future that year by year recedes before us', and observes that 'we beat on, boats against the current, borne back ceaselessly into the past'. Such elegiac notes have their rightful place in our imaginations, narratives and discourse. But neither they nor the experiences of failure and disappointment in which they are embedded are 'une raison de cesser de lutter': they are no reason to stop struggling, no reason to stop resisting.

Notes

1 The Culloden School episode of summer 1991 was described in 'Culloden – the real story', *ACE Bulletin*, 41, May/June 1991, published by the Advisory Centre for Education.
2 The press coverage relating to Brent's DPRE is described in further detail in Richardson, R (1992) 'Race policies and programmes under attack: two case studies for the 1990s' in Gill, D, Nayor, B and Blair, M (eds) *Racism and Education: Structures and Strategies*, Sage Publications, London.
3 The campaign is described in my article in *Racism and Education: Structures and Strategies* (see note 2).

References

Benjamin, W 'The Storyteller' in Arendt, H (ed) (1968) *Illuminations*, Harcourt Brace, New York.

Camus, A (1947) *The Plague*, Penguin Books, Harmondsworth, p 108.

Fanon, F (1952) *Black Skin White Masks*, Paladin Books, London, p 13.

Scott Fitzgerald, F (1926) *The Great Gatsby*. Available in Penguin.

Greene, M (1990) 'The passion of the possible: choice, multiplicity and commitment', *Journal of Moral Education*, 19, 2, p 69.

Kitwood, T (1990) 'Psychotherapy, postmodernism and morality', *Journal of Moral Education*, 19, 1, pp 10-11.

Rest, J R (1989) 'With the benefit of hindsight', *Journal of Moral Education*, 18, 2, p 93.

Richardson, R (1990) 'Manifesto for inequality' in *Daring to be a Teacher: Essays, Stories and Memoranda*, Trentham Books, Stoke on Trent, pp 79-82.

Yeats, W B 'The great day', in *Last Poems* (1936-1939).

Chapter 5

On Not Being White in Britain: Discrimination, Diversity and Commonality

Tariq Modood

Abstract

The antiracism which focuses on colour and class is only a partial basis of understanding and opposing racial discrimination. This becomes apparent when one notes that racial stereotypes are rarely about 'black' people as such but about groups such as Asians and West Indians and that we may currently be witnessing the racialisation of Muslims. I draw attention to the 'ethnicity paradox', the idea that social integration is best achieved through secure ethnic identities and argue that diversity can only flourish where there are, as in America, clear means of expressing and affirming commonality. I argue that we need a symbol of Britishness as well as to bring out the common values in what may seem to be alien and divisive cultural forms. I conclude with some implications for education entailed by this ethical perspective.

Introduction

I would like to raise some issues to do with not being white in Britain and having an ethnic identity that most British people, including members of ethnic minority groups, feel is in some sense not properly 'British'. The presence of ethnic identities of this sort in Britain is a legacy of ex-Empire immigration, and, as such, even where they do not evoke direct hostility, they are taken to be identities that need some justification or adaptation if they are to cohere with the more accepted ways of living and belonging in Britain.

These subjects cannot be approached without a discussion of race and racial discrimination. Our concepts of race (which largely means what white people think of those they think are not white) and all that flows from them are powerful determinants of social processes and ethnic identities, but also because forms of opposition to racism can distort ethnic identities and our understanding of ethnicity.[1] I believe this to be the case at the moment, so I shall begin with a discussion of race before going on to the issues of identity and pluralism. In discussing the latter I shall mention some important issues in political theory and ethics which arise out of this discussion but are all too rarely discussed sensibly and are left to the mercy of right-wing tabloid populism such as Norman Tebbit's disparaging of Asians who do not cheer for England in the cricket stands. I conclude by pointing out some of the implications of my view of race and pluralism for educational policy.

Race and racial discrimination

I find that much contemporary discussion is informed by rather simplistic concepts of race and racism which are largely influenced by British sociology and sociology in general (Modood, 1990a). The prescriptive, practical perspective of the sociological outlook often calls itself 'antiracism'; there are more sophisticated forms of antiracism than I will be addressing here, so I will call what I am talking about crude antiracism. I choose to concentrate on the cruder version for I believe it is of some influence in reformist educational and social policy at various levels.

There are two things antiracism brings to the fore but does so rather simplistically:

1 The nature of racial discrimination, which is held to be something that white people do, through actions and social processes, to 'black' people. While 'white' here refers to a self-perception, 'black' refers to what white people ascribe to others, to the victims, who are powerless to resist the ascription.[2] The perception of colour by white society and the significance it places on it is, on this view, the defining feature of race and racial discrimination. It follows that 'black' is not a chosen identity but an identity constructed and imposed by the oppressor. For crude antiracism it does not logically matter whether the victims accept or reject this identity; for all practical purposes, however, antiracists accept 'black' on the grounds that it has the weight of reality behind it: educators are therefore asked to teach 'black culture' to children who may not define themselves as black. On this view of racial discrimination in contrast to the concept of racial discrimination in British law, it also follows that white people can never be the object of discrimination. The critical point, however, is that race and racial discrimination are understood to be about white people's ascription of *colour*.
2 The insistence that racial discrimination does not consist of free-floating prejudice, or merely of individual acts, but of social processes and structures which link up with wider socioeconomic inequalities.

I hope, in what I say below, it will become clear why I regard these ideas as only a partial basis of understanding and opposing racial discrimination.

My own understanding (which accords with the 1976 Race Relations Act, but is not narrowly legal) is that there are different levels and dimensions of racial discrimination (Modood, 1990b and 1992a). The first level is what could be called colour discrimination, for all British studies show that face-to-face discrimination at first encounter is usually on the basis of colour. People whom white people think are white get treated in one way, while people whom white people think are something other than white get treated in a less favourable way. For instance, studies over the last two decades show that in carefully monitored tests one-third of the non-white people enquiring about job vacancies or rooms to let, but not white enquirers, were falsely told that there was no longer a vacancy or a room to let (Brown and Gay, 1985; CRE, 1990). This was vividly illustrated a few years ago by the popular BBC television series 'Black and White', in which two journalists, one black and the other white, went to Bristol in search of jobs and accommodation, using hidden cameras to record what happened. This level of discrimination is the 'ground floor' of what we might call the building of racism: in any case, it is not the building as a whole. The next level up is discrimination to do with class and socioeconomic inequalities, as captured in the concept of indirect discrimination. This form of discrimination takes place when a practice or procedure has a certain requirement, neutral by itself, but whose effect is that some racial groups will be more disadvantaged than others, and when the requirement cannot be justified with reference to, for example, the job. Applicants for a job may be asked for two 'A' levels when this requirement is excessive; this may mean that fewer people from a particular racial group can actually go forward and make the application.[3] In effect, the requirement will screen some groups out, although it is racially neutral in form. Clearly, in a society like ours which is so class-conscious and where the individuals' life-chances depend upon the education they have had, some racial minority groups will have the least opportunities. While white majority people will be affected by class inequalities, certain racial minority groups will be disproportionately affected to a greater degree. Thus, in Britain, with its imperial history of discrimination and oppression, even were colour discrimination to disappear tomorrow at the press of a button, there would still be indirect racial discrimination. The different advantages and opportunities enjoyed by different people and racial groups would continue, simply because they would piggy-back on to the other kinds of inequalities. Historical discrimination, having created a particular socioeconomic profile for racial minorities, is able, unless counteracted, to generate that profile of inequality into the future even if colour discrimination were to disappear. Class inequalities, like the distribution of educational opportunities, are part of what I and the law understand as a source of racial discrimination.

Stereotypes and cultural-racism

My disagreements with crude antiracism begin to emerge more clearly with the third level of discrimination. That is to say, where racial stereotypes begin to operate, so a person is not simply dismissed on the basis of their skin colour, but where people – individuals or groups – are judged in terms of certain stereotypes. Fertile areas for this kind of racial discrimination are job selection into higher education, where one is assessing something over and above paper qualifications or some other objective criteria such as social and personal skills (CRE, 1987, pp 19–21). As far as I know, although much has been said about it, there has only been one serious in-depth, empirical study of how racial stereotypes work in job selection. In his book, *Racism and Recruitment*, Richard Jenkins (1986) undertook a study of middle managers across a range of public- and private-sector organisations. Through interviews, he identified eight stereotypes in the things the managers said (the percentage indicates the number of times this comment came up in the interviews):

1 West Indians are lazy, happy-go-lucky, or slow   4%
2 Asians are hard workers   3%
3 Asians are more ambitious and academic   14%
4 West Indians are aggressive and excitable   12%

5 West Indians mix better with whites	13%
6 Asians are clannish and don't mix	13%
7 West Indians have a chip on their shoulder	11%
8 Asians are lazy, less willing	11%

This list is not surprising, because these are the kinds of stereotypes we would expect. What is interesting, and often goes unremarked, is that none of them is about – to use the managers' favoured terms – 'coloured people'. They are not about 'coloured people' as such, but some other grouping. Stereotypes usually work at some other level than that which I call the ground floor of racism, namely, colour. There has to be another consideration that identifies the group that is being stereotyped. In the above study, what emerges are basically two groups, Asians and West Indians: and what is interesting is that there is only one stereotype that applies to both (cf 1 and 8), and there the votes cast suggest a contrast rather than similarity. Jenkins did not seek to present it in this way, but the stereotypes come across as a contrast between these two groups and the same is found in Mac an Ghaill's study of teachers' attitudes to ethnic minority pupils (Mac an Ghaill, 1988).

Both these studies took place in the mid 1980s and are probably accurate for that time. For I think it is true that during that time in white people's minds, or in the minds of British society as a whole, there were these two groups. It may be that at present a third racial group is being formed: Muslim. Were the exercise with middle managers to be repeated in the mid-1990s, we would probably have three categories. Even though strictly speaking 'Muslim' denotes a religious affiliation yet, as the example of the Jews shows, religious groups can be racialised by how they are treated and by how they come to view themselves. For racism is normally not just unequal treatment on the basis of a difference in physical appearance; there is usually a linkage between a difference in physical appearance and a difference in group attitudes and behaviour. In contemporary settings the linkage is unlikely to be crudely genetic or biological, but is likely to rest on history, social structure, group norms, values and culture. Whole groups of people can be stereotyped in terms of pathological social behaviour, such as trouble with the law, street crime, use of violence and so on. It is easy to see how this form of 'demonising' which received considerable analytical attention at one time can be highly suggestive and, feeding off existing or latent prejudices, can create racist treatment, including policy and institutional response, of the group in question (Hall *et al*, 1978).

Other kinds of group stereotypes that can be associated with colour or differences in physical appearance are to do with a community's structures, norms and values. Whole communities can be objects of suspicion and hate because they are deemed to be backward or illiberal, unduly religious, oppressive of women or unwilling to mix socially with other groups. The price of 'acceptability' may be for minority individuals to exhibit signs of rejecting their origins and disassociating themselves from their communities. France is an example of where this sort of cultural racism can be stronger than colour racism, where the hostility, for instance, against relatively light-skinned Arabs is far more intense and ruthless than against Francophone West Indians and West Africans. Cultural-racism is likely to be particularly acute if the minority community actually, and not just defensively, wants to maintain some of the essential elements of its culture or religion; if, far from denying their difference (beyond the colour of their skin or exacerbated social deprivation) they want to assert it and demand respect just as they are. On the basis of this analysis it comes as no surprise that a recent European Commission survey showed that of all minorities in Britain, Asians are the most disliked (*Today*, 14 March 1990). This was also the finding of Dervla Murphy in her sojourns in Bradford and Birmingham (Murphy, 1987); of a Scottish–Nigerian writer on race in his travels around Britain (Maja-Pearce, 1990, p 72),[4] and most recently of an opinion survey commissioned by the Runnymede Trust (Amin *et al*, 1991).

Indeed, even without reference to the existence of these kinds of aggressive stereotypes, we would have to broaden our concept of racial discrimination. For, if we link the concept of indirect discrimination to ethnic groups, we have a deep concept of ethnic discrimination since our society (and in fact any society) is full of all kinds of ways of doing things (customs, norms, cultural preferences and rewards), which reflect a majority view or that of a particularly prized cultural group. Any group deviating from that norm will find it increasingly and consistently difficult to be able always to meet the requirements of that norm. For example: the day of the week schools and shops should be closed or what counts as acceptable, professional and appropriate clothes, or accent and manner of speech. To be disadvantaged by such norms in virtue of one's ethnicity where the norm is not strictly justifiable (eg by reference to the needs of the job) is to suffer discrimination. Employment, for example, that requires staff to work on Fridays, the day of collective worship for Muslims, but recognises that it is unreasonable to demand work on Sundays, may have no ground of justifiability other than custom, and thereby quite unintentionally creates an obstacle to employment for some Muslims.

It is very important, therefore, to recognise that racial discrimination is not the same as colour discrimination. Colour discrimination is part of racial discrimination, but it is only the ground floor of a bigger building. This is partly why I use the term *crude* antiracism. For crude antiracism tends to overstate the importance of colour discrimination within the whole area of racial discrimination. Moreover, we cannot assume an automatic, necessary or long-term link between racial discrimination and socioeconomic disadvantage; that is to say that the discriminated will occupy a worse position than the discriminators. The link in question is a contingent one. Historically, it has existed at various times but, as we know in the cases of the USA, Canada and Australia, there can be non-white minority groups who exceed (in terms of most socioeconomic performance indicators) the levels of white average achievement. The evidence, while not decisive, suggests that this is or will be so for Indians in Britain, a fact that is usually obscured when data about that group are aggregated with the below-average performance of Pakistanis and Bangladeshis to produce a single Asian figure (Modood, 1991).[5] And yet Indians do not experience less discrimination than other ethnic minorities and may suffer more as they come to be perceived to be successful; in any event, the sociological links emphasised by antiracists will increasingly be seen to be exaggerated.

The final thing which has to be said about discrimination and groups – and discrimination and identities – is that nearly everything I have said so far is about how groups are discriminated against, and, therefore, how white people look at and treat other people. However, ultimately the discriminator, the racist, must not be allowed to have the final word. People cannot be simply what the racists think they are.

People thought to be 'black' may turn round and demand to be recognised as Muslims – with all that that implies for educational and welfare policies. We are probably only at the beginning of a difficult period of adjustment of this kind; to see our way through which we should hold to the idea that it must be part of our concepts of racial equality and the dignity of minority groups that their public identity and their role in British society must come from them and not from the historical perceptions and stereotypes of white people. This principle of primacy of collective self-identity may in some ways seem obvious but it is one which many anti-racists have overridden in favour of the creation of a united 'black' political identity. Mac an Ghaill (1988) is a good example. While in many ways extremely sympathetic to the situation of working-class non-white pupils, 'and insightful into the workings of racial stereotypes', he himself uncritically used a counter-stereotype of what he calls 'the black community'. Indeed, it is only in the last few years that this coercive and unethical aspect of antiracism has been seriously challenged (Modood, 1988 and 1990a).

Pluralism and commonality

At this point I would like to commend a particular view about minorities and pluralism, which some have called the 'Ethnicity Paradox'. This is the idea of integration through pluralism rather than assimilation, as has been observed and advocated in the first quarter of this century by the American sociologists Park and Thomas (Park and Miller, 1921).[6] They made a study of the European and Southern black immigration to such cities as Chicago. The ethnicity paradox refers to their conviction that allowing ethnic communities to take root and flourish in the new soil was the most satisfactory way of promoting long-term integration and participation in the institutions of the wider American society. They argued that not only did immigrant institutions meet the special cultural needs of a community, but also provided a basis of continuity for people who were particularly caught up in severe and destabilising change. More importantly, they were a source of individual self-esteem and status, which otherwise suffered from the sense of devaluation that the immigrant experienced. Moreover, these institutions can enable group pride to develop and lead to a rise in the status and respect for the group as a whole, thereby stemming the need for the individual to disown their origins in order to succeed in the new society where enormous pressure, both overt and subtle, is often put upon minority people to disown their parents and their community origins and adopt ways which damage their sense of self-respect and self-esteem.

Park and Thomas also recognised that ethnic group organisations bring control to areas of urban life that might lack it and, more importantly, give immigrant groups some control over their own adaptation to the new society. Such control allows them to adapt in an atmosphere of relative security as opposed to one of rootlessness and powerlessness, where each individual is forced to come to terms with a new society in relative isolation and thereby does so exclusively in terms of the majority, which can make stronger demands upon individuals than it can upon groups. In many ways the respect that individuals seek is tied up with the respect their group receives, so it is very difficult for individuals to have some sense of their own worth when the group they belong to is being systematically denigrated and devalued. For members of minorities, individual self-esteem critically hangs upon group dignity and group status. Some of the dimensions of the Salman Rushdie affair reflect this kind of besieged insecurity on the part of Muslims who feel they are not valued or respected. They are uncertain how to adapt to the new social and cultural environment in which they find themselves and feel that this adaptation is going to lead, within one or two generations, to the loss of important group identities and values (Modood, 1990c). Forcing people to change faster than they are ready to and faster than the natives are willing to accept is pointless, because assimilation cannot take place when minorities experience rejection. British people, the white majority, must decide to be consistent, because it is the majority which has to do the accepting. Asking the minority to assimilate in the context of widespread racial discrimination is asking for conflict and destabilisation and the fragmentation of communities that are currently the sources of stability, group pride and self-esteem. Even ignoring the question of rights, it is therefore bad social policy to insist upon assimilation. What we really need are new concepts of Britishness.

We could here learn something from the Americans who have come to have a notion of *hyphenated nationality*. They take pride not just in their Americanness but in asserting that they are Irish–American, Black–American, African–American, Greek–American and so on. And when a presidential candidate can make the assertion of being a Greek–American an explicit part of his campaign, it is clear that a hyphenated nationality does not imply that one is only half-American or any detraction from patriotism. Rather, it is seen as the claiming of an ethnic identity within the framework of a common nationality that is open to all forms of ethnic difference that do not challenge the overarching bonds of nation and citizenship. Of course, for reasons of history, power and number, ethnic groups are not equally represented in the compound and changing quality of Americanness, but the nation is not tightly identified by any one, or a limited number of ethnicities. 'British' by contrast is virtually a quasi-ethnic term, and being closely identified with whiteness, it excludes other ethnic terms, so it is not surprising that descriptions such as British Black or British Pakistani are at present not much more than courtesy titles and carry limited conviction. Moreover, people who describe themselves as, for example, British Pakistani often speak of themselves as 'neither one nor the other, a bit of both', whereas hyphenated Americans have no doubt that they are fully American. What we need, therefore, contrary to the reinforcement of ethnocentricity in the national curriculum, are ways to move towards a concept of Britishness that is not frozen in history and identified with only one or a narrow set of ethnicities, such as English, Welsh, Scottish and Irish, but can highlight the grounds of our commonality, past and present, as well as our contribution through our differences.[7]

Those who, like myself, emphasise diversity and pluralism have, however, a particular duty to point out commonalities and how these can be built upon, and it is to this that I would like to attend in the remainder of this chapter.

We need a symbol of belonging

An explicit form of our commonality is our common citizenship, that we are members of the same national state or commonalty. I think we make too little of this and need to give more valued expression to this than we do. We need a demonstrative expression of commonalty and national loyalty that can serve as a symbol of belonging. The Americans have this in the American Constitution and in the acceptance of this constitution as the condition of citizenship. They also insist upon single nationality. Quite contrary to what I was saying about being Greek–American, which is a form of being American, you cannot be Greek and American in the sense of holding a Greek passport and an American passport.[8] For us to have exactly what the Americans have got would be too simplistic because there is genuine value in having dual-nationality for it allows individuals and families to straddle countries and link economies. What is important is that the Americans have had – and recognise the importance of having – the means whereby people can say: 'I, too, am American because I go along with that, so don't tell me about loyalty tests. I am American just like you because there is something we can point to as the basis of our commonality and nationality.' In this sense, Americans are more open to diversity than the British and yet are very definite about there being unity, everyone being able to assert that their being American means more than happening to live inside the borders of the USA. Laurence Fuchs, in a masterful survey of ethnicity in America, celebrates the impulse to diversity in American society, arguing that contemporary America is probably one of history's best examples of a society making diversity work (Fuchs, 1990). Yet an important strand of his argument is that the acceptance of the American Constitution and the political culture that goes with it has been such a powerful vehicle for demonstrating allegiance to America by new groups that it has neutralised the forces of majoritarian cultural intolerance.[9] In short, a demonstrative loyalty to the republic and its constitutional principles created the space for religious and cultural diversity and the visible formation of tight ethnic residential communities and ethnic-origin based interest groups at all levels of American society. Britain is too different from the USA in its political culture, immigration, demography and much else for us to attempt US solutions here in any crude sense. While America has proclaimed itself to be a new world, a country in the making, Britain is what has been called an 'old' country (Wright, 1985). Yet this in itself points us to important issues in ethics and political theory which have hardly been addressed to date. If groups with distinctive historical identities have a right to seek social arrangements which preserve their identities, presumably this applies to majorities as well as minorities. This raises further questions about the nature and extent of rights a society has to preserve various aspects of its culture; which aspects may be buttressed by the state and in particular to what extent may the state education system be used for the purpose of transmitting a particular culture; how are the rights of minorities, in particular their right to preserve their cultural identities, to be reconciled with the previous mentioned rights (assuming there are such rights) and what special safeguards are necessary? Some years ago Bhikhu Parekh pointed inquiry in this direction when, in conjunction with arguing for the need to redefine what it means to be British, he maintained that

> British society, like any other society, has a certain definite conception of the good life to which its members subscribe and which influences the way they live . . . [it] is entitled to insist that everyone of its members, immigrant as well as native must conform to . . . [those] basic, minimal, values . . . that it regards as constitutive of its conception of the good life. (Parekh, 1974, p 229–30).

The value questions that flow from this have hardly been discussed at all or only in terms of a tabloid populism such as Norman Tebbit's notorious 'cricket loyalty test' in 1990. The responsibility for leaving the field open to such political mischievousness must partly lie with those who have failed to raise these issues in a more constructive manner.

There may be some romanticism in Fuchs' view but there is also some sense in the idea that by insisting on adherence to the national ideology that informs the political institutions one makes the commonalty a secure basis for the expression of commonality and thereby takes the pressure off new minorities to exhibit loyalty through sociocultural conformity in everyday life. For ethnic minorities in Britain there is bound to be some attraction in the idea that one Loyalty Test should replace numerous less explicit loyalty tests. For the pressures to conform in Britain are greater than they are in America, even though, admonitions from Home Office ministers notwithstanding, there is little official pressure that people must become 'British'.[10] The pressures are social and cultural rather than legal, political or institutional. On the one hand, we are more culturally intolerant towards minority differences. On the other hand, we are wholly unspecific about forms of loyalty, even at a symbolic level. This is perhaps a result of the English being secure in their own ethnic and national identity and giving little attention to what 'Britishness' means. The Welsh, the Scottish, the Irish are expected to make some adjustments because Britishness is a concept which applies to them, whereas the English carry on being English. Minority and immigrant communities, therefore, face a lack of cultural tolerance alongside an absence of a stated and specified concept of what it means to be British (other than holding a passport). This leaves communities vulnerable: they know they are not respected and yet are given little opportunity to express 'Britishness'. It is sometimes said that 'British' is a term without content, but if this is so it cannot be true only of Britishness but must be true of all such kinds of concepts. Why should not the same problem beset, for example, 'Pakistani'? However, most advocates of multiculturalism do not seem to have difficulty with saying people ought to be allowed to be Pakistani. Moreover, one cannot say both, as is sometimes heard, that Britishness has no content and that it should not be imposed upon minority groups, for that is contradictory. Clearly, various terms can have different content and ranges of meaning, but there is a naivety when native Britsh people rely upon an unstated concept of their own identity, while assuming that to be Pakistani, Greek or Norwegian and so on is unproblematic. This may be a useful kind of political rhetoric on behalf of multiculturalism insofar as it resists the political pressures of assimilationism. Intellectually, it is inadequate.

One possible symbol of belonging is the Crown. My father, a fervent royalist, views the monarch as the symbolic unity of Britain to whom respect must be shown and loyalty given. This ideal is not only held by people of my father's generation. When I recently visited IQRA, a Muslim educational charity in London, I was surprised to find a portrait of the Queen in the entrance hall.[11] Yet, the fact of my surprise was a reflection of our current assumption that the new British minorities are ill-fitted to identify with the historical institutions of the country that they have made their home; that they need to be 'protected' from Britishness. Indeed, there is nothing unusual in Muslims having loyalty to the head of state, whether that person is Muslim or not, when they belong to a particular country. In this sense Muslims (and I use

Muslims as an example) can be fully British; they can actively make a core British institution their own. For this to happen there has, of course, to be acceptance by other British people that the new community is indeed British.[12] The Crown is offered here as no more than an illustration, for the time has probably passed when it could be used as an expression of commonality. If so, it should at least be noted that white British people's preoccupation with colour and with developments such as the European Community have led them to waste the contribution to national integration that could have been played by the sentiment for the Crown that settlers from the Commonwealth brought with them. The point I wish to make is that to talk of symbols of nationhood and the integration of new communities and cultures into an existing ongoing society is not to concede everything to a narrow-minded assimilation. And that the absence of a definition of what it means to be British creates its own problems for new communities that seek acceptance but wish at the same time to preserve areas of difference.

We need to recognise how much we have in common

Despite the American example or, as it may be, the idealised version of it, it is unrealistic to suppose that the burden of community should be placed upon allegiance to the commonalty. Social life cannot be so easily compartmentalised. But nor can social groups. There is fortunately a shared morality despite religious, cultural and other differences when it comes to personal conduct, though, we can be deceived by appearances to believe the contrary. Let me illustrate what I mean by an example that I hope will not be regarded as too quixotic. My father has long been of the view that the idea of an English gentleman comes very close to what the Qur'an requires from the individual and his idea of an English gentleman is not unconnected with the royal family which he sees as a model for his ideals.[13] One of his favourite sayings, however, is 'God made man but a tailor makes a gentleman'. This led to ongoing rows between us over my style of dress, especially in my teens and when I was a student. Some years later – and this is the point of the example – when I was still dressing as a layabout as he saw it, he said to me: 'You haven't turned out too badly.' He came to see that while I did not share his sartorial standards, we shared many common values and that I held some of the standards of conduct that he sought to inculcate. That under my hippie exterior there was courtesy, gentleness in speech and sobriety; there was a commitment to honour one's word and fulfil one's obligations, to not defame others or act out of malice or ulterior motive; and, as a further example, there was a valuing of education for its contribution to one's soul and for the opportunities it gives to serve others less talented or socially fortunate. Common values can therefore belie differences in outward appearance. The example may also illustrate the many cases of inter-generational culture-clash in immigrant families capable of resolution. My example is idiosyncratic but it should not be dismissed.

Recently, I was involved in a programme for BBC Radio 4 and the producer challenged me to take my ideas back to my former school in the London Borough of Brent. It was a secondary modern and in many ways a typical inner-city school. It had always been working class, but when I first went there it was very much a white, working-class school. Now only 10 per cent of the pupils are white and over 50 per cent are from an Afro-Caribbean background. Radio 4 arranged for an 'A' level

English literature class to discuss a passage which I thought embodied some English values, but which it was possible for anyone to make their own. I chose the ideal of a 'parfit gentil knyght', knowing that it would seem remote, and with which the students would find fault and which would immediately raise Muslim hackles – and yet which I believed was capable of appreciation on reconsideration. The passage was from the General Prologue of Chaucer's *Canterbury Tales* and can be summed up in the following extract:

> A Knyght ther was, and that a worthy man
> That fro the tyme that he first bigan
> To riden out, he loved chivalrie,
> Trouthe and honour, freedom and curteisie.
> Ful worthy was he in his lordes werre,
> And therto hadde he riden, no man ferre,
> As wel in cristendom as in hethenesse,
> And evere honoured for his worthynesse.

They thought it was sexist, Euro-centric, Christian-centric, highly classist and harking back to an England that had never existed. I then asked them to tell me their values which they started to list: truth-telling, respect for elders, courtesy, consideration for others, self-control, being true to oneself; interestingly, they blamed the television for too much sex, violence and swearing. For a moment I closed my eyes and could hear my father talking. My point is that multiculturalism must rest on an affirmation of shared moral certainties: it cannot just be about differences. We have a lot in common and must work to bring this out. Some of the moral certainties would be to do with the family, community, religious or quasi-religious ethics. The Swann Report, the major British document on multiculturalism, emphasised the importance of developing a common framework of values (GB, P, H of C, 1985: para 4); while it took too antipathetic a view on the contribution of religious schools to this end (McLaughlin, 1987) and gave no thought to how we were to move from values we *do* share to the values it believed we *should* share if a rational pluralist society is to be established (Halstead, 1988, p 215–19), the emphasis on common values is too much neglected by the Report's admirers and detractors, and needs far more attention than it has received hitherto.

If it was possible for my father to think of me, long-haired, tie-less and in my tight, faded jeans as a gentleman then, although outward appearances may change, there can be a continuity of values. Even at the time when Chaucer wrote the *Canterbury Tales* people would have said that his concept of gentilesse was very aristocratic. He was, however, attempting to lift it out of its social setting and to show it had nothing intrinsically to do with aristocracy. Likewise, it is the case with our concepts of Britishness, Hinduness, Muslimness, Africanness, or whatever else that people think is under threat as an identity in existing contemporary Britain. We have to find a new way of affirming what is worthwhile and of value to us, but which cannot survive in outdated forms without seeming to exclude or create separatism.[14]

The image of old wine in new bottles – although slightly conservative – is not inappropriate for recommending multiculturalism. It is not enough, but nevertheless is an important image. There also has to be creative thinking and synthesis. For instance, the syntheses which come from the perception that Islam, Judaism and

Christianity are not just three religions with a single source, but three traditions within a single Abrahamic faith. This example is for me one of the profoundest and most hopeful of insights in contemporary discussion. The capacity for creative synthesis is crucial but alongside this is the need for an anchor; not just an anchor for Britishness, but also an anchor for minority identities. We need the wisdom to know what we can conserve and what needs to be changed, or even given up. Above all, it is the surface of our cultural forms – like suits and ties – that we have to be ready to change, but at least some of the values they embody will need to be held onto if we are to be a worthwhile society.

Concluding implications for education

We need an educational philosophy which recognises that individuals and communities have a right to be culturally different from their neighbours and to be understood in their own terms and not in terms of racist and antiracist stereotypes. This inevitably means creating a positive awareness of multiculturalism in all pupils, majorities and minorities. This implies a recognition of the inadequacy of an antiracism in education which narrowly focuses on colour and class and fails to engage with cultural-racism. The right to cultural difference also means creating the educational space for minorities to do their own thing. This extends to policy decisions such as the inclusion within the state sector of Muslim and other minority-faith denominational schools where they satisfy the requirements of the national curriculum and of DES standards of efficiency. Those worried by the low educational standards of some private Muslim schools should bear in mind that there is nothing inevitable about this. There are Muslim schools in America which have quickly established themselves as superior to the education provided by the public school system (Haddad, 1986, p 5). In any case if private Muslim or other religious schools are proving to be educationally inadequate that surely is an argument for allowing them into the more regulated sector. There are unlikely to be many such schools but they will meet the needs of the particularly orthodox, remove a community grievance of unequal treatment by the authorities, and, like all educational experiments, provide a resource for the rest of the system to learn from and selectively use. This development carries a risk of communalism which can be countered by the development of some genuine multifaith schools; if such schools are to be more than just nominal Christian or secular schools with multifaith rolls they will need to be part of a larger multifaith movement. Educational rights for cultural minorities also extend to the provision of community languages within the timetable. Giving those children who want it the option of, for example, Urdu instead of French, may be to decrease their subsequent career opportunities in the post-1992 world, but this is a choice that pupils and their parents should be able to make. Yet the aim of multiculturalism as an educational and social philosophy should not be to reinforce separate identities but to give enough confidence to all not to be ashamed of one's ethnic background, to be able to celebrate it while respecting that of others, and, above all, to give to each person enough confidence in their group identity so as to be able to cross boundaries and to share each others' cultures.

If this aim seems contradictory in itself, or with the examples I have given in the previous paragraph, I remind the reader of the ethnicity paradox: one needs a certain amount of conservative autonomy in order to create the psychologically and sociologically secure identities which will be open to change and synthesis and will be able to contribute something of their own to the wider society and not be swamped by it.[15] The pluralism that should be our goal must be open to change and should allow individuals some degree of choice. For not only are most minority individuals bi-cultural or even multicultural but most people do not want to be tied to the culture of their origins or families in accordance with the preconception of others, especially outsiders to that community. Many Asian and black people are at home in and identify themselves with majority British cultural styles and this too is part of a natural diversity. It can be no part of pluralism that individuals are pressed into narrow pigeon-holes which others believe they should be in because of their ethnic origins or appearance.

The right to be culturally different, to be a minority, has, I have argued, to be balanced against the fact of being a society. One of the most basic functions of education is induction into the common society. This must go well beyond the imparting of a standard of English, numeracy and all the other skills necessary for adult employment and basic social survival. It is sometimes suggested that what is needed is preparation for democratic citizenship. While there is something right in this, it cannot be interpreted too abstractly for after all one is talking about *this* democracy and *this* citizenship. Just as American citizenship rests on a particular constitution with its own particular founding myths and a historically developed political culture, so similarly our commonality, our common future, has to be shaped by our understanding of and commitment to our commonalty. Differences can only flourish where one can take a certain amount of commonality for granted: it must be the task of our schools to make both these things possible. To do so is to extend and enrichen our understanding of our Britishness, a sense of belonging capable of embracing a number of hyphenated nationalities; but contrary to those for whom Britishness is a reactionary, meaningless or irrelevant concept, I doubt if progress can be made without taking the concept seriously and engaging with it. Nor can this progress be made without the assistance of the moral and religious traditions that at least partly constitute what we mean by ethnicity. These traditions are not about to fade away and must be co-opted into the classroom as into our social order (Sacks, 1991). They are, underneath their alien and divisive appearance, part of our commonality which is in the making and cannot be ghettoised into some private realm. Together with the challenge of eliminating racism, they offer the basis of a morally strengthened social order. Indeed, these are at bottom not two separate tasks: multicultural education is a significant way to challenge racism, especially cultural racism, by tackling its intellectual and moral roots (Parekh, 1986, p 31). Educationalists have a leading role in moving the perception of ethnic minorities in terms of colour and class to voices in a moral dialogue. They will need to proceed by doing some listening themselves.

Notes

1 This paper is based on a lecture given at a World Congress of Faiths' Conference on Education and Identity in a Plural Society in Birmingham on 30 October, 1990.
2 Of course this is not the only meaning of 'black' in contemporary discourse, it also, for

example, refers to the self-identity of the African diaspora. As the latter usage was established through the American 'Black is Beautiful' movement it is worth noting that in recent years that movement has abandoned the term 'Black' in favour of the hyphenated term 'African–American'.

3 It is now clear that just at the time in the 1980s that it became equal-opportunities wisdom that reliance on academic qualifications in selecting job applicants is discriminatory, Indians and some other ethnic groups were beginning to achieve above-average results in GCEs, especially in inner London. This has now become visible in higher education where in the first year of monitoring, 1990, ethnic minorities, who form about 6 per cent of the 16–24 year olds, secured nearly 8 per cent and 16 per cent of the university and polytechnic places respectively. Some of these groups could well argue that to reduce the importance of academic qualifications as a criterion of selection, without it being strictly necessary in terms of the post to be filled, is to indirectly discriminate against them. Some ethnic minority groups are indeed arguing so in America and it may well become a contention here.

4 He writes: 'this obsessive hatred of people from the Indian subcontinent is paralleled in recent history by a well-known event in central Europe' (Maja-Pearce, 1990, p 72).

5 It is only by so manipulating the term 'Asian' one can write articles with titles such as 'the myth of South Asian Achievement levels' (Tanna, 1990).

6 The term 'ethnicity paradox' is Barbara Lal's and I am indebted to her for my understanding of Park and Thomas; see, Lal, 1983, reworked as Lal 1990. For an alternative and perhaps more conventional reading of Park and Thomas see Kivisto, 1990.

7 Interestingly, while very few ethnic minority, at any rate, Asian, individuals speak of themselves as being English, some Asians in Scottish public life claim they are proud to be Scottish and some are even politically active in the SNP without attracting any of the Uncle Tom opprobrium that their English Asian counterparts would risk.

8 There may now have come to be certain exceptions to this, most notably in the case of Jews who acquire Israeli passports without renouncing US nationality.

9 Fuchs, on a visit to a school in Denver in 1980, pointing to a picture of George Washington on the wall asked a Vietnamese pupil, 'What did he do?' . . . His reply, in the tradition of Mary Antin, 'he was the father of our country', came as no shock to the other children or teachers standing close by. His claim to membership in the American polity was taken as a matter of fact, a situation that probably could not have occurred in any other country in the world (Fuchs, 1990, p 358).

10 See, for example, the letter of 4 July 1989 from John Patten, Secretary for State at the Home Office, to Muslim leaders, together with a Muslim response (Ahsan and Kidwai, 1991, p 321–30). The following from the latter, incidentally, is a good example of 'the ethnicity paradox': 'While we acknowledge that we have responsibilities to the society we live in, we feel that these responsibilities will be better discharged if the community's need to preserve its ethos is recognised and if the facilities and where necessary the legal provisions for doing so are accorded, not grudging or as a result of a process of attrition, but willingly and in a spirit of goodwill and harmony' (p 327). See also Asad (1990) for a penetrating analysis of Home Office anxieties about assimilating Muslims into some core features of Britishness.

11 The Arabic word 'iqra' means 'recite' and is the command by which the archangel Gabriel's revelation to Muhammad began.

12 I believe that legal protection against incitement to hatred and group defamation is necessary for Muslims and other minorities to be symbolically and actually accepted and made a part of Britain (Modood, 1992b).

13 My father's views on British morals are less rosy today than they once were (Modood, M

S, 1990, p 92–3). Such views are relevant to the reservations Muslims and others have about assimilation.

14 Some descriptions of minority cultures that educationalists are asked to consider are superficial (of the 'steelbands, saris and samosas' variety); for an antidote, see Christie, (1991).

15 The term 'conservative' should not mislead; compare Susan Mendus' view that a socialist conception of tolerance must welcome people's ethnic and other group loyalties, for while socialism aims to create new solidarities, it sees a sense of belonging as an important value in itself (Mendus, 1989, pp 154–62).

References

Ahsan, M M and Kidwai, A R (eds) (1991) *Sacrilege Versus Civility: Muslim Perspectives on 'The Satanic Verses' Affair*, the Islamic Foundation, Leicester.

Amin, K, Gordon, P and Richardson, R, (1991) 'Race issues opinion survey', *Race and Immigration*, 247, pp 1–4.

Asad, T (1990) 'Multiculturalism and British identity in the wake of the Rushdie affair', *Politics and Society* 18, 4, pp 455–80.

Brown, C and Gay, P (1985) *Racial Discrimination: 17 Years After the Act*, Policy Studies Institute, London.

Christie, C J (1991) 'The rope of God: Muslim minorities in the West and Britain', *New Community*, 17, 3, pp 457–66.

Commission for Racial Equality (1987) *Chartered Accountancy Training Contracts; Report of a Formal Investigation into Ethnic Minority Recruitment*, CRE, London.

Commission for Racial Equality (1990) *Sorry it's Gone: Testing for Racial Discrimination in the Private Rented Housing Sector*, CRE, London.

Fuchs, L H (1990) *The American Kaleidoscope: Race, Ethnicity and the Civic Culture*, University Press of New England, USA and London.

Great Britain, Parliament, House of Commons, (1985) *Education for All; Report of the Committee of Inquiry into the Education of Children from Ethnic Minority Groups,* (Swann Report, cmnd 9453), HMSO, London.

Haddad, Y (1986) 'A century of Islam in America', The Muslim World Today Occasional Paper no 4, The Middle East Institute, Washington.

Hall, S, Critcher, C, Jefferson, T, Clark, J and Roberts, B (1978) *Policing The Crisis*, Macmillan, London.

Halstead, M (1988) *Education, Justice and Cultural Diversity*, Falmer Press, Lewes.

Jenkins, R (1986) *Racism and Recruitment*, Cambridge University Press, Cambridge.

Kivisto, P (1990) 'The transplanted then and now: the reorientation of immigration studies from the Chicago School to the new social history', *Ethnic and Racial Studies*, 13,4, pp 455–81.

Lal, B B (1983) 'Perspectives on ethnicity: old wine in new bottles', *Ethnic and Racial Studies*, 6, 2, pp 154–73.

Lal, B B (1990) *The Romance of Culture in an Urban Civilisation: Robert E. Park on Race and Ethnic Relations in Cities*, Routledge and Kegan Paul, London.

Mac an Ghaill, M (1988) *Young, Gifted and Black*, Open University Press, Milton Keynes.

McLaughlin, T H (1987) '"Education For All' and religious schools' in Haydon, G (ed) *Education for a Pluralist Society*, Bedford Way Papers 30, Institute of Education, University of London.

Maja-Pearce, A (1990) *How Many Miles to Babylon?*, Heinemann, London.

Mendus, S (1989) *Toleration and the Limits of Liberalism*, Macmillan, London.

Modood, M S (1990) 'My faith: a personal statement' in Gumley, F, and Redhead, B *The Pillars of Islam*, BBC Books, London, pp 90–93.

Modood, T (1988) ' "Black", racial equality and Asian identity', *New Community*, 14, 3, pp 397–404.

Modood, T (1990a) 'Catching up with Jesse Jackson: being oppressed and being somebody', *New Community*, 17, 1, pp 87–98.

Modood, T (1990b) 'Colour, class and culture: the 3 Cs of race', *Equal Opportunities Review*, 30, pp 31–3.

Modood, T (1990c) 'British Asian Muslims and the Salman Rushdie affair', *Political Quarterly*, 61, 2, pp 143–60; also in Donald, J and Rattansi, A (eds) (1992) *'Race, Culture and Difference'*, Sage, London.

Modood, T (1991) 'The Indian economic success: a challenge to some race relations assumptions', *Policy and Politics*, 19, 3, pp 177–89.

Modood, T (1992a) 'Cultural diversity and racial discrimination in employment selection' in Hepple, B and Szyszczak, E (eds) *Discrimination: The Limits of Law?*, Mansell, London.

Modood, T (1992b) 'Muslims, incitement to hatred and the law', in Horton, J (ed) *Liberalism, Multiculturalism and Toleration*, Macmillan, London.

Murphy, D (1987) *Tales from Two Cities*, John Murray, London.

Parekh, B (ed) (1974) *Colour, Culture and Consciousness*, Allen and Unwin, London.

Parekh, B (1986) 'The concept of multicultural education' in Modgil, S, Verna, G, Mallick, K and Modgil, C (eds) *Multicultural Education: The Interminable Debate*, Falmer Press, Lewes.

Park, R E and Miller, H A (1921) *Old World Traits Transplanted*, Harper, New York.

Sacks, J (1991) *The Persistence of Faith: Religion, Morality and Society*, The Reith Lectures 1990, Weidenfeld, London.

Tanna, K (1990) 'Excellence, equality and educational reform: the myth of South Asian Achievement levels', *New Community*, 16, 3, pp 439–68.

Wright, P (1985) *On Living in an Old Country*, Verso, London.

Chapter 6
Moral Dilemmas of Societal Myth Making

Bruce Gill

Abstract

This chapter examines moral and ethical problems posed by societal 'myth', in particular those relating to views of British national characteristics. It is suggested that the myths serve a necessary function and to that extent are indispensable, but that they require urgent review in the context of a modern multicultural society if social cohesion is to be achieved. It is suggested that a new myth incorporating values and qualities to which the whole of society could relate should actively be created and that education should play a central role in this.

The ethical and moral dilemmas posed by seeking to manage and control this process are considered as are some of the implications of not taking action. Official stances on multicultural education are examined and an assessment made of the likelihood of their being implemented effectively. A rationale for a new myth is offered and an indication given of the range of contributions that would need to be made to the process of generating it.

Myths and multicultural education

An analysis of the sets of values that are commonly equated with 'national identity' raises a range of considerations. One of these is the fact that these values, positive though they may be, nonetheless are selective, and, as such, represent a distortion of reality. Another consideration is that such selective value clusters appear to serve important functions in fostering social coherence and may in fact be necessary elements of any attempt to achieve coherence. The stability and durability of these values over time are just two of the complexities that follow from an analysis of this order when the phenomenon of rapid societal change is taken into account. As one of these changes, the apparent increased cultural diversity in society poses serious questions of its own about the relevance and accuracy of the sets of values and, not least, questions of how competition between oppositional value sets (themselves seemingly intended to achieve social coherence but of a different order) will be resolved.

The implication that the circumstances so described are open to a degree of social management provokes dilemmas around the ethics of deliberately using selective value sets, of actively promoting these and of using education as a main means of effecting this social management. However, a compelling moral imperative may demand that steps of just this kind be taken and be taken urgently.

March 1985 saw the publication of the long awaited Swann Report entitled *Education for All* (GB, P, H of C, 1985). The report had its beginnings in the acute concerns of the black community about the significant numbers of children of West Indian background who were being failed by the schooling system. In 1979 a committee of inquiry was set up by the then government to examine the issues of the educational attainments of children from ethnic groups, the value of instituting arrangements for keeping educational performance under review and to consider the most effective use of resources for these purposes. The terms of reference required all this to be done:

Recognising the contribution of schools in preparing all pupils for life in a society which is both multi-racial and culturally diverse.

The interim report, *West Indian Children in Our Schools* (the Rampton Report, GB, P, H of C, 1981) was published in June 1981 and caused great interest and raised the hopes of the black communities because it openly discussed the belief of those communities that the factor of racism was the major reason for their children's underachievement. The Committee concluded that while racism alone could not account for the underperformance of West Indian children it was nevertheless an important factor.

By its acknowledgement of the factor of racism the Rampton Report became a particularly significant document. Against the background of some controversy there was a change of chairman and the outcome of the final report was eagerly awaited. When it came, the Swann Report received a mixed reception. There was anger and consternation on the part of those who felt that the Rampton position on racism had been undermined and that the 'blame' for underachievement had been shifted to the homes and parents of those children seen as underperforming. There were those who were pleased that such a weighty government tome was at least giving recognition and credibility to an area of education that had long been marginalised. There were others who, for similar reasons, were enraged, castigating the Swann Report for being one of the most subversive documents ever to emanate from a government agency. It is interesting to note that for proponents of this latter position, even to give credence to the tenets of multicultural education, to argue for cultural diversity and racial equality opened one to being cast in the role of 'subversive'.

Against this background, in February 1986 Birmingham Education Committee held a day-long seminar to discuss the findings of the Report as part of the process of producing the first phase of their equal opportunity policy for education. The opportunity for members and officers to discuss openly a major policy initiative of such sensitivity was itself seen by many as both a significant and positive step. Three days before the seminar, however, an article written by a member of the Education Committee and attacking 'multicultural myth makers' appeared in the local press (Coombes, 1986). To those involved in planning and presenting the seminar it was apparent that the article was timed to inflict maximum damage to the key intended outcome of the seminar; namely to establish unequivocally the multicultural education policy in that LEA. The strategy adopted by the member of the education committee attested to the impact politicians can have in wrecking educational policy and the work of education professionals. The article itself is significant not so much in the quality of the arguments it contains but in their widespread credence; the fact that popular assumptions underpin many of the points that are made and that the myths that it addresses (the first explicitly and the second implicitly) are connected by the principle of selectivity on which they are founded.

While the article accepted that the British had a responsibility to see that, 'Commonwealth citizens were free from racial discrimination or lack of opportunity', and conceded that most people might accept the wisdom of monitoring recruitment, providing English language support in schools and perhaps even employing home-school liaison workers and multicultural advisers and inspectors, its attack was directed at what it portrayed as a particular variant of the multicultural lobby.

> At first, Race Relations, or multicultural policy as the educationists call it, was non-contentious and constructive. But recently, the driving out of Ray Honeyford from his head teacher's post and the pillorying of Jonathan Savery of Bristol are clear signs that these formerly balanced racial policies have been hijacked and in many schools are being insidiously replaced by a new unthinking and dictatorial multi-cultural orthodoxy.

The analysis is interesting on a number of counts. First, there is the apparent acknowledgement that multicultural education, at some point in the past, was positive and non-contentious. This raises the further question of why, if this were the case, was multicultural education not taken up more rapidly by schools, colleges, universities, colleges of education and other educational establishments? Indeed Troyna and Carrington (1990) suggest that there are many who might testify that there was clear hostility to the very idea of this constructive and non-contentious development in the early years of its inception.

Second, attention is drawn to cases where individuals have been at the centre of race-related controversies but details of those cases are not provided. Halstead's discussion of some of these controversial cases (see pp 39–56) offers perspectives and interpretations that differ (markedly, one suspects), from those of Councillor Coombes and those projected by the news media. The greater part of the press reporting presented images of an insidious and shadowy 'antiracist lobby', which was overly critical of traditional custom and practice and which either victimised the lone individuals who dared to criticise antiracism or injected conflict and discord into situations where no trouble had existed before. It would be fair to say that this type of negative press reporting of these and subsequent race-related cases had a significant impact in shaping as well as reflecting public views on race and multicultural education.

Third, school policies are seen as being 'hijacked' and 'insidiously' transformed by a 'dictatorial' brand of multicultural education.

It is clear that the attack is being directed at the development of antiracism in education and those upholding the tenets of antiracist education are portrayed as being the 'multicultural myth makers'. At issue is a view of Britain that the antiracists are alleged to promote. Whether the particular characterisation of antiracism is accurate is a matter that merits further scrutiny but this is not my main interest at this point. Rather, I wish to consider mythic dimensions of that article that remain implicit but which are important to its central theses. These dimensions include the sets of values (which, in the main, are ethical qualities) that people ascribe to themselves and the issue of the extent to which these sets accord with reality.

The article opens,

> Modesty may prevent their admitting it, but the British have long been regarded as a pretty tolerant, fair-minded bunch with a genius for sometimes hazy, but generally canny compromise.

At once, we are presented with a view of the essence of being British which indeed is not only widespread but also remarkable in that it so easily passes unquestioned. It is far from clear who, apart from the British themselves, actually view the British in this way.

The 'distinctly British traits' of tolerance, fair-mindedness and compromise are then given as the reason why countless ethnic groups over the centuries have been enabled '. . . to settle here happily'. Difficult questions of who 'the British' are and when, 'over the centuries', did other ethnic groups become absorbed into 'the British', again are not addressed. What is presented is a view of certain social values, seen as persisting over centuries, embodying distinct national characteristics and carrying the implication of contributing to social cohesion.

Antiracism, as characterised in the article, becomes a threat to social cohesion because it,

> pretends you can pull society in Britain together by the arbitrary categorisation and promotion of multicultural groups while studiously avoiding reference to anything that is intrinsically British.

Both cases of myth as presented in the article fail to address the factor of the actual experiences of black people in Britain; what the article refers to as 'the black experience' and disparagingly dismisses as a slogan. It is precisely by addressing the fact of discrimination in housing, employment, policing, the working of the judiciary, immigration policy and in education itself, of racial attacks and harassment that a critique of the selectivity of the 'distinctly British traits' is sharpened and from which antiracist education derives the objective of securing social justice and equality.

The failure of opponents of multicultural and antiracist education to address the facts of the actual experiences of black people in Britain, and the concerns that arise from these, contributes to the situation where myths alluding to an imperial past have to be clung to like straws as the nation struggles to assert an identity in the face of changes wrought by time.

National Curriculum

Discussions about the shape and content of the National Curriculum brought to the surface different threads of the debate about national identity and the role the curriculum should play in achieving social cohesion. Writing in *The Telegraph* in February 1988, Donald Naismith observed that, despite its name, the National Curriculum made no mention of 'love of one's country as a legitimate study'. He equated this with patriotism which he saw as posing the question of personal and national identity. Early in his discussion he identifies what he calls national characteristics:

> distrust of emotion; natural reserve; a preference for understatement; a willingness to allow things to be 'understood' rather than written down.

In his discussion of personal and national identity he adds,

> inseparable in my mind from being British are, on the better side, such qualities as tolerance, willingness to compromise, fairness, seeing the other person's point of view – even taking the newspaper you don't agree with.

The same issue of selectivity is apparent. Here, however, there is an implicit acknowledgement of this. Naismith concedes that these traits are taken from the 'better' side and the reader is left to guess what the other side might contain. He, too, makes connections between Britain's decline and the need to assert a new identity. He attributes the loss of identity to internal and external factors; the growth of internationalism abroad, 'the settlement of many peoples with different cultures' at home, and changes in educational philosophy and practice are seen as playing a part.

He observes with sadness that, since World War II, Britain has quietly repudiated its past and in so doing lost its self-respect. A vigorous intervention is recommended to help remedy the situation.

> The National Curriculum offers an opportunity to reinforce Britain's recovery and to restore a justifiable pride in its achievements. The Government should be bolder in two respects. It should regard the National Curriculum more as a national syllabus, specifying among all the other necessary things, in a balanced way, the contribution Britain has made to history and the world.

Obviously much would hang on the 'balanced' way in which this might be achieved, but the thrust is clear. History, the stories societies tell about themselves, the tales of how they got to be where they are, is seen as central to the process of social identity. But whose story will be used? Will it be her-story (that is, will it reflect women's perspectives and experiences rather than merely his-story)? Whose version of the same events? How will they take account of the racially and culturally diverse context of Britain today? The need for an urgent review and reworking of the stories, myths and telling of history so as to ensure a shared sense of 'who we are' and 'where we have come from' is beyond doubt. Salman Rushdie (1982) makes this observation in pointed fashion in his analysis of the famous victory address made by Margaret Thatcher following the Falklands War. In it she referred to the 'waverers and the fainthearts' who at the start of the war were,

> the people who thought we could no longer do the great things which we once did . . . that we could never again be what we were. There were those who would not admit it . . . but – in their heart of hearts – they too had their secret fears that it was true: that Britain was no longer the nation that had built an Empire and ruled a quarter of the world. Well they were wrong.

Rushdie wryly comments that the 'we' to which Margaret Thatcher referred could hardly have meant black people (who have a different perception and experience of that history) and therefore the speech in a powerful and dramatic sense instantly excludes part of the population from 'belonging' to Britain. But what of the basis on which individuals are asked to see themselves as included? The speech demonstrates an appeal to 'traditional' values underpinning 'patriotic' sentiment, values which reveal strengths and yet frightening limitations.

The increased rate of social change is putting severe strain upon all those institutions and mechanisms that have served to lend a sense of coherence to society. Among these are the myths designed to effect bonding in terms of national identity. Current conditions of change demand that the bonds be redefined to be inclusive of more groups of people. The boundaries which distinguish those who are 'insiders' from those who are 'outside' have to be recast so as to enable society to value and celebrate all its peoples or pursue a path of ostracism and injustice.

The implications of not taking action to achieve this add force to the moral imperative that would demand that myths be managed.

A modern, multicultural society needs to clarify and proclaim the values that unite it and give it a sense of direction and a sense of purpose. Above all, these values need to be appropriate for *all* the people.

The solution to the national identity question advocated by Naismith is the inclusion of civics as a compulsory subject in the National Curriculum, with a view to enabling pupils to identify with their country and the ideals it embodies. He suggests that this might be substituted for religious education which he views as a divisive rather than cohesive force in Britain's multicultural society. Quoting the French approach he notes,

> 'Above all civics is concerned with morality: it develops honesty, courage, a rejection of racism and a love of the Republic. Civics never takes the form of indoctrination or incitement. It invites responsibility: it is always an education for liberty.'

The remarks about indoctrination should not pass without comment. Palmer (1986) contains a collection of articles typifying the arguments advanced in the attack upon multicultural and antiracist education. The titles of some of these ('Here be witches! "Antiracism" and the making of a new inquisition', 'Preference and prejudice: the mythology of British racism', 'Antiracist rhetoric') are illustrative of the main thrust of this opposition which criticises multiculturalism and antiracism for alleged doctrinaire stances and philosophies. This particular point is connoted in the reference to 'dictatorial orthodoxy' in the Birmingham article. In itself this is a many-layered dilemma. Multiculturalists and antiracists have debated and are continuing to debate the morality and ethics of simply supplanting an old orthodoxy with a new. Like Naismith, who notes that the French, too, would place 'teaching pupils to think for themselves' at the top of their educational priorities, so would antiracists. Difficulties arise when 'thinking for oneself' leads one to question authority. Indeed, Naismith himself suggests that education contributed to the weakening of British identity when it

> became more concerned with challenging authority than with its other main purpose of passing on one generation's inheritance to another (1988).

It does not necessarily follow that fostering enquiring minds will cause social fragmentation. Nor does it automatically follow that the act of questioning constitutes unpatriotic behaviour or subversion. However, the fact that there seems to be widespread feeling that this is precisely what would result merits investigation so that the reasons may be examined as to why this should be the case.

People able to think for themselves would not be confined by received knowledge and understandings and would be interested in verifying for themselves what they are told or led to believe. This would apply equally to traditional content as to newer material such as antiracist perspectives. If societal myths cannot stand up to such scrutiny then the structures and belief systems built upon such foundations are indeed likely to fall and fragmentation will occur. The question arises as to whose interests are being served by having structures and belief systems that cannot withstand such scrutiny.

Educationally, this is explosive territory because, despite having the aim of 'teaching pupils to think for themselves' as a priority, there appears consistently to be spectacular failure in providing the requisites for achieving this goal. The failure of the educational system to meet the learning needs of children of African–Caribbean background exemplifies this phenomenon, provoking consideration of: the underperformance of pupils of other ethnic backgrounds, pupils who are working class, and, the unrealised potential of many girls and young women.

The question should perhaps be better put another way. Whose interests might be served by *not* enabling pupils to think for themselves? Is it possible that the main aims of education, as Naismith puts it, are in tension? To what extent is 'thinking for oneself' compatible with receiving the 'heritages' given the way in which these heritages are currently constructed and communicated?

The linguistic paradigm

The suggestion is that values embodied in certain approaches to education have the effect of undermining authority and the established, perhaps traditional, process in which the national identity is formed. Naismith suggests that the identity-forming process is part of the 'hidden curriculum' in which the values school and society share are 'instinctively' understood. He offers study of national heroes, historic events and knowledge of great works of English literature as possible means by which this understanding could be promoted. He is probably correct for multicultural educationists and teachers committed to race equality also cite the 'hidden curriculum' as significant in achieving a non-racist education with a view to challenging Eurocentric, not to mention sexist, world views.

There are however, more explicit examples of the tension between education and authority as lived through the education system. Deborah Cameron and Jill Bourne (1989), in their paper 'Grammar, Nation and Citizenship: Kingman in Linguistic and Historical Perspective', examine the heated reactions provoked by the debate about whether grammar should be taught in the National Curriculum and uncover what can be seen to be the basis of the sense of threat that contributes to fears about linguistic diversity. They argue that the violent response is understood when the social significance of grammar in our culture is examined. In their analysis the ostensibly innocuous concept of grammar becomes inextricably linked with less innocuous concepts such as authority, hierarchy, tradition, order and rules. They suggest that attitudes to grammar are connected with attitudes to authority and that anxieties about grammar are at some deeper level anxieties about the breakdown of order and traditions not just in language but in society at large.

They cite John Rae who in an article, written for the *Observer* in 1982, entitled 'The decline and fall of English grammar', asserted:

> There is a further claim that can be made for the restoration of the teaching of correct English. Attention to the rules of grammar and care in the choice of words encourages punctiliousness in other matters. This is not just an intellectual conceit. The overthrow of grammar coincided with the acceptance of the equivalent of creative writing in social behaviour. As nice points of grammar were mockingly dismissed as pedantic and irrelevant, so was punctiliousness in such matters as honesty, responsibility, propriety, gratitude, apology and so on.

The very title carried by Rae's article alludes not only to a lost golden age, but also to a lost imperial past. Resonances such as these go to the foundations on which the 'myth' of the national identity is constructed.

Cameron and Bourne (1989) suggest that an authoritarian state frequently uses the 'national language' as a point of unity and social cohesion, and analogously finds linguistic diversity threatening, a force to be contained or even eliminated. This view point is perhaps one way of accounting for the opening of Chapter 7 of the Swann Report which begins: 'The English language is a central unifying factor in "being British"....'. Swann appears to adopt a milder approach because the English language is posited as just one factor. The chapter goes on to state,

> In order to lay the foundations for a genuinely pluralist society, the education system must, we believe, both cater for the linguistic needs of ethnic minority pupils and also take full advantage of the opportunities offered for the education of all pupils by the linguistic diversity of our society today.

These positive statements can be cast as embodying true multicultural and antiracist ideals but then the chapter proceeds to argue against bilingual education, against mother-tongue provision and mother-tongue maintenance in primary education, largely on the grounds that the arrangements for such provision would contribute to educational separatism. There is a strong sense in which diversity is perceived as threatening to social cohesion, to stability, perhaps even to law and order. Swann's rhetoric is one of cultural pluralism yet the practice being prescribed is essentially assimilationist. It is as if the deep structure meaning of the opening sentence to that chapter is that the English language is *the* central unifying factor in 'being British'.

Cameron and Bourne note that whereas in many parts of the world the equation of belonging to a nation and speaking a particular language would appear absurd, in England it is taken as obvious. Furthermore, they distinguish between two related but different meanings of 'standard', noting that in discussions of Standard English there is often slippage between these two meanings. In one sense 'standard' means uniform, ordinary, common to all, or normal. In the second sense it connotes excellence, the best, something to aspire toward. In this sense, 'standard' is not normal but normative. An effect of the slippage between the two meanings is that, the normative is passed off as the merely normal; . . . the language of a class is passed off as the common tongue of a whole people.

As well as illustrating the deep-rooted nature of fears of diversity there is an implied explanation for the cause of the fear, namely the unstable basis on which the identity is predicated. The slippage between normal and normative uses of the word 'standard' does appear to reflect the slippage between the purposes attributed to the stories we tell about ourselves (the history, the myths) in order to create a sense of identity. Are they merely factual, dispassionate accounts of events and personalities, things as they happened? Are they simply edited highlights of the best parts, the unsightly elements removed, in order to represent an ideal to which we might aspire, a goal to attain? Are they fact or artefact?

In a similar fashion to that in which slippage permitted the language of a class to be passed off as the language of the people, so, the edited myth of 'what we were' risks slipping into becoming the myth of 'what we are'. The qualities people claim as being 'British', especially those to do with fair play, resonate with experiences of the cricket field, public school education and, I would suggest, a social class and particular historical context. It is interesting to note the regularity with which images of the cricket field are alluded to both in times of perceived crisis and as measures of national identity. Norman Tebbit's notorious reference to the 'cricket test' in the context of the debate about admitting Hong Kong Chinese into Britain was not only a reference to an indicator of 'Britishness' (ie which cricket team was supported by people of minority ethnic background), but also an oblique reference to qualities of loyalty and fair play associated with sportsmanship and which themselves are seen as being 'British' qualities. Yet the basis for this cricket myth, by virtue of its history and social context, does not appear to refer to significant sections of the population in terms of social class, gender or ethnicity. At the outset the foundation of this myth was probably unstable and this condition has been exacerbated by contemporary circumstances. The instability of the myth lay in the fact that it was founded on premises or assumptions that for most people were probably untrue in the first place. Yet, this normative view was being projected as normal for the whole nation. The instability is moved into a state of crisis by the conditions of cultural diversity (which demand that the ideals embodied in the normative view be seen to be actually operating) and close scrutiny (which raises questions as to whether those ideals were ever realised in the first instance). How is it possible to claim to be tolerant and compromising when there exists a history of intolerance, antisemitism and racism? Where is fair play and justice when the experiences of minority sections of the population are dismissed or held to be inadmissible?

The dilemma

The myths under discussion are inevitably artefact in that selection must occur when constructing an account. Generally, all the facts cannot be presented because the sheer amount of detail itself tends to be overwhelming, making it difficult for a clear and coherent theme to be discerned and understood. The question is more one of which facts are included and for what purposes?

The 'multicultural myth makers' are attacked because they present a view of life in Britain which speaks of people experiencing discrimination in employment and housing, subjected to unjust treatment at the hands of the police, the judiciary and the penal system, receiving poor education and the targets of harassment and racist attacks. This view of life does not accord with the view which holds that British characteristics of fair play, tolerance and compromise predominate and so the different views are set in false competition, each contending that it represents the true reality. The attackers use the term 'myth' pejoratively to indicate that the perspective labelled 'myth' is false, the implication being that it is a lie. It is considered false because it contains no elements that those attacking it recognise, or perhaps wish to recognise, as their own view of British society. Furthermore, the 'myth' is not merely different. Because the 'myth' points to shortcomings in British society it inevitably exposes the fact that in too many instances the ideals expressed in terms of the 'British characteristics' of tolerance, compromise and fair play are nothing more than that; ideals not characteristics. This relevation is threatening because it forces the conclusion that the notion of such characteristics is itself false, a 'myth', a lie.

The viewpoints appear to exist in an inverse relationship. The need for the antiracist stance increases in proportion to the extent the majority ethnic group refuses to acknowledge the lived experience of minority ethnic groups. The majority view interprets the antiracist critique as threatening and unpatriotic, making it easier to justify treating minorities less favourably. The antiracist 'myth' serves the purpose of drawing attention to those experiences that have tended to be ignored and which demand action. Other more positive experiences of individuals and groups from racial minorities may also be presented. The dilemma is that in doing so the main theme would be lost because the racial majority would only respond to what it recognises as itself.

The 'myth' of being British has presented values and ideals to which any society should aspire. The problem seems to be that this artefact has been presented as fact. Widespread acceptance of these notions of the 'British character' suggests that it has made some contribution towards forming a sense of identity but a consequence appears to have been that the racial prejudice, discrimination and racism experienced by racial minorities has taken a long time to have begun to be believed.

A solution might be to dispense with 'myths' of all kinds, but this seems impractical even were it desirable. The 'myths' reflect viewpoints charged with moral and ethical dimensions. One view demands social justice and equality of opportunity, the other asserts commitment to fairness, compromise and tolerance. Perspectives of this kind will always be selective in some way and could never claim to tell the whole truth. But that should not mean that they are lies. Intentions behind the perspectives are, perhaps, critical. It is more a matter of how economical society chooses to be with the truth and the reasons for this. Perhaps society needs a new 'myth' appropriate for the modern world.

The old 'myth' needs to be altered to permit a proper view of things as they are. The dilemma is that it is probably impossible to achieve this without radically transforming the view 'the British' (whoever this means) have of themselves. There can be little doubt that racial dimensions are fundamental to the identity question. While it has become relatively more frequent to hear someone described as being 'black British' it seems that the concept of a black Englishman, or black Welsh woman or black Scot has further to go in becoming incorporated into this emerging transformed view.

'Myths' of this type pose the moral dilemmas arising from having to make choices that could distort truth, the consequences of those choices for individuals and society, and provoke the moral question of whether there should be attempts actively to create new 'myths' to fit new circumstances. Furthermore, while education may well have a major role to play in transmitting the new 'myths' should education be involved in developing these?

Education cannot escape involvement; so the issue is whether involvement will happen by design or by default. Yet again education is called upon to address an area which society finds to be one of great difficulty. The National Curriculum approaches multicultural education not as a 'subject' but as a dimension which permeates the entire curriculum. The expressed intention is that multicultural thinking would influence curriculum planning, development and implementation. *Curriculum Guidance 8: Education for Citizenship*, produced by the National Curriculum Council (1990), deals most explicitly with multicultural education, and, in one of the eight essential components which it addresses, the following possible areas of study are suggested:

- the interdependence of individuals, groups and communities;
- similarities and differences between individuals, groups and communities and their effects;
- the existence of differences in perception and the ways in which these may be reconciled;
- Britain as a society made up of many cultures, ethnic groups, faiths and languages;
- the diversity of cultures in other societies;
- a study of human development and culture from different perspectives;
- the origins and effects of racial prejudice in British and other societies.

Within the National Curriculum, multicultural education is not a compulsory subject in the sense Naismith advocated for civics. Instead, as a dimension its delivery is interwoven through the work of other subjects and cross-curricular dimensions. This presents problems in that the status of multicultural education is implicitly diminished by its not being a 'subject' and effective delivery of dimensions requires greater coordination and so greater commitment on the part of teachers and school managers.

The February 1991 edition of *NCC News* carried a piece entitled 'A pluralist society in the classroom and beyond'. It stressed that multicultural education is concerned with more than the needs of pupils from minority ethnic backgrounds and that it seeks to prepare all pupils for life in a society, and a world, of cultural and ethnic diversity. It observes, 'Multicultural education is the professional responsibility of all teachers in all schools.'

If education can so influence the processes in which views of self and national identity are formed, so that progress toward a non-racist society is accelerated, this is to be welcomed. Whether this can be achieved by the education system alone is another matter. The question of the heritages that need to be passed on, the perspectives from which they are seen, quickly takes the discussion back to the urgent need for a new 'myth'.

The permeation of the curriculum with multicultural elements is expected to occur in a climate of negative attitudes towards multicultural education reflected and in part moulded by the press. Furthermore, any guidance offered by the National Curriculum Council is undermined by statements made by politicians critical of multicultural approaches and which see multicultural education as inconsistent with raising standards in education. Taken in conjunction with the organisational difficulties that coordinating the curriculum presents, it would seem that the desirable objectives suggested by the National Curriculum Council are unlikely to be realised. The changes arising from the implementation of the Education Reform Act seem set to increase the unlikelihood of further progress in securing multicultural education objectives. The reduced power and influence of LEAs mean that opportunities for LEA intervention in terms of equality of opportunity are also reduced. The increased powers of governing bodies and parents places greater responsibility upon individuals who have to contend with the climate of attitudes reflected in the media. Local Management will mean tough decisions having to be taken about priorities on resourcing with damaging effects if, as likely, the importance of multicultural issues in education is not recognised.

An opportunity to begin to attend to the urgent task of creating the new 'myth' risks being lost.

At stake is the prospect of a new approach which promotes understanding of the purposes, values and limitations of past 'myths' and in which the set of values, mainly ethical qualities, selected for social coherence are posited as the common goal to which individuals in society aspire and are exemplified by examples taken from the past. To develop this will require the help of many including journalists, the broadcasting media, those involved in the arts, academics, politicians, and, not least, teachers.

References

Cameron, D and Bourne, J (1989) *Grammar, Nation and Citizenship: Kingman in Linguistic and Historical Perspective*, Department of English and Media Studies Occasional Paper no 1, Institute of Education, University of London.

Coombes (1986) 'Multicultural myth makers'. *Birmingham Post*, 3 February, 1986.

Great Britain, Parliament, House of Commons (1981) *West Indian Children in Our Schools*, Interim Report of the Committee of Inquiry into the Education of Children from Ethnic Minority Groups (Rampton Committee), HMSO, London.

Great Britain, Parliament, House of Commons (1985) *Education for All*, report of the Committee of Inquiry into the Education of Children from Ethnic Minority Groups (Swann Report), cmnd 9453, HMSO, London.

Naismith, D (1988) 'My country right or wrong'. *The Telegraph*, February, 1988.

National Curriculum Council (1990) Curriculum Guidance 8, *Education for Citizenship*, NCC, York.

National Curriculum Council (1991) *NCC News*, no 5, February, 1991.

Palmer, F (ed) (1986) *Anti-Racism an Assault on Education and Value*, Sherwood, Woodbury, NJ.

Rae, J (1982) 'The decline and fall of English grammar', *Observer*, 7 February, 1982.

Rushdie, S (1982) 'The new empire within Britain', *New Society*, 9 December, 1982.

Troyna, B and Carrington, B (1990) *Education, Racism and Reform*, Routledge, London.

Chapter 7

The Misrepresentation of Religious Education

Robert Jackson

Abstract

This paper argues that the portrayal of contemporary religious education in England and Wales advanced by critics during the debates associated with the emergence of the Education Reform Act was misleading. The variety of religious education proposed by critics from the radical right and by some theologically conservative Christian writers is found to raise serious moral questions about the aims and conduct of the subject. An alternative 'conversational' mode of religious education is introduced which attempts to accommodate certain criticisms of modern RE while recognising the integrity of the different religious traditions present in British society.

Introduction

During the debates about religious education surrounding the publication of the Education Reform Bill there emerged a point of view combining the interests of the radical right in politics and some forms of conservative Christian theology. This lobby argued for a stronger place for RE in schools but against a religious education reflecting the religious pluralism of the UK. The argument was for 'predominantly Christian' RE rather than 'multifaith' RE, which was regarded as the norm among many Local Education Authority syllabuses. 'Multifaith' RE was, for example, associated by this lobby with secularism, was regarded as inherently relativistic and not concerned with issues of truth, and was considered to have a confusing 'mishmash' of subject matter and to betray Britain's cultural heritage. 'Predominantly Christian' RE, on the other hand, would offer close attention to the Christian faith and its role in shaping 'British culture', and would also provide a particular brand of moral instruction with the aim of reducing social problems among the young.

Through publications (especially *The Crisis in Religious Education* (Burn and Hart, 1988)) and through the activities of individuals, the lobby succeeded in influencing Parliamentary debates about religious education. The legislation on RE and collective worship embodied in the Education Reform Act (ERA) can be seen as a compromise between the views of liberal educators and those of the radical right of education in alliance with some theologically conservative Christians. The latter have continued to campaign against 'liberal' interpretations of ERA on RE and collective worship and have encouraged parents to make use of complaints procedures established under the terms of ERA.

This chapter argues that the characterisation of religious education by the 'predominantly Christian' lobby is largely mistaken. Many of its arguments have been in the form of generalisations from anecdote or assertions unsupported by evidence. While replying to these critics, the chapter shares with them a concern that in some cases schools have lacked sensitivity to parents and children from conservative religious backgrounds. A more 'conversational' view of RE is proposed which is operable within the terms of ERA.

Specifically ethical issues raised by the chapter are the radical right's proposed use of certain interpretations of Christian teaching, in deliberate isolation from alternative views, in order to achieve certain social goals. Their views on authority in relation to personal autonomy also raise moral issues about the nature of the person and of education. With regard to ethnic and religious pluralism, their association of morality with one religious tradition ignores the moral concerns and contributions of other traditions within British society.

The background

In 1988, following the publication of the Education Reform Bill, a pamphlet was published called *The Crisis in Religious Education* (Burn and Hart, 1988). The document was not written by professional religious educators but by members of an Evangelical Christian education pressure group (Christians and Tyneside Schools, CATS) and published by the politically right-wing Educational Research Trust.[1] The paper was sent to all MPs and members of the House of Lords before the key debates on the Education Reform Bill's clauses on religious education. Many of the arguments and assertions contained in the pamphlet continue to be reiterated as disputes about the interpretation of the 1988 Act on religious education and collective worship erupt from time to time.

The authors polarise two forms of religious education which are labelled 'multifaith' and 'predominantly Christian'. The pamplet mounts a vigorous attack on the former while calling for the restoration of the latter. The document influenced the Parliamentary debates about religious education and collective worship which took place in 1988 and the writings and utterances of politicians who support its case. Some aspects of the story of the debates and their outcome in law is documented elsewhere (eg Alves, 1991; Brown, 1989; Hull, 1991a). There are also a number of published discussions of the legislation (eg Cox and Cairns, 1989; Hull, 1989). With regard to religious education (as distinct from collective worship[2]) the essence of the compromise is contained in Clause 8(3) of the Education Reform Act which states that new agreed syllabuses for religious education must:

> reflect the fact that the religious traditions in Great Britain are in the main Christian whilst taking account of the teaching and practices of the other principal religions represented in Great Britain.

Disputes continue over the interpretation of this clause by those agreed syllabus conferences which have been set up by LEAs since the publication of ERA. The trend has been for right-wing pressure groups (such as PACE, the Parental Alliance for Choice in Education) to support individual parents in making full use of complaints procedures established under ERA in order to challenge the legality of new agreed syllabuses for religious education or particular interpretations by schools of the legal requirements for collective worship. A recent publication from CATS is a guide for parents to the legislation on RE and collective worship, offering advice on how to complain (Hart, 1991).[3]

Rather than discussing the political and theological conflicts which are presently taking place over the interpretation of law, this chapter argues that the analysis of developments in religious education in England and Wales by writers such as Burn and Hart is largely mistaken. Thus a distorted and misleading account of religious education in English and Welsh schools has been presented to politicians and to many parents.

The chapter also recognises, however, that some of the concerns expressed by the critics of 'multifaith' RE need to be addressed in order to arrive at a form of religious education which is both theologically sound and culturally fair. In this sense it makes a plea for better communication between groups with different interests in religious education.

Secularisation and secularism

Baroness Cox in her foreword to *The Crisis in Religious Education* juxtaposes points about multifaith religious education and secularisation.

> Many of our children are in schools . . . where teaching about Christianity, has either been diluted to a multifaith relativism or has become little more than a secularised discussion of social and political issues. (p 4)

That its opponents see 'multifaith' RE as a step in the direction of secularism is confirmed by Anthony Coombs MP in a letter to *The Times*:

> During the passage of the bill, during the winter of 1987–8, Mr Michael Allison MP, Baroness Cox and others, including myself, wanted to ensure that religious education reflected a Christian view and that the kind of relative comparative religion shading into blatant secularism was banished from the classroom. (*The Times*, 12 April 1991)

This interpretation ignores the fact that secularisation had made an impact on religious education well before multifaith RE had become a widely discussed issue. Harold Loukes' work with teenagers, for example, confirmed that young people were disenchanted with a Bible-based RE that assumed the truth of Christianity (Loukes, 1961; 1965). What they wanted was for the controversial nature of religion to be recognised and the opportunity to discuss openly issues of deep concern. Similarly, in the early 1960s Edwin Cox's research with sixth formers revealed an antipathy towards an RE which made assumptions about the truth of Christianity (reported in Cox, 1967). Cox's book *Changing Aims in Religious Education* (Cox, 1966) was not a radical attack on religious education as a medium for instruction or nurture in the Christian faith. Rather, it put into words not only Cox's changing views influenced by his research but also the direct experience of many teachers and pupils; namely, that if the subject was to retain any credibility, it had to acknowledge that religious claims were a matter of intellectual dispute. It needs to be emphasised that RE was shifting away from Christian instruction or nurture before the religious pluralism of Britain had become a major issue and before movements to give education a more global perspective were showing any significant influence. To associate a multifaith approach to religious education with secularism, especially by suggesting that the former has a causal relationship with the latter, at the least distorts the history of religious education in England and Wales and is misleading.

Christianity and public morality

It is in the domain of values that the real intentions of this group of critics become clear. They rightly draw attention to the marginalisation of Christian perspectives in many school personal and social education courses. Indeed, many such courses tend to marginalise religions in general. These critics go further, however, in relating social and moral problems to the decline of a particular form of Christian morality.

> Many of the guidance and personal and social development courses in schools have been so secularised that Christian values are not considered at all. This is a tragic situation and one that goes a long way towards explaining the increasing violence in our society . . . (Burn and Hart, 1988, p 9)

The writers go on to assert their commitment to a particular form of Christian ethics and then imply that exposure of young people to alternative views of morality is undesirable.

> The Christian faith provides God-given moral absolutes for personal and social conduct. It also emphasises human responsibility and rejects determinism. We believe that explanations of conduct as being determined by the environment alone are now seen to be bankrupt. . . . We are concerned that some of the new Locally Agreed Syllabuses with their emphasis on non-theistic life stances have already opened the door to the possibility of exposing the young to political ideologies which deny human freedom, human responsibility and the reality of sin. (ibid, p 31)

The authors appear to be seeking to deny the controversial nature of Christian claims by ruling out any consideration of alternative views in religious education. Their concurrence with this view is confirmed by their quotation (on p 27) of a passage from a book called *Education and Indoctrination* which includes the sentences:

> The exposure to alternatives may defeat the purpose of religious education as much as it defeats the purpose of morality: it offers to place idle curiosity where there should be certainty and truth. The crucial feature of religious belief is that, unlike political belief, it is essentially addressed to the individual, his conscience and his salvation. It is a guide to life and a source of confidence. (Scruton *et al*, 1985).

These passages reveal a number of assumptions.

1   There is a complete disregard for the home and community background of children and young people. Given the undoubted plurality of religious and secular commitments in British society, it is very difficult to see why the decision whether or not to raise children within a particular religious way of life should be a matter for publicly funded schools and not for parents. There seems to be an assumption that children are not nurtured in faith and morality in the home and community. For many children from a variety of religious backgrounds this is simply not the case. Research evidence shows something of the range of variety of formal and informal religious nurture, not only among the different traditions in Britain, but *within* each one.[4]

2   There is a mistaken assumption about the unity of Christianity with regard to its approach to human conduct. There are ongoing variations of interpretation within the Christian tradition which reflect different theological views of scripture and doctrine (eg Outka and Ramsey, 1968). Many committed Christians would, for example, reject the view of authority implicit in the above passages. The pluralism of Christian ethics and theology is reflected in the variegated character of informal and formal nurture in homes and churches (Jackson and Nesbitt, 1992).

3   There is the ethically dubious assumption that it is proper to deny students access to information on the grounds of achieving an instrumental goal. At the very least this assumption raises serious moral and theological questions about civil liberties as well as about the nature and aims of education.

There is an interesting difference in the two passages concerning the effects of exposing young people to more than one view. For Scruton *et al*, exposure to more than one view engenders 'idle curiosity', while exposure to one view can bring about 'certainty and trust'. No evidence is offered to support this assertion. On the other hand, for Burn and Hart, exposure to different views (namely views they do not hold) is dangerous for the contrary reason that young people might adopt them. Again, no evidence is offered in support of this claim. What they both agree on is the exposure of children only to one view of one tradition with the intention that children should adopt it. One obvious objection to this approach is that there are plenty of examples of its failure. Many people who have had a highly specific form of religious schooling have not continued to believe what they were brought up to believe by teachers or indeed by parents.

More importantly, the view that the writers adopt reveals a view of education that rejects the principle that in areas of experience that are legitimately a matter of public dispute, individuals should be encouraged to make decisions for themselves on the basis of the available evidence. This view is inconsistent with the argument, also advanced forcefully by these writers, that religious education should not be relativistic and should take seriously the issue of truth claims in religion (eg Burn and Hart, 1988, p 15). If young people are to be taught the skills necessary to make judgements about the claims of religions they can hardly be insulated from these claims or be expected to accept, on someone else's authority, that certain claims are true and others false.

One can understand the psychological force of an argument that seeks to leave young people cocooned within a particular world view. However, not only do the authors of the quoted passages ignore the range of religious positions represented in

British society, they also fail to recognise that young people do not grow up in a world where such cushioning is possible. The young are exposed to the influences of their peers at school and of the media. Further, in their lessons they ask critical questions, give voice to prejudices, deliberate, make judgements and express opinions. Is it not better to provide an educational environment in which the skills of deliberation and evaluation are well taught and where high standards of argument and discussion are expected rather than to leave young people to learn by default?

The question raises a general issue about the relationship between religious education and religious upbringing or nurture. There are some situations in which certain forms of religious upbringing appear not to be compatible with the educational goal of encouraging young people to make decisions autonomously. Some of the clashes between more narrow forms of religious nurture and the educational processes of critical discussion and analysis are less problematic than they seem to be at first sight. Not only those children who are brought up narrowly in certain religious contexts are socialised into having particular beliefs, values and judgements. *All* children are socialised within the family in an informal and often unconscious way. Many arrive at school with strongly held beliefs and prejudices which have been acquired in the context of the family, peer group and local community. Most children – not just those from particular religious backgrounds – will be challenged through the introduction of a broader range of knowledge and through the development and transfer of critical skills.

Further, the fears of some religious groups about the pursuit of autonomy are often groundless. The perception of members of certain religious groups is that schools encourage children to be a 'law unto themselves' in matters of religion and values. Children, it is alleged, are encouraged to choose beliefs and values rather in the manner of selecting cans of beans or fruit from the shelves of a supermarket. This, of course, is distortion of what educators mean by autonomy. In the educational context autonomy usually means the capacity to make decisions on the basis of a reasonable scrutiny of available evidence (Gardner, 1991). There is no contradiction, then, in deciding autonomously to adopt a position that one has hitherto accepted on authority. Further, autonomy does not imply complete individualism, for a consideration of others in relation to oneself is an important factor in autonomous decision making. In this sense all autonomy is 'relative'. Many apparent clashes between autonomy and religious nurture might be resolved by good conversation between parents, pupils and staff at the school. The educational environment in which these skills are learned needs to be one in which religious positions are treated in an informed and serious way, and where other areas of the curriculum – science, for example – are discussed with the same critical rigour.[5] There will, however, from time to time, be disputes where no reconciliation is possible and in these cases parents have the right under the law to withdraw their children from religious education.

Relativism and phenomenology

The quotations above, from Baroness Cox and Anthony Coombs both refer to relativism – 'multifaith relativism' and 'relative comparative religion'. I take both examples to mean that multifaith religious education is assumed to be approached in such a way that questions of the truth or falsity of religious claims are avoided or that all religions are regarded as being equally true. Burn and Hart relate this to phenomenology, an approach which they claim: 'denies children the opportunity of examining counter claims to truth in religion'. (Burn and Hart, 1988, p 15).

Burn and Hart regret that the Swann Report, *Education for All* (GB, P, H of C, 1985), endorsed the phenomenological approach to religious education. The Swann Report (which seems to be the only source for their account of phenomenology) favoured a phenomenological approach in order 'to teach children to understand the nature of beliefs and a range of belief systems' (3.19) and as seeking 'to "inform" rather than "convert" pupils' (5.4). The Report's characterisation of phenomenology is dependent on *Schools Council Working Paper 36* (Schools Council 1971). This itself is strongly influenced by the work of Professor Ninian Smart, who was the Director of the Schools Council Project whose findings the working paper reports. In the words of *Schools Council Working Paper 36*, the phenomenological approach:

sees the aim of religious education as the promotion of understanding. It uses the tools of scholarship in order to enter into an empathic relationship with individuals and groups. (Schools Council, 1971, p 21)

The essence of the approach as it has been described so far is to help students to suspend temporarily their own judgements in order to understand the faith, beliefs and practices of people of different religions. Phenomenology is not, however, a total method. A look at *Secular Education and the Logic of Religion*, Professor Smart's main theoretical contribution to religious education, confirms that he envisaged young people developing critical skills for forming judgements about the truth or falsity of religious claims (Smart, 1968). Gaston Berger, a French phenomenologist of religion, sums up well the role of phenomenology in the study of religions:

The phenomenologist ... stops confusing truth and meaning. He does not necessarily regard everything he describes as true or good, but through various examples, he applies himself to the task of discovering deep-lying structures, the meaning of which becomes clear to him. He is like a faithful translator who is prepared to respect the thought of his author, also when he is aware that he does not approve him. Later, perhaps, he will be his judge, but for the time being, he only wants to be his friend. (Berger, 1957; English translation in Waardenberg, 1973, p 665)

A phenomenological approach then does not entail relativism. This is not to say that there have not been teachers who have avoided issues of truth and falsity or have considered their discussion inappropriate for younger children. Nor is there any suggestion that all phenomenological materials for schools have been good ones. These are separate issues.

Phenomenology is not only characterised by critics of multifaith religious education in terms of its supposedly inherent relativism. The phenomenological approach to religious education, it is claimed:

is to study religion through its observable expressions. It is argued that as children learn about sacred places, festivals, rites of passage and customs, they are led to a more authentic understanding of faith. But such an approach devalues the vital ingredients of faith, belief and practice and so leads to the trivialisation of all faiths. (Burn and Hart, 1988, p 15)

Once again no evidence is offered to support the assertion. It should already be clear that phenomenology involves much more than studying the 'observable expressions' of religion. The Dutch scholar Pierre Chantepie de la Saussaye, the probable originator of the term 'phenomenology of religion', points out that the method is not only concerned with religious practices and arts, but also with 'religious impressions, sentiments and states' and he comments on the dialectical relationship between the mental activity in religion and its outward expression (Chantepie de la Saussaye, 1891; reproduced in Waardenburg, 1973, p 110). For Gerardus van der Leeuw, probably the most influential twentieth-century phenomenologist of religion, a 'phenomenon' is not a religious object, ritual or custom, nor is it the faith or spirituality of a religious person. It is the relationship between the two (van der Leeuw, 1938; reproduced in Waardenburg, 1973, p 412). Many more examples from the literature could be given. Rather than trivialising faiths, phenomenology sets out to grasp the power and meaning of faith within its appropriate religious and cultural context. If any teachers or syllabuses simply require their students to describe the externals of religion then they are not using a phenomenological approach.[6]

Thematic teaching

A further criticism is focussed on thematic teaching. It is asserted that material drawn together from a number of different traditions and centred on a theme or topic produces a mishmash or a hotchpotch, a confusing mixture of material which is dangerous in its syncretism and confusing to children. There is some validity in this criticism in that there are some published textbooks which include far too much material from a wide range of religious traditions and expect teachers and pupils to be edified by it. This is not a criticism of a thematic approach in principle, however. Themes need to be chosen carefully so that illustrative material from religious traditions does not distort those traditions. Further, it is sensible not to draw on more than, say, three traditions in illustrating a theme. This is a practical way of ensuring that children are not overloaded with material.[7] Also thematic work, like any other work in religious education, needs to be carefully assessed and teachers need to be sure that children have understood the material before moving on to new work. Similar principles apply in considering the integration or combination of religious education with other subjects.

As John Hull points out, however, the attack on thematic teaching from opponents of multifaith RE goes further than pointing out the dangers of confusing children. His analysis of the use of food metaphors, particularly their association with disgust and purity, shows the intention to vilify a thematic approach to religious education (Hull, 1991a).

Cultural arguments

A recurring theme in the rhetoric opposing multifaith RE is the idea that children are deprived of their cultural heritage if Christianity is not emphasised in religious education. Some take the argument further, wanting to exclude all alternatives, denying that Britain is a multifaith society (Burn and Hart, 1988, p 25) and/or using the cultural argument to justify Christianity as true (eg McIntyre, nd). Burn and Hart in *The Crisis in Religious Education* state that:

All citizens irrespective of creed or culture need an understanding of the influence of Christianity upon our literature, laws, customs, architecture and art forms. (p 26)

Anthony Coombs states the argument in this form:

unless RE is set in a Christian context it cannot fulfil its academic role of ensuring pupils have a sufficient understanding of the British way of life (Coombs, 1988).

At one level it is right to agree with these writers. As the tradition which has interacted with the personal and social lives of people in this country for well over a millennium it would be unthinkable not to give the study of Christianity an important place in religious education. At another level one must be cautious. The relationships between personal faith and religious traditions and between religious traditions and the wider cultural milieu in which they are set are dynamic and not static. Christianity indeed has helped to shape 'the British way of life', but a Christianity already deeply influenced by Hellenic thought, and open to the influences of social and cultural movements within 'British' culture and within the many cultures in which it now flourishes. Christianity should have an important place in religious education, but not on the grounds that there exists a fixed and unchanging culture or 'British way of life' that requires a study of an equally static Christianity for its preservation. Christianity and the other faiths need to be seen as living entities, relating, responding and reacting to one another and to the secularism they all encounter. Christianity also needs to be presented as theologically and ethnically pluralistic (Jackson and Nesbitt, 1992).

Christianity will generally warrant more space on the timetable than the other traditions, not to preserve a particular way of life but because of its historical and contemporary presence in our society together with its significance as a global religion. It stands open to academic discussion, however, on the same terms as any other religious tradition.

The future of religious education

The rejection of many of the arguments of the critics of multifaith RE does not imply that present arrangements are ideal nor that the critics have no important points to make. The 1991 report of the Senior Chief Inspector of Schools on standards in education points out low quality of work in the subject (DES, 1991). Papers from the Religious Education Council of England and Wales (REC, 1988, 1990) and the National Curriculum Council's first analysis of the reports of Standing Advisory Councils for Religious Education (NCC, 1991) highlight the shortage of well-qualified teachers of the subject. These are indicators that for whatever reasons, many schools attach little importance or value to religious education. While religious education, in theory, seeks to help pupils to understand religious traditions and to explore basic questions of meaning and value, the general ethos of many schools conveys the message that religions are private pursuits of limited educational interest rather than total ways of life embodying universal claims about truth. This is an observation sometimes made by critics of multifaith religious education.

The solution offered (eg by Scruton *et al*, 1985) of teaching Christianity as true and avoiding exposing children to alternative views is hard to defend in the publicly funded schools of an open society which embodies a range of deeply held religious and secular commitments.

Another solution might be to encourage religious communities to operate their own schools, a way favoured by some Muslims and supporters of New Independent Christian Schools who have argued for voluntary aided status for their independently run religious schools, partly on the grounds that their children's religion has not been taken seriously, or indeed has been the subject of abuse or derision, in county schools (eg Deaking, 1987; Halstead, 1986). The arguments for and against such schools are rehearsed elsewhere in this book (see chapters by McLaughlin pp 114-36 and Connolly pp 137-45). My own principal argument against separate schooling lies in the loss of contact and interaction between young people from different backgrounds. Young people have the potential for learning about and from one another's religious cultures, though a necessary condition for this is a policy of sensitivity towards religious groups agreed by all parties within the school.

A third solution might be to remove religious education from the curriculum of state-funded schools, as in the USA, France or India. The religious instruction of the young would then be solely the responsibility of parents and their religious communities. One unfortunate corollary would be that most children would be less informed about religious matters than they are under the present system. The implicit assumption that religions are unworthy of serious attention and study would be the price to pay for excising a controversial area from the curriculum.

A fourth solution is less tidy than any of the above and is both pragmatic and ethical. It would entail that those claiming the universal truth and application of a particular way of life would have to acknowledge that there were others who held different beliefs equally sincerely or lived according to different ways of life. There would be need to be *some* body of shared values for this approach to work. For example, a basic principle of the open society – freedom to follow a particular religious or secular way of life under the constraints of the law – would have to be accepted as a pragmatic if not a theological or epistemological basis for religious education. The sensitive application of academic methods and standards would also have to be agreed, though those methods would themselves be open to the critical scrutiny of commentators within religious and secular traditions. For example, the debate about the relationship between personal autonomy and varieties of religious upbringing could be informed and enriched by different religious and secular perspectives on individualism, responsibility and authority.

Resources reflecting the understandings of different academic disciplines would need to be balanced by those presenting the perceptions of different kinds of 'insiders' from the religious traditions. For pupils the development of skills necessary to gain an understanding of different ways of life would be vital as would the capacity to form judgements consistently from each person's perspective.

Specialist teachers would be needed at all levels to teach, to coordinate contributions from members of religious communities and to arrange in-service training. The school would need to have an agreed policy on recognising the centrality of religious faith and practice in the lives of some of its pupils, and of affirming the worth of all children, regardless of their religious or secular background.

There would be some who could never take part in such a conversational approach, though I suspect that educators and parents from a wide range of religious positions – particularly some of the conservative ones who currently feel marginalised or excluded from policy making in religious education – might decide to contribute to it.

Some religious educators will recognise in this outline sketch an approach to their subject which they have already been trying to develop, albeit constrained by a lack of resources and other forms of support. I would argue that Clause 8(3) of the 1988 Education Reform Act, in spite of infelicities of drafting, permits this kind of religious education. Further, although the structural arrangements are not ideal, the formation of local authority Standing Advisory Councils for Religious Education, representing different religious, educational and community perspectives provides, in principle, an opportunity to influence and develop forms of religious education which are genuinely conversational (Taylor, 1991). Would it be too much to hope that all parties might work together to achieve the proper levels of resources and training needed to bring about the success of this form of religious education?

Notes

1 By no means all Evangelical Christians are opposed to 'multifaith' religious education. See, for example, Wilkins (1991), for arguments not only for the compatibility of evangelicalism and multifaith RE teaching, but also giving reasons why evangelical Christians can bring distinctive qualities to their professional work as teachers of a religious education which draws on several religious traditions.

2 Disputes about ERA's stipulations on collective worship centre on interpretations of the term 'worship' and the notoriously unclear wording 'wholly or mainly of a broadly Christian character'. Discussions of ERA on collective worship include Brown (1989); Bysh (1990); Cooling (1990); Hewitt (1990); Hull (1989); Jackson (1990); National Society (1989); Slee (1990). Complaints made in 1990 about the 'multifaith nature' of collective worship provided at a Wakefield first school and two Bradford primary schools, forwarded to the Department of Education and Science by the Parental Alliance for Choice in Education, were rejected by the Secretary of State in July and August 1991 respectively (Richardson, 1991). Letters from the Department of Education and Science rejecting the complaints both emphasise that 'broadly Christian worship under the Act is clearly intended to be such that pupils of a non-Christian background can take part'.

3 A complaint about the Ealing Agreed Syllabus resulted in the Department of Education and Science sending a letter to all Chief Education Officers in England and Wales. This contained a substantial extract from legal advice sought by the Secretary of State on what conditions would have to be met in order for an agreed syllabus to be consistent with Section 8(3) of ERA. The letter was sent out on the grounds that the Secretary of State 'believes it would be helpful to make this information available more widely'. According to the opinion, an agreed syllabus which meets the requirements of Section 8(3) 'must devote a reasonable amount of attention to teaching based on Christian traditions'. That the majority of religious traditions in Britain are Christian would be, in most cases, 'properly reflected by devoting most attention to Christian traditions'. However, *no* agreed syllabus

conforming to section 8(3) can only include material on Christianity. Further, *no* agreed syllabus should 'exclude from its teaching any of the principal religions represented in Great Britain'. The precise balance of content is a matter for local determination by the agreed syllabus conference.

The legal opinion makes further general points about agreed syllabuses:

- they must not be denominational;
- they must not aim to convert pupils or to promote among them a particular religion or religious belief;
- they must be based on Christianity and other major religions, indicating appropriate material for different ages;
- they should include exploration of ethical issues within religions and not be purely informational; and
- they should have regard to the national as well as the local situation, though decisions about content are to be made locally with due regard to local circumstances.

Finally, the opinion states that shorthand phrases such as 'mainly Christian' or 'multifaith' are inadequate for testing the legality of syllabuses, since neither embodies all the various requirements of Section 8(3). In confirming the local determination of RE syllabuses, the opinion implicitly rejects crude formulae for establishing their content, such as specific percentages of time allocated to Christian and other material, as advocated by some pressure groups. Christianity should be covered, but so should all the other major religions represented in Britain. In most cases more time will be given to Christianity than the other traditions, but the balance is a matter for local agreement.

The Secretary of State's response to the opinion was to declare that he expected syllabuses to give readers 'sufficient guidance' about what content from Christianity and the other principal religions is supposed to be taught. In other words his concern was *not* whether syllabuses are 'mainly Christian' or 'multifaith' but whether they provide enough detail for schools to design clear and coherent schemes of work. DES letters which went separately to Ealing and Newham gave lack of 'sufficient particulars' as the Secretary of State's reason for being unsatisfied that their syllabuses conform with Section 8(3). For a discussion of the DES letter see Hull (1991b).

Ironically, opponents of a broadly based RE attempted in the press to claim the publication of the DES letter as a victory over the 'multifaith' approach (eg Michael Allison MP's letter to *The Times* of 12 April, 1991). The contents of the legal opinion clearly show this not to be the case.

4 The Religious Education and Community Project based at the University of Warwick is conducting ethnographic studies of religious upbringing in a number of traditions. The varied patterns of formal and informal nurture in one British city, and in Christianity and Hinduism respectively, are described in Jackson and Nesbitt (1992) and Jackson and Nesbitt (forthcoming).

5 The positivistic view of science which has been partly responsible for a dismissive attitude towards religion in society has been superseded at the academic level. Its legacy lingers in some schools, however, and explains to some extent their insensitivity to children from religious backgrounds or their incapacity to take religious world views seriously.

6 What the literature of phenomenology fails to offer students is the practical skills for understanding religious faith and tradition from the point of view of insiders. For a discussion of this issue see Jackson (1989).

7 Support for the view that material drawn from several traditions need not be confusing to children comes from an analysis by Stephen Orchard of HMI reports on RE published between 1985 and 1988. Orchard remarks, 'If religious education was becoming confusing or ineffective since the introduction of a multifaith approach the inspectorate seem to regard

such failures as failures in competence rather than a consequence of the additional content' (Orchard, 1991, p 20).

References

Alves, C (1991) 'Just a matter of words? The Religious Education debates in the House of Lords', *British Journal of Religious Education*, 13, 3, Summer, pp 168–74.

Berger, G (1957) 'Religion', in *Encylopaedia Francaise*, vol XIX.

Brown, A (1989) 'Religious Education and worship in schools: flexibility, frustration, foibles and fallacies', *Resource*, 12, 1, Autumn, pp 1–3.

Burn, J and Hart, C (1988) *The Crisis In Religious Education*, Educational Research Trust, London.

Bysh, J (1990) 'One eye view of school worship', *Resource*, 13, 1, p 6.

Chantepie de la Saussaye, P (1891) *Manual of the Science of Religion*, (English translation of *Lehrbuch der Religionsgeshichte*, Freiburg, 1887).

Cooling, T (1990) 'Collective worship – one Christian perspective', *Resource*, 13, 1, pp 2–3.

Coombs, A (1988) 'Diluting the faith', *Education*, 26 August.

Cox, E (1966) *Changing Aims in Religious Education*, Routledge, London.

Cox, E (1967) *Sixth Form Religion*, SCM, London.

Cox, E and Cairns, J (1989) *Reforming Religious Education*, Kogan Page, London.

Deakin, R (1987) *Report on the New Independent Christian Schools*, Christians in Education.

Department of Education and Science (DES) (1991) *Standards in Education: the Annual Report of HM Senior Chief Inspector of Schools 1989–90*, Department of Education and Science, London.

Gardner, P (1991) 'Personal autonomy and religious upbringing: the "problem" ', *Journal of the Philosophy of Education*, 25, 1, pp 69–81.

Great Britain, Parliament, House of Commons (1985), *Education for All*, (Swann Report), cmnd 9453, HMSO, London.

Halstead, J M (1986) *The Case for Muslim Voluntary Aided Schools*, Islamic Academy, Cambridge.

Hart, C (1991) *Religious Education: From Acts to Action*, CATS Trust, Newcastle Upon Tyne.

Hewitt, I (1990) 'Muslims and the ERA: the after-effects', *Resource*, 13, 1, pp 4–5.

Hull, J (1989) *The Act Unpacked*, Birmingham Papers in Religious Education, Christian Education Movement, Derby.

Hull, J (1991a) *Mish Mash: Religious Education in Multi-Cultural Britain: A Study in Metaphor*, Birmingham Papers in Religious Education, Christian Education Movement, Derby.

Hull, J (1991b) 'Agreed syllabuses and the law', *Resource*, 14, 1, pp 1–3.

Jackson, R (1989) 'Religious education: from ethnographic research to curriculum development', in Campbell, J and Little, V (eds) *Humanities in the Primary School*, Falmer Press, Lewes.

Jackson, R (1990) 'Religious education after the Reform Act', in Jackson, R and Starkings, D (eds) *The Junior RE Handbook*, Stanley Thornes, Cheltenham, pp 3–13.

Jackson, R and Nesbitt, E (1992) 'The diversity of experience in the religious upbringing of children from Christian families in Britain', *British Journal of Religious Education*, forthcoming.

Jackson, R and Nesbitt, E (forthcoming) *Hindu Children in Britain*, Trentham Books, Stoke on Trent.

van der Leeuw, G (1938) *Religion in Essence and Manifestation*, Allen and Unwin, London.

Loukes, H (1961) *Teenage Religion*, SCM Press, London.

Loukes, H (1965) *New Ground in Christian Education*, SCM Press, London.

McIntyre, J (nd) *Multi-Culture and Multifaith Societies: Some Examinable Assumptions*, Occasional Papers, Farmington Institute for Christian Studies, Oxford.

National Curriculum Council (NCC) (1991) *Analysis of SACRE Reports 1991*, National Curriculum Council, York.

National Society (1989) *School Worship*, National Society, London.

Orchard, S (1991) 'What was wrong with religious education? An analysis of HMI Reports 1985–1988', *British Journal of Religious Education*, 14, 1, pp 15–21.

Outka, G H and Ramsey, P (eds) (1968) *Norm and Context in Christian Ethics*, SCM, London.

Religious Education Council (REC) (1988) *Religious Education: Supply of Teachers for the 1990s*, The Religious Education Council of England and Wales.

Religious Education Council (REC) (1990) *What Conspired Against RE Specialist Teacher Supply?*, The Religious Education Council of England and Wales.

Richardson, R (1991) 'Religious Education 1991: letter and spirit', *Race and Immigration: Runnymede Trust Bulletin*, no 249, October, pp 1–3.

Schools Council (1971) *Religious Education in Secondary Schools*, Schools Council Working Paper 36, Evans/Methuen, London.

Scruton, R, Ellis-Jones, A and O'Keeffe, D (1985) *Education and Indoctrination*, Education Research Centre, London,

Slee, N (1990) 'Developments in school worship: an overview', *Journal of Beliefs and Values*, 11, 1, pp 5–9.

Smart, N (1968) *Secular Education and the Logic of Religion*, Faber, London.

Taylor, M J (1991) *SACREs: Their Formation, Composition, Operation and Role on RE and Worship*, National Foundation for Educational Research, Slough.

Waardenburg, J (1973) *Classical Approaches to the Study of Religion*, Mouton, The Hague (vol I).

Wilkins, R (1991) 'How can an Evangelical Christian teach multi-faith RE?', *Resource*, 13, 3, Summer, pp 1–3.

Chapter 8
The Ethics of Separate Schools

T H McLaughlin

Abstract

It is widely felt that in a pluralist liberal democratic society which is both multiracial and culturally diverse, ethical considerations point decisively against separate schooling, particularly when it is based on the ethnic, cultural and religious identities of pupils. In this paper it is argued that there is a less strong and direct connection between liberal educational principles and the notion of the common school than is often supposed. This is due in part to ethical and philosophical complexities in the principles which are often overlooked. It is claimed that arising from these complexities are arguments which are worthy of serious attention concerning the legitimate plurality of schooling arrangements, including certain sorts of separate school, acceptable within, and demanded by, a framework of liberal educational values. It is further claimed that an open mind should be kept concerning arguments in favour of separate schools which appear to come from outside the tradition of liberal education.

Introduction

The case for 'separate schools' is now the subject of increasing theoretical and practical debate and controversy in which ethical considerations have a significant place.

Much of this debate is located, explicitly or implicitly, within the context of the sort of culturally and racially diverse and pluralistic democratic society outlined in Chapter 1 of the Swann Report (GB, P, H of C, 1985; hereinafter referred to as Swann). At the heart of this view of society is the need for a careful balance to be struck between social and cultural cohesion and diversity. In this context, separate schools of whatever sort are viewed with considerable suspicion, and there is a widespread view that common schools represent the only ideal, or in some cases acceptable, form of educational environment.

In this chapter I shall argue that opponents of separate schools have a harder case to argue than is commonly supposed, and that greater recognition needs to be given to the demands of diversity in schooling. My intention here is not to engage in a full-scale defence of separate schools, much less an attack upon the common school. My aim is rather to map some of the major contours of the ethical territory on which debates about separate schools are conducted and to draw attention to some neglected and complex features of the terrain which opponents of separate schools often overlook. Exploration of these features should result not only in a renewed appreciation of the force of the concerns underlying demands for separate schools, and a consideration of some new lines of argument in relation to them, but should also have implications for the illumination of a defensible concept of common schooling.

This chapter has two main sections. The first deals with issues concerning separate schools which arise within what I shall loosely refer to as a 'liberal' conception of education, with its commitment to notions such as critical rationality and rational autonomy. Such a view of education is closely associated with the kind of society delineated by Swann, and can be argued to be a central feature of it. In the second section I shall turn to more intractable problems concerning private schools involving educational principles at odds with those of the liberal tradition.

Before proceeding, however, it is important to note that there can be no simple, general treatment of 'The Ethics of Separate Schools'. This is at least for two reasons.

First, the concept of a 'separate school' is complex. 'Separate schools' (proposed or actual) can be of many different kinds. There is a wide range of (explicit and implicit) criteria for separation based on a variety of characteristics of the students attending the school. These include: ability, disability, gender, ethnicity, race, religion, culture, class, and willingness and capacity of the family to pay school fees. These criteria are often related to each other in complex (explicit and implicit) ways. Each case for separation will employ different criteria (or a different mixture and weighting of them) and the ethical considerations will vary accordingly. A further difficulty is that the notion of 'separation' in schooling can only be understood in contrast to what 'separation' is *from*. The alternative to 'separate schools', 'the common school', gives rise to its own problems.

This first point should dispel a temptation to see the question of separate schooling as arising uniquely in relation to the needs and demands of ethnic minorities. Ethnic diversity provides just one focus upon, and dimension to, a matter of more general educational concern.

Although there can be many kinds of separate school, I shall focus somewhat in this chapter on the specific case of religious schools. This is not only because of the prominence of such schools in recent debate, but also because they raise particularly interesting ethical questions which are of significance with regard to ethnicity.

A second factor preventing a simple treatment of our question is that, even if the kind of separate school at stake is more precisely defined, ethical and philosophical considerations alone cannot settle whether, and in what way, such institutions should be established. Many other issues (for example, of a practical, pedagogic, psychological, sociological, political and demographic kind) need to be considered in a full assessment of practical educational policies. Ethical and philosophical reflection must be conducted in relation to this fuller range of complex considerations and not in an abstract way independent of them.[1] It is rash, for example, to condone or condemn certain kinds of separate school solely on grounds of philosophical principle. Much depends on how the institutions actually operate, and what their effects actually are on students and the broader community.

Liberal education and the separate school

A good example of the conception of education I have in mind here is contained in Richard Pring's chapter in this volume, 'Education for a Pluralist Society' (see pp 19-30), which resonates with, and can only be fully understood in relation to, the fuller tradition of liberal education of which it is a part.

What is meant by 'liberal education'? Leaving to one side narrow conceptions of the notion,[2] I shall offer as an illustration a broad conception developed by Charles Bailey in his book *Beyond the Present and the Particular: a Theory of Liberal Education* (1984 – hereinafter CB). For Bailey, a general liberal education is characterised by four main features:

1 Most importantly, it aims at *liberating* those who receive it. Bailey expresses this in terms of the classic distinction between freedom *from* and freedom *to*. What a liberally educated person is freed *from*, according to Bailey, are the limitations of the 'present and particular' – 'specific and limited circumstances of geography, economy, social class and personal encounter and relationship' (CB, p 21). The education of such a person has not sought to 'entrap or confirm' him or her in these circumstances but to 'widen . . . horizons, increase . . . awareness of choice, reveal . . . prejudices and superstitions as such and multiply . . . points of reference and comparison' (CB, p 21). What a liberally educated person is freed *for*, on Bailey's view, is 'a kind of intellectual and moral autonomy, the capacity to become a free chooser of what is to be believed and what is to be done . . . a free chooser of beliefs and actions . . . a free moral agent, the kind of entity a fully-fledged human being is supposed to be' (CB, p 21). The precise characterisation and defence of this central notion of 'autonomy' in liberal education has given rise to a great deal of discussion, and I shall return to this issue in due course.
2 A commitment in learning and teaching to what is *fundamental* and *general*.
3 A concern to 'locate' – activities in . . .' aspects of knowledge and understanding which can become ends in themselves . . . likely to have intrinsic value rather than *only* capable of serving as means to other ends' (CB, p 20, emphasis in original).
4 A concern for involvement with the life of reason, since this is a necessary condition for the individual achieving anything in 1-3 above. For Bailey 'A general liberal education is necessarily . . . the development of the rational mind . . . simply because nothing else could be so liberating, fundamental or general' (CB, p 20).

Bailey's version of liberal education, with its clear Kantian influences, is, of course, open to a number of lines of query and criticism[3] and is only one of several broad conceptions of liberal education that can be pointed to. Theorists of liberal education differ quite widely in the interpretation and emphasis that they give to elements of the sort outlined by Bailey.[4] It is not necessary here to undertake a detailed mapping of the precise positions of the range of philosophers committed to liberal education or to discuss in any detail the epistemological, ethical and political underpinning of the concept.[5] For my purposes in seeking a basic account of liberal education to inform subsequent discussion, it is sufficient to draw attention to a recognisable family of conceptions including:

(i)   the aim of developing autonomy;
(ii) an emphasis on fundamental and general knowledge;

not GNP or "convok"?

(iii) an aversion to mere instrumentality in determining what is to be learnt; and
(iv) a concern for the development of critical reason which, notwithstanding the complex issues (not least of interpretation) to which they give rise, constitute fundamental elements in the basic concept of liberal education.

Such a conception of education can be clearly discerned in the Swann Report.[6]

It must be remembered that presupposed to this conception of education is a related conception of the sort of society in which it is located. Roughly speaking, this is the pluralist democratic society of which Swann speaks, with its balance of diversity and cohesion. I shall have more to say below about the distinctively liberal principles which underpin such a conception.

In exploring the attitude of liberal educators to separate schools it is helpful to begin by illustrating briefly the implications of this conception of education for a particular area of the curriculum – education (as distinct from catechesis)[7] in religion. These implications are contained in many influential discussions of the subject which, while offering different emphases, share a common viewpoint.[8]

The central implication of this view is, of course, arising from (i) above, that in education in religion, children must not have their religious commitment (or lack of it) determined in any way, but must be allowed to make their own judgements on the basis of appropriate reasoning and evaluation. Arising from (ii) is a notion that a broad introduction to the religious domain is required, not merely the teaching of one religion, and certainly not as if it were true. The implication of (iii) is that education must not see itself as having the merely instrumental aim of producing religious persons and (iv) gives rise to the insistence that appropriate *reasoning* be involved in the judgements made by individuals, and that education should develop this capacity.[9]

What attitude to separate schools is likely to result from such a conception of education? While there is an important gap between the conception and particular schooling arrangements, it is easy to see that each of its features generates a *prima facie* suspicion of separate schools in the mind of the liberal educator. These suspicions can be briefly sketched. With regard to (i) a concern for developing the autonomy of the child, can and will separate schools embody this adequately? Bailey, for example, expresses his concern about religious schools which educate and train their pupils into a predetermined set of beliefs and attitudes (CB, pp 227–28). With regard to (ii) can a separate religious school, with its commitment to the truth of a particular religion, meet the requirement that students be given a broad exposure to the religious domain as whole? Related to these concerns is a doubt about whether a separate religious school can foster adequately the kind of reasoning demanded in (iv). With regard to (iii), liberal educators are sensitive to the possibility that separate religious schools will act as agents not of non-instrumental general education but of specific religious formation.

Liberal concerns of this sort about separate schooling are general ones, and extend to many contexts beyond the specific case of religious schooling. They arise in relation to all separate schools whatever their criteria of membership. A liberal educator will be similarly concerned about threats to autonomy, breadth of curriculum, non-instrumental general education and appropriate reasoning capacity arising for other categories of pupil as a result of their being segregated from the mainstream of pupils in a potentially restrictive educational environment. These include the disabled, gifted, girls, working class and ethnic minority pupils in addition to those who are members of particular religious faiths. In these other cases, the sources of restriction may be seen as arising not only or necessarily from the explicit transmission of a particular view of the good life (as in the case of religious schools) but from (say) implicit assumptions about the character and destiny of the group of pupils in the school and the effects of isolation from the majority of pupils on aspiration, self-perception and opportunity.[10] There is an egalitarian thrust in the liberal position in the sense that *all* children are seen as having a right to a liberal and liberating education, and separate schools can be seen as a threat to this.

Yet these concerns about separate schooling are only *prima facie* in character. This is often overlooked in treatments of liberal education. Discussions of the notion, and its associated ideas and difficulties, have tended merely to assume its institutionalisation in one basic form: common 'pluralist' schools. This has provided the main context for discussions of concepts such as objectivity, neutrality, bias and so on.[11]

But is it possible to conceive of considerations which would lead a liberal educator to see separate schools in certain circumstances as consistent with his or her basic educational commitments? A liberal educator might reply to this that while *in principle* separate schools are unacceptable *in practice* they may need to be tolerated. This is because of the gap that exists between educational principles and their actualisation in any given society. In the formulation of practical educational policy, compromise and practical judgement are necessary, and this may include the acceptance of certain kinds of separate school given practical constraints.[12]

But do liberal educational *principles* licence (certain forms of) separate schooling? There are, of course, a number of levels of principle here, which practical considerations have a role in forming. At the fundamental level are principles concerning the basic aim and character of the liberal educational enterprise, of the sort indicated in (i) – (iv) above. At a subsidiary level are related means principles[13] concerning, say, forms of schooling.

What liberal educational principles might lead to a principled acceptance of (certain sorts of) separate schools? I shall examine four categories of argument, each appealing to a different ground on which distinctive educational provision, including separate schooling, might be claimed. These categories are, of course, not wholly unrelated to each other. (For example, on the common ground that Muslims and Radical Feminists might share in seeking single-sex schools, see Halstead, 1991.) I shall claim that some of the strongest and most neglected arguments for separate schools within the liberal educational tradition are to be found in the final category.

(a) Ethnicity and cultural membership

What significance does membership of an ethnic minority group have from the point of view of liberal education? Bearing in mind the caution that is needed in the use of terms such as 'ethnic minority group' (Swann, p vi), I shall begin by referring generally to 'cultural membership', separating out considerations relating distinctively to ethnicity in due course.[14]

From a liberal point of view, membership of a distinctive cultural community is no ground for claiming that a form of education *radically in conflict* with liberal principles is justified, particularly principles relating to the development of autonomy. This is because the sort of society and community characteristically stressed by liberals gives salience to the political, rather than the cultural, community. The political community is the context or framework in which individuals are fellow citizens, governed by the principles of justice. It is articulated by an insistence upon state neutrality in relation to perfectionist or substantial conceptions of the good life, and seeks to sustain a 'culture of freedom' necessary for individuals to pursue their freedom in choice of lives.[15] The cultural community is the context (involving such shared features as language and history) where individuals live their lives in a fuller sense, forming and putting into practice their substantial conceptions of the good life. Although political and cultural communities may be identical, in culturally plural societies they are not, and the issue of 'minority' cultures arises, together with possibilities for conflict.

That liberalism has neglected the significance of cultural community, plurality and the collective rights of minority cultures is a charge developed by Will Kymlicka, (Kymlicka, 1989), who seeks to provide an appropriate treatment of these matters from within a liberal perspective. He criticises Rawls for failing to include cultural membership as a 'primary good' with which justice should be concerned. However, it is important to note that what emerges from this argument is not a defence of cultural membership *per se*. Such membership is only seen as valuable because individuals need a rich and secure cultural structure to serve as a 'context of choice' in which they become aware of meaningful options and develop the capacity seriously to evaluate them (ibid, ch 8). Certain forms of cultural membership are inimical to liberal ideals, given (say) Rawls' claim that an essential precondition for our being able to pursue our essential interest in leading a good life is that we have the freedom to form and revise our beliefs about value. The 'shared ends' of existing community practices therefore come up for assessment against this criterion. For liberals, cultural membership or ethnic identity *as such* has no moral significance or weight independent of, or in conflict with, its significance for individuals. Nor can it take precedence over the values implicit in political membership, most notably the rights of individuals to full and equal consideration and participation in the political, economic and cultural spheres without regard to race, sex, religion, disability, and so on. Kymlicka therefore uncompromisingly defends the right of individuals within minority cultures (ibid, ch 9). The major educational implication of this view is that membership of a particular cultural community or ethnic group does not in itself generate educational rights fundamentally at odds with the liberal tradition.

However, there is clearly room within liberal principles, and indeed a demand within them, for cultural membership to be *taken into account* in educational arrangements. The most obvious sense in which this is so is in relation to disadvantage. This is where ethnic (and more specifically racial) characteristics assume a particular significance, given their visibility and unalterability and their tendency to lead to disadvantage to individuals and groups because of phenomena such as racism. These characteristics constitute an important set of unchosen, and therefore morally irrelevant, grounds on which disadvantage, an inequality in the 'context of choice', can arise. I shall discuss in (c) below, arguments relating to disadvantage, together with the question of the extent to which *separate schools* are justified on this kind of ground.

In addition to arguments relating to the countering of disadvantage, ethnic and cultural membership should also be taken into account in educational provision because of what is involved in educating *all* children, including children from minority backgrounds, in a fair and adequate way. This generates, among other things, the familiar but important principles relating to the aims, curriculum and practices of the common school contained in Swann's philosophy of *Education for All* (Swann, especially parts II and III).[16]

But can ethnic and cultural membership constitute a ground, within liberal principles, on which *separate schools* can be justified? The Swann Report's misgivings about separate schools catering explicitly to ethnic minority groups encapsulates a mainstream liberal educational response to this proposal. (See Swann; especially ch 8, section II). A similar range of anxieties is evident in the Commission for Racial Equality document *Schools of Faith* (1990).

However, in (d) below, I develop a line of argument relating to complexities in what is involved in the development of autonomy and liberal citizenship, which may offer a broader perspective on the matter.

(b)   The educational rights of parents

The second category of argument yielding a principled ground on which separate schools might be seen as acceptable within a liberal framework of educational values concerns the educational rights of parents, which are often appealed to in the defence of separate schools, and in favour of greater variety of educational provision generally. This category overlaps with (a) but is clearly separable from it.

What attitude to parental rights emerges from the point of view of liberal education?

It seems clear that *unlimited* parental rights are incompatible with such a perspective. Bruce Ackerman, for example, claims that parents have no 'basic right' to determine the education of their children. What is basic here is the right of the *child* to a liberal and liberating education which will provide him or her with the tools for autonomy and self-definition; the opportunity to assess (and perhaps deviate from) parental norms. For Ackerman, such a liberal education is one of the conditions for a liberal political community. Ackerman thus rejects Friedmanite suggestions that schools compete for pupils in the marketplace, with parents having complete freedom of choice of schools via a 'voucher' system. He claims that since parents are likely to spend their vouchers on schools which reinforce their existing values, the plan

> legitimises a series of petty tyrannies in which like-minded parents club together
> to force-feed their children without restraint. Such an education is a mockery of
> the liberal ideal. (Ackerman, 1980, p 160).

Ackerman accuses Friedman of being blind to the moral indoctrination of children undertaken by parents – a process which infringes 'the dialogic rights of the powerless'. As I shall indicate below, this basic position is shared by a large number of philosophers committed to liberal educational principles.

It stands in sharp contrast to much recent advocacy of the rights of parents, for example by the Hillgate group in their manifesto, *Whose Schools?* (Cox *et al*, 1986) and by philosophers such as Antony Flew (Flew, 1987, especially chs 1, 4).

However, the Hillgate Group nowhere *defends* its commitment to parental rights, and nor does it discuss or acknowledge the character and significance of the concept of the autonomy of the child. *Whose Schools?* merely asserts, for example, that – 'Children *need* to be instructed in religious doctrine, in accordance with the wishes and the faith of their parents' (Cox *et al*, 1988, p 2, my emphasis). What is the justification for this need claim? An attempt by Anthony O'Hear to provide a philosophical justification for the Hillgate Group's proposals in an article in *The Times Educational Supplement* (O'Hear, 1987) is deficient. O'Hear claims that the proposals 'allow just the sort of genuine flexibility and diversity in education that true liberals ought to cherish', and he welcomes the notion of different kinds of school in each area promoting its own vision of what a good education should be. He supports this view by invoking J S Mill's strictures in *On Liberty* (Mill, 1859) against the necessarily despotic and homogenising character of a general system of state education. But Mill himself inadequately considers both the significance of the autonomy of the child and the possibility that a certain form of general, common, educational provision might promote it. This inadequacy is inherent therefore in O'Hear's Millian defence of the Hillgate Group proposals. The absense of a convincing justification for parental rights is also a feature of Flew's discussion.[17]

The claim that a (certain sort of) non-parentally determined national curriculum is required by liberal education is a strong one. Both Flew and the Hillgate Group see a national curriculum as compatible with their plans. Indeed, the Hillgate Group sees such a curriculum as 'essential'. However, this is conceived very sketchily in terms of a core of 'reading, writing and arithmetic' and 'a settled range of proven subjects', constituting 'a testable and coveted body of knowledge which it is the duty of any educational system to pass on from generation to generation' (Cox *et al*, 1986, p 7). There is no consideration given to the possibility that what might be required in terms of a core or entitlement curriculum for all young people is a richer diet determined by what is needed as preparation for life as a rationally autonomous person in a pluralistic democracy.[18]

Views such as those of the Hillgate Group and Flew seem to invoke a conception of society such as that described by Amy Gutmann in *Democratic Education* as 'the state of families', where educational authority is placed exclusively in the hands of parents (Gutmann, 1987, pp 28–33). The essence of the arguments which Gutmann develops against this conception echoes Ackerman's and is captured by Gutmann in her principle of 'non-repression'; one of the two principled limits to parental and political authority over education which she specifies (see Gutmann, 1987, pp 44–5).

It is important to note, however, that this denial by liberal educators of *unlimited* parental rights does not involve a denial of *all* parental rights, or their unqualified transferral to (say) the state. It involves merely a denial that parents have a right to determine *exclusively* the educational experience of their children.[19]

The principles of liberal education establish merely in very general terms a *tension* in the determination of schooling between 'rights of parents' and 'rights of children to liberal education'. This 'principled tension' is visible in the positions of many philosophers sympathetic to liberal education.[20] However, Ackerman himself observes that such a principle does not enable us to determine the particular kind of parental control that is justified within a particular institutional setting (Ackerman, 1980, p 148).[21] Agreement at the level of basic principle is compatible with quite wide-ranging dispute about the scope of parental rights thereby licensed. Leaving aside complexities,[22] and arguments from within the liberal tradition arguing for more wide-ranging parental rights,[23] can an argument for certain sorts of separate school be developed within the principles relating to parental rights adopted by the majority of liberal educators?

One source of such an argument concerns disadvantage, which I shall explore in the next section. In section (d) I shall outline my view that, given a defensible 'core' concept of liberal education, there can be a number of forms of it, including certain kinds of separate school, each compatible with the development in the child of fundamental liberal capacities such as autonomy and liberal citizenship, but approaching that development in different ways. In relation to such alternatives, parents can be conceded, within the principles of liberal education, legitimate rights of choice.

(c) Countering disadvantage

I shall discuss this category of justification for separate schools briefly, since, although it often contains strong arguments, its detailed working out and justification involves mainly practical considerations.

The essence of arguments in this category is that certain kinds of pupils are disadvantaged by their attendance at common schools in virtue of the inability of such schools to overcome obstacles to the satisfaction of their specific needs, including their capacity for achieving the kind of autonomous agency enshrined in the aims of liberal education. Thus girls may be thought to flourish better in a single-sex educational environment because of the negative influence on their attitude and achievement by the behaviour of boys and other aspects of sexism; certain categories of able and disabled pupil may require special provision, and pupils from certain ethnic or racial minorities may be thought to benefit from being removed from common schools in which they meet hostility and a failure to address their distinctive cultural and other needs. It might be thought that, at least in certain circumstances, these measures *could* include the justification of certain sorts of separate school.

Arguments of this general sort vary in the extent to which they see the considerations invoked as short term, arising (for example) from the contingent features of existing common schools, or more permanent in character. The detailed justification of arguments of this sort, especially the claim that the need for distinctive provision requires separate *schools*, depends upon fairly extensive empirical argument in the light of powerful countervailing arguments concerning the value of common provision. Such separate schools would, of course, need to satisfy certain conditions relating to the fundamental principles of liberal education, not least those relating to the development of critical rationality and independence.

Liberal principles create room for such a line of argument, because it concerns justice, which is a central liberal ideal. The detailed working out and justification of the argument in particular cases is, however, essentially an empirical task, given an alertness to the value judgements that may be involved in the categorisation of pupils and the delineation of their needs. I turn now to a category of argument in which philosophical considerations have a more direct role to play.

(d) *Alternative starting points for autonomy and liberal citizenship*

This final category of justification for separate schools may overlap with the others but is not uniquely associated with any one of them. The central claim here, which has a more distinctively philosophical flavour to it, is that there are a number of legitimate educational starting points[24] for the child's journey towards autonomy and liberal citizenship. In relation to these, both ethnic/cultural identity and parental rights have significance.

One such starting point for a child is indeed from the basis of experience in a common school, and the various values to which it is committed.[25] However, another possible and legitimate starting point is from the basis of experience of a particular 'world view' or cultural identity; a substantiality of belief, practice and value, as in (say) a certain sort of religious school. Such schools, in relation to which parents can exercise legitimate rights of choice, would not seek to entrap their pupils in a particular vision of the good, but to provide a distinctive starting point from which their search for autonomous agency can proceed.

I have developed elsewhere the view that there are a number of different schooling contexts in which the demands of 'openness' and 'stability' in the conditions required for the development of autonomy can be variously balanced (McLaughlin, 1987)[26] and have indicated a number of the complex conceptual and practical issues to which it gives rise. The argument is parallel to one concerning the rights of parents within a liberal framework of values to give their children certain sorts of religious upbringing.[27]

Although my development of the argument elsewhere refers to the notion of a 'liberal religious school', I see no reason why a similar argument could not be developed in relation to a number of the other kinds of distinctive school that might be advocated.

The motivation for such an argument stems not merely from the need for practical compromise in the formation of educational policy, but from complexities inherent in the basic principles of both liberalism and liberal education. These difficulties are related to the neglect by liberals of cultural aspects of community which was mentioned earlier, but are also associated with more wide-ranging concerns about liberalism. I shall illustrate these by indicating briefly some of the philosophical challenges which have been made to the principles. Points have been made such as the following:

- the danger of invoking an unduly abstract and a-historical conception of autonomy, rationality and the human agent;
- a possible neglect of the rootedness of persons in particular cultural traditions of belief, practice and value and of the significance of involvement and engagement in such traditions for the ability to achieve identity and critical independence;
- use of an unreal model of the child as an abstract, rootless chooser, unchanged by choices made;

- the need to encourage initial stable beliefs, reflective commitment and a range of determinate dispositions and virtues in the development of autonomy;
- lack of specification of the character and range of autonomy, and of critical reflection;
- the impossibility of determining a single optimum route to the achievement of autonomy;
- the problem of specifying general criteria for choice and value;
- difficulties in distinguishing between 'public' and 'private' values.

Such difficulties are elaborated and discussed not only by philosophers of education,[28] but also by philosophers sympathetic to the values and benefits of tradition and by communitarian critics of liberalism.[29]

Difficulties of this sort are seen by some as requiring the rejection of liberalism and liberal education. However, another response is to see them as requiring not abandonment of these notions but their restatement in a more nuanced way.[30] Part of this, I suggest, involves acceptance of the notion of a plurality of legitimate forms of liberal education and schooling. At the very least, the difficulties indicated cast doubt on the suggestion that there is anything straightforward about the conditions in which liberal education can best take place. For example, they indicate the complexities involved in outlining significantly non-controversial ethical and other principles for the conduct of the common school, even within a liberal framework of values. Among the issues here are dangers of superficiality in learning, or disorientation, arising from a 'babel of values' in the common school, and doubts about whether the fairness of such a context can be sufficiently established to enable it to be insisted upon as the only context in which liberal education can take place. There are also concerns about whether the values of the common school can be 'thick' enough to generate a deeply humanising education.[31]

While all these issues require further discussion, the onus lies with liberal educationalists opposed to all forms of separate schooling to show that the difficulties mentioned above can be resolved in such a way that only one starting point and institutional form of liberal education can be specified, and the one I suggest as an alternative for parental choice be ruled out either on grounds of incoherence or incompatibility with the liberal ideal. Part of this task would be to show that philosophical difficulties concerning the significant neutrality of the common school can be overcome.[32]

A crucial question here concerns the sorts of conditions that would need to be satisfied by acceptable separate schools. These conditions relate to the role of the school in achieving a balance between 'openness' and 'stability' in such a way that the development of both autonomy and liberal citizenship are not frustrated. I have attempted to say something about these conditions elsewhere (McLaughlin, 1987, pp 77–83).

A full defence of this notion would require a detailed treatment of such matters. In the case of religious schools, it would need to take account of the wide ranging debate concerning them which has been in progress for some time.[33] Another issue requiring attention concerns the *status* and *funding* of such schools, which is in turn related to the distinction between the state and private provision of education, and the right of parents to pay for the education of their children privately. Given the egalitarian thrust of liberal education principles, this is an issue which is troubling for liberal educators. I cannot, however, pursue it here.[34]

It is appropriate to refer to two lines of criticism which relate particularly to issues of ethnicity. Both concern the point that, although there may be some doubt about the precise sense and extent to which liberals generally are committed to a vision of community, there is an undeniable need for society to be held together by communal bonds, commitments, loyalties and the like, which go beyond mere toleration.[35] While a pluralist society must be *diverse*, it must also be *cohesive*, and separate schools may be seen as a significant threat to the achievement of this in at least two ways.

First, separate schools may fail to develop in their students the range of qualities demanded by liberal citizenship. These include an understanding of, and commitment to, the publicly recognised principles of justice together with qualities of understanding, imaginative sympathy and the like.[36] However, schools justified within the liberal framework of values will have as one of their conditions that they engage in an appropriate programme of civic education, not limited (for example) by a lack of critical thrust.[37] The strongest forms of criticism of this claim require justification of the view that there is something inherent in the very notion of separateness which makes the achievement of certain of these objectives very difficult, impossible or incoherent. It is also important to bear in mind that common schools, in virtue of the 'thin' character of the values which underpin them, may have their own difficulties in achieving their civic aims.[38]

The second concern, of particular significance for ethnicity, involves the fear that separate schools may lead to segregation of different ethnic, cultural and racial groups within society, with its attendant evils such as the spread of prejudice and discrimination. While this is a genuine concern, there is insufficient evidence to make a clear judgement about this matter.

It is important to note that considerations relating to all these issues requires a judgement to be made about the *balance* to be drawn between the legitimate demands of diversity and cohesion, openness and stability. A strong case against separate schools requires that balance to be drawn in a very confident way in a situation of considerable complexity.

A major concern about separate schools among liberal educators is that acceptance of them will lead to the establishment of schools of a distinctly illiberal character. I turn now to problems relating to schools of this kind.

Non-liberal education and separate schools

I have argued in the first section of this chapter that separate schools *of a certain sort* may be compatible, at least in principle, with liberal educational principles. In this second section of the chapter, I shall explore some of the questions concerning separate schools which emanate from, and are associated with, conceptions of education in conflict with the liberal view.

The presence in societies such as Britain of ethnic or religious minorities who do not value the autonomous life poses a major practical and theoretical challenge to liberal education and to liberal democratic theory generally.[39] Our earlier discussion has illustrated how individual autonomy and critical independence are non-negotiable elements of the liberal point of view. Thus liberal philosophers such as Joseph Raz hold that communities not supporting autonomy, even if they are 'morally worthy' in the sense that they do not harm or restrict the freedom of non-members and provide a life for its members which is adequate and satisfying, have a culture inferior to liberal ones. In relation to such cultures, options of coercion, assimilation and (mere) toleration arise (Raz, 1986, pp 423–4). Susan Mendus claims that in such cases liberalism will see toleration not as a good, but as a necessary evil (1989, ch 4). This principled position applies also to non-liberal educational views, proposals and practices. Thus John White insists that in an 'autonomy-supporting' society, *all* children must be protected against true believers who wish to impose on them a non-autonomous conception of the good life' (1990, p 105, emphasis in original). Similarly Pring insists that not every cultural tradition is educationally acceptable. Those which, in various ways, close the mind to reflection and critical enquiry are anti-educational and therefore not to be given equal status.

A host of *practical* difficulties arise for liberals from such views. What is actually done about illiberal cultural traditions and groups? Because of the range of negative effects associated with policies of coercion, caution is invariably urged in relation to them (see, for example Raz, 1986, p 424).[40] Such caution can be seen also in the educational domain in White's acceptance that 'gentle' methods of persuasion should be adopted, avoiding open conflict between different cultural groups and respecting the integrity of the child's psychological development (White, J, 1990, p 105). Pring, however, rules out negotiation as a means of dealing with such educational disputes, so it is difficult to know how he would proceed in a situation of conflict.

It may be felt, therefore, that this general problem is one to be settled by practical politics, in an untidy process of struggle, compromise and, perhaps, democratic vote.[41] One element in such a process is the political difficulty of conceding separate schools to some cultural groups and not others. It may be thought politically impossible to render explicit the grounds for refusal, which may lead to the surfacing of other profound sources of conflict in a multicultural society.[42]

Leaving political and practical considerations to one side, it is by no means obvious, however, that the issues of *principle* are clear here. How are the non-liberal cultures at issue to be *identified*? This is not merely a practical matter. The theoretical difficulty with this question for liberals can be illuminted by reference to obscurities concerning the meaning and justification of their central notion of autonomy.

I shall approach this point by looking first at matters of justification. Both White and Raz advance a justification for autonomy which at first sight seems powerful. They both concede that such a justification which applies to human beings in general, those in both 'tradition-directed' and 'non tradition-directed' societies, cannot be provided, but that in a non-tradition directed society, but not necessarily in any other, autonomy is necessary to flourishing.[43] Such a claim is attractive in that it offers the possibility of avoiding controversial fundamental value disputes by appealing to practicality. For us, claims Raz, 'The value of autonomy is a fact of life. Since we live in a society whose social forms are to a considerable degree based on individual choice . . . we can prosper in it only if we can be successfully autonomous' (1986, p 394).[44] This claim needs, however, to be treated with considerable caution, which becomes clear when questions about the meaning of autonomy are turned to.

What is the *nature* and *extent* of the kind of autonomy that is justified on this view? White appeals to a distinction between *autarchy* and *autonomy* (White, J, 1990, p 97).

The rational deliberation and self-determination of the (merely) autarchic person is limited in extent and scope, not extending, for example, as far as calling into question fundamental matters of belief or convention (such as prevailing social structures). Thus, one can be autarchic within the confines of a tradition-directed society or cultural group. In contrast, the rational deliberation of autonomous persons must extend much further. They must achieve a distanced critical perspective on all important matters, and their belief and action must result from principles and policies which they have themselves 'ratified' by critical reflection. A distinction of a similar sort between kinds, levels or degrees of autonomy has been drawn by a number of writers.[45]

The crucial question here is whether the 'practical' justification demonstrates only the value of autarchy,[46] given the underdetermined and ambiguous character of the term 'autonomy.'[47] Mendus complains that the attempt by liberals to articulate concepts of autonomy and rationality independent of the background or assumptions (relating to, say, metaphysics or the teleology of human nature) invoked by philosophers such as Kant, Locke and Mill makes it impossible to assess and use them. They become vacuous (1989, pp 88-109).

It is clear that every cultural group and tradition will value and embody certain forms of reason and individual thought.[48] Can criteria be outlined to indicate the degree and kind of critical thought that is constitutive of acceptable autonomy? There are a number of difficulties here concerning not only the specification of these criteria (in the light, for example, of problems about the limits of fundamental questioning) but also the correct identification of their absence or presence in the cultural groups and traditions at issue (given, for example, problems of knowledge, understanding and interpretation). Care is needed, for example, in the use of the notion of fundamentalism in relation to certain cultural groups (see CRE, 1990, pp 16-18).[49] This is particularly true in the case of Islam.[50] These problems are carried over into educational proposals made by the various groups.[51] It is also important to remember that potentially illiberal views and proposals should not be uniquely identified with minority cultural groups.

It is difficult to draw a very sharp line in practice between views which fall inside, and those which fall outside, the liberal education tradition. The suggestion here is that it is also difficult to draw such lines in theory.

In the light of this it is appropriate for liberals to regard all proposals for separate schooling as falling *prima facie* within the framework of principles outlined in the previous section of this chapter. This will have a number of benefits. As well as being even handed and a defence against the misunderstanding, misrepresentation and alienation of minority cultures and their educational demands,[52] such an approach offers the best hope for the defensible liberalisation of such proposals and the avoidance of the development and entrenchment of patently illiberal attitudes.

It may well be that certain proposals will be unacceptable. If so, one benefit of this strategy will be to focus discussion on the concrete issues at stake, rather than matters of elusive abstract principle.

An important factor in creating a climate for the discussion of issues of separate schooling which is both just and likely to promote the most satisfactory solutions overall is for liberal educators to acknowledge that, given their complexity, there is a less strong and direct connection than is sometimes supposed between their educational principles and the notion of the common school.

Acknowledgements

An earlier version of this chapter was presented as a paper to a meeting of the London Branch of the Philosophy of Education Society of Great Britain. I am grateful to the participants in that discussion for helpful comments. I am also grateful to my colleague, Madeleine Arnot, for the benefit of her remarks on an earlier draft of this work. The chapter was completed during my fellowship at the Centre for Philosophy and Public Affairs at the Department of Moral Philosophy at the University of St Andrews. I am very grateful to Dr John Haldane, Director of the Centre, for his offer of the Fellowship and for making my stay so fruitful and congenial.

Notes

1 For a further discussion of this, and related matters, see Hirst (1983).
2 I shall therefore be using the term in a broader way than Hirst does in his well known and influential paper, 'Liberal education and the nature of knowledge' and related discussions (Hirst, 1974a, chs 3, 6). Hirst sees liberal education as providing only a *part*, albeit for him an important part, of the total experience of the child. He claims that in addition to liberal education, but distinct from it, are aspects of education such as specialist education, physical education and the development of moral character. This is because Hirst sees liberal education as the unconstrained development of the mind in rational knowledge. It is concerned solely with crucial (non-instrumental) aspects of the cognitive elements of the achievements of rational autonomous agency, the necessary dispositions and capacities crucial to the child actually *functioning* as an autonomous person, and the additional knowledge necessary, being supplied from outside it. Hirstian liberal education may provide a necessary basis for these other achievements, but is not itself directly concerned with them. In my view, there are good reasons for rejecting this 'narrow' conception of liberal education in favour of a broader one. (See, for example, Bailey, 1984, pp 79–80; White, J, 1982, p 70).
3 For comment upon, and criticism of, Bailey's view, see, for example, Gibson, (1986); O'Hear, (1985).
4 For example, Bruce Ackerman significantly plays down (ii) and (iii) in his account (Ackerman, 1980, ch 5). John White's view of liberal education is in conflict with Bailey's interpretation of (iii) and (iv). With regard to (iv), White's later writings have tended, without denying the significance of the development of critical reason, to place more emphasis on the shaping of dispositions, virtues and qualities of personhood more generally. (See, for example, White, J, 1982, ch 6; 1990; White and O'Hear, 1991). Relevant also here is Patricia White's work on the nature and educational significance of democratic virtues such as self-esteem, self-respect, courage, friendship, trust, hope and confidence. (White, P, 1987a, 1987b, 1989, 1990, 1991a, 1991b). Philosophers of education of a more existentialist persuasion, such as Michael Bonnett, whom Bailey considers to be a liberal educator, offer a distinctive interpretation of both (i) and (iv). (See, for example, Bonnett, 1986.) In relation to (iii) a number of liberal educators have attempted to achieve a reconciliation of liberal and vocational aims (Pring, 1985; Wallace, 1986). For Pring's reservations about certain construals of (i) see Pring, 1984, pp 72–5.
5 On these matters see, for example, Crittenden (1982), Hirst (1985), White, J (1990).

6 See McLaughlin, (1987).

7 On the distinction between education and catechesis, see, for example, Hirst (1981).

8 See, for example, Cox and Cairns (1989), Hirst (1972, 1974a, especially ch 3, p 12, 1974b, 1981, 1984, 1985), Hull (1984), Schools Council (1971), Sealey (1985), Smart (1968), Swann, Ch 8.

9 These claims involve related claims about the character and status of the religious domain. These include such claims as: it is possible to engage in reasoning in some form in the area of religion; that no one set of religious claims can be *shown* to be true; that there is controversiality about their status; that important distinctions between the religious and moral domains need to be acknowledged, and so on.

10 These concerns may, of course, arise in relation to religious schools also. See Clara Connolly's chapter in this volume, pp 137-45.

11 Despite an otherwise comprehensive and wide-ranging approach to the subject, Bailey seems to assume throughout that the 'common school' is the only context in which liberal education can take place, and religious schooling, for example, is characterised in rather a crude way and ruled out (see, for example, CB, pp 227-8). On general issues concerning objectivity, neutrality and bias see Bridges (1986).

12 An example of this approach is the position of the minority report in Swann on the question of religious schools (Swann, p 515), where such schools are seen as contingently valuable and necessary because Swann's conception of *Education for All* is not yet a reality, and existing common schools do not yet meet the needs and concerns of minority groups. The minority report concedes that when *Education for All* is enacted, separate religious schools will be unnecessary (Swann, p 515).

13 The distinction between ends and means in the educational context needs to be treated with considerable caution. On this, see, for example, Sockett (1973).

14 On the notion of 'ethnic identity' see Swann, ch 1, para 2.

15 For an outline of the liberal position in more detail see, for example, Brown (1986, ch 3); Kymlicka (1990, ch 3); Mendus (1989, ch 4); White, P (1983, chs 1, 2). At the heart of liberalism is a kind of agnosticism, or at least a lack of certainty, about what the good life, in any substantial sense, consists in. In the light of this, Rawls, at any rate in the original version of his theory (Rawls, 1971), invokes a non-perfectionist 'thin' theory of the good, putatively free of significantly controversial assumptions and judgements, to distribute to individuals in a just way 'primary goods' (such as liberties and opportunities). These primary goods, neutral between particular, or substantial, conceptions of the good, enable individuals to pursue, within a framework of justice, many different ways of, and conceptions of, life. (For Rawls' later views, which involve what has been described as a 'communitarian turn' see Rawls, 1985, 1987, 1988. For some specific criticisms of Rawls see Haldane, 1985, 1991a. The explicit commitment of liberalism to the value of autonomy is apparent in Rawls' later work. See also Raz, 1986.)

16 For a discussion of central concepts concerning education and cultural diversity see Halstead (1988, ch 6-8).

17 Flew claims that his view of education 'follows as a corollary from a recognition of the most fundamental and universal human rights' (Flew, 1987, p 14), but the rights in question are never analysed, and there is no detailed treatment of the tension and potential conflict between the rights of parents and of children.

18 On such a requirement, see, for example, White, J (1990); White and O'Hear (1991); White, P (1988a); Crittenden (1988, ch 5, 7); Peters (1981); Swann, part II.

19 Gutmann, for example, holds that neither parents nor the state have a right to complete authority over the education of children. Ackerman acknowledges that the child's family will typically exercise continuing powers of 'legitimate control and guidance' over their children and that this will have implications for the rights of professional educators

(Ackerman, 1980, ch 5). See also the various educational duties, including duties of coordination and monitoring, which Patricia White lays upon parents (White, 1983, ch 5). For a general treatment of parental choice in education see Johnson (1990).

20 See, for example, Bishop (1980); Bigelow (1988); Callan (1985); Chamberlin, R (1989); Crittenden (1988); Feinberg (1980); Fisher (1982); Gutmann (1987); Hamm (1982); Henley (1979); Hobson (1984); Walzer (1983); White, J (1990); White, P (1983, 1988a, 1991c); Young (1980).

21 For an illustration of this general point see Gutmann (1987, ch 3, 5).

22 One question which can be raised about this 'tension' is whether it is a tension between conflicting *rights*. It has been argued that the parent has no educational rights which are independent of the child's right to liberal education (see, for example, White, P, 1983, ch 5). If all parental rights are seen as subserving the educational rights of children in this way, then no real tension between *rights* can arise; the tension is one between conflicting *duties*.

23 See, for example, Cohen (1981), Coons and Sugarman (1978).

24 Clarification of the notion of a 'starting point' is required here. This might be understood in one of two senses. In a weak sense, it might refer to the beliefs (etc.) that the student actually brings into the classroom from his or her background, previous reflection and so on. These existing beliefs are the 'starting point' for the educational enterprise in that (roughly expressed) it is the 'material' that must be acted upon. There must clearly be a plurality of 'starting points' in this sense, especially since the range of beliefs brought to the class by students in the common school might be very wide. However, I have in mind a stronger sense of 'starting point'. This is where the educational process itself starts off with the presupposition of the truth of (say) a particular religious position which is presented as the 'norm' of belief and practice initially and from which the search for critical independence proceeds.

25 For an outline of these see, for example, Hirst (1974b; 1981; 1985).

26 For a similar general point expressed in terms of the need to achieve a balance between distance and proximity to the surrounding world in the development and exercise of autonomy see Mendus (1989, ch 4).

27 See McLaughlin (1984, 1985, 1990); Callan (1985); Gardner (1988; 1991).

28 See, for example, Callan (1989); Crittenden (1988); Godfrey (1984); Haydon (1986, 1987b); Jones (1987); Lloyd (1980, 1986); Thiessen (1987); Ward (1983); White, J and P (1986); White, J (1990).

29 For emphasis on the importance of tradition see, for example, Almond (1990); Bambrough, (1987); Cooper, (1987); Hampshire (1983); Kekes (1988, 1989); Kerr (1986); MacIntyre (1981, 1987, 1988, 1990); Midgley (1980, especially ch 12); Nagel (1979, ch 9); Oakeshott (1962, especially the essays 'Rationalism in politics', 'The tower of Babel', 'Rational conduct', 'On being Conservative'); O'Hear (1981, ch 5, 1985, 1986, 1988); Quinton (1971); Scruton (1980a, 1980b, 1983); Weil (1952). On the communitarian critics of liberalism, see, for example, Gutmann (1985); Sandel (1982); Sacks (1991); Kymlicka (1989, especially ch 4, 8; 1990, ch 6); Macedo (1990); Rasmussen (1990).

30 See, for example, Kymlicka (1989, especially ch 4, 8); Macedo (1991).

31 See Strike (1991).

32 On this see, for example, Crittenden (1988: esp 120-128; 206-218), Callan(1989); McLaughlin (1987: especially 75-77; 1991).

33 For criticisms of religious schools see, for example, Ball, S (1988); Ball, W and Troyna (1987); Commission for Racial Equality (1990); O'Keeffe (1988c); Socialist Educational Association (1981, 1986); Swann, ch 8.

For arguments in favour of religious schools see, for example, Ashraf (1988); Commission for Racial Equality (1990); Deakin (1989a, 1989b); Duncan (1988); Halstead (1986); O'Keeffe (1986: esp ch 5, 6; 1988b); Socialist Educational Association (1981: Appendix C).

34 On the general issue of whether religious schools should be supported by public funds see, for example, Almond (1988); Callan (1988); Crittenden (1988, especially ch 8); Flew (1968); Strike (1982, ch 5). For a broad perspective on issues relating to public and private provision of education see Walford (1990).

35 On this see, for example, Callan (1991); Haldane (1991b); Mendus (1989).

36 For an outline of the 'democratic virtues' and their educational significance, see White, P (1983, 1987a, 1987b, 1988b, 1989, 1990, 1991a, 1991b).

37 Compare Galston (1989).

38 See Strike (1991, p 30).

39 On this, see, for example, White, J (1990: pp 24-6; 103-5); Mendus (1989, especially ch 4-6).

40 Alternative policies can involve attempts to liberalise such traditions and groups without destroying them (see, for example, Kymlicka, 1990, p 170).

41 For a celebrated recent example of a pratical conflict see the case of *Wisconsin* v. *Yoder* in the USA, which concerned the desire of parents from the Old Order Amish community not to send their children to school beyond the age of 14 because of its corrosive effects on their traditional way of life. For the text of the judgements see O'Neill and Ruddick (eds) (1979, pp 280-305). For discussion see, for example, Feinberg (1980).

42 On such conflicts see, for example, Harris (1982).

43 See, for example, White, J (1990, pp 25-6, ch 6).

44 For a similar argument about the implications of the fact of pluralism for the immunity of holders of traditional views from reflection, see Fitzmaurice (1992).

45 See, for example, Ward (1983); Barrow (1974, especially 123-4); Phillips (1975).

46 White concedes that Raz's judgement justifies merely the value of autarchy and not autonomy. For his attempt to support Raz's conclusion with a supplementary argument see White, J (1990, 98-103).

47 For an annotated bibliography of sources relating to the concept of autonomy and its significance for education see Karjohn (1989, pp 104-10). See also Haworth (1986); Young (1986); Dworkin (1988).

48 See, for example, MacIntyre (1988, especially ch 17, 18).

49 On the notion of fundamentalism, see, for example, Barr (1977); Sacks (1991: ch 5).

50 On Islam, critical thought and post-enlightenment culture, see, for example, Akhtar (1990).

51 On some of the philosophical complexities involved in proposals for Muslim schools, see Halstead (1986).

52 See, for example, Straw (1989).

References

Ackerman, B, A (1980) *Social Justice in the Liberal State*, Yale University Press, New Haven and London.

Akhtar, S (1990) *A Faith for All Seasons. Islam and Western Modernity*, Bellew Publishing, London.

Aiken, W and LaFollette, H (eds) (1980) *Whose Child? Children's Rights, Parental Authority, and State Power*, Littlefield, Adams & Co, Totowa, New Jersey.

Almond, B (1988) 'Conflict or Compromise? Religious and moral education in a plural context', in McClelland, V A (ed) (1988).

Almond, B (1990) 'Alasdair MacIntyre: the virtue of tradition', *Journal of Applied Philosophy* 7, 1, 99-103.

Ashraf, S (1988) 'A view of Education – an Islamic Perspective', in O'Keeffe, B (ed) (1988a).

Bailey, C (1984) *Beyond the Present and the Particular: a Theory of Liberal Education*, Routledge and Kegan Paul, London.

Bambrough, R (1987) 'The roots of moral reason' in Straughan, R and Wilson J (eds) *Philosophers on Education*, Macmillan, London.

Ball, S (1988) 'A comprehensive school in a pluralist world – division and inequalities' in O'Keeffe, B (ed) (1988a).

Ball, W and Troyna, B (1987) 'Resistance, rights and rituals: denominational schools and multi-cultural education', *Journal of Educational Policy*, 2, 1, pp 15–25.

Barr, J (1977) *Fundamentalism*, SCM Press, London.

Barrow, R (1974) *Plato, Utilitarianism and Education*, Routledge and Kegan Paul, London.

Bigelow, H, Campbell, J, Dodds, S M, Pargetter, R, Prior, E W and Young, R (1988) 'Parental autonomy', *Journal of Applied Philosophy*, 5, 2, pp 183–96.

Bishop, S (1980) 'Children, autonomy, and the right to self-determination', in Aiken, W and LaFollette H (eds).

Bonnett, M (1986) 'Personal authenticity and public standards: towards the transcendence of a dualism', in Cooper, D E (ed) *Education, Values and Mind. Essays for R S Peters*, Routledge and Kegan Paul, London.

Bridges, D (1986) 'Dealing with controversy in the school curriculum; a philosophical perspective', in Wellington, J J (ed) *Controversial Issues in the Curriculum*, Basil Blackwell, Oxford.

Brown, A (1986) *Modern Political Philosophy: Theories of the Just Society*, Penguin, Harmondsworth.

Callan, E (1985) 'McLaughlin on parental rights', *Journal of Philosophy of Education*, 19, 1, pp 111–18.

Callan, E (1988) 'Justice and denominational schooling', *Canadian Journal of Education*, 13, 3, pp 367–83.

Callan, E (1989) 'Godless moral education and liberal tolerance', *Journal of Philosophy of Education*, 23, 2, pp 267–81.

Callan, E (1991) 'Pluralism and civic education', *Studies in Philosophy and Education*, 11, 1, pp 65–87.

Chamberlin, R (1989) *Free Children and Democratic Schools: A Philosophical Study of Liberty and Education*, Falmer Press, Lewes.

Cohen, B (1981) *Education and the Individual*, George Allen and Unwin, London.

Commission for Racial Equality (1990) *Schools of Faith. Religious Schools in a Multicultural Society*, CRE, London.

Coons, J E and Sugarman, S D (1978) *Education by Choice: the Case for Family Control*, University of California Press, Berkeley.

Cooper, D E (ed) (1986) *Education, Values and Mind. Essays for R S Peters*, Routledge and Kegan Paul, London.

Cooper, D E (1987) 'Multi-cultural education', in North, J (ed), *The GCSE: An Examination*, The Claridge Press, London.

Cox, C, Douglas-Hume, J, Marks, J, Norcross, L, Scruton, R (1986) *Whose Schools? A Radical Manifesto*, The Hillgate Group, London.

Cox, E and Cairns, J M (1989) *Reforming Religious Education: The Religious Clauses of the 1988 Education Reform Act*, Kogan Page, London.

Crittenden, B (1982) *Cultural Pluralism and Common Curriculum*, University Press, Melbourne.

Crittenden, B (1988) *Parents, the State and the Right to Educate*, Melbourne University Press, Victoria.

Deakin, R (1989a) *The New Christian Schools*, Regius Press, Bristol.

Deakin, R (1989b) *New Christian Schools: The Case for Public Funding*, Regius Press, Bristol.

Duncan, G (1988) 'Church schools in service to the community', in O'Keeffe, B (ed) (1988a).

Dworkin, G (1988) *The Theory and Practice of Autonomy*, University Press, Cambridge.

Feinberg, J (1980) 'The child's right to an open future', in Aiken, W and LaFollette, H (eds).

Fisher, D (1982) 'Family choice and education: privatizing a public good', in Manley-Casimir, M E (ed).

Fitzmaurice, D (1992) 'Liberal neutrality, religious minorities and education', in Horton, J (ed) *Liberalism, Multiculturalism and Toleration*, Macmillan, London, forthcoming.

Flew, A (1968) 'Against indoctrination' in Ayer, A J (ed) *The Humanist Outlook*, Pemberton, London.

Flew, A (1987) *Power to the Parents: Reversing Educational Decline*, The Sherwood Press, London.

Galston, W (1989) 'Civic education in the liberal state', in Rosenblum, N L (ed).

Gardner, P (1988) 'Religious upbringing and the liberal ideal of religious autonomy', *Journal of Philosophy of Education*, 22, 1, pp 89–105.

Gardner, P (1991) 'Personal autonomy and religious upbringing: the "problem" ', *Journal of Philosophy of Education*, 25, 1, pp 69–81.

Gibson, R (ed) (1986) *Liberal Education Today?*, Institute of Education, Cambridge.

Great Britain, Parliament, House of Commons, (1985) *Education for All*, The Report of the Committee of Inquiry into the Education of Children from Ethnic Minority Groups, (Swann Report) cmnd 9453, HMSO, London.

Godfrey, R (1984) 'John White and the imposition of autonomy', *Journal of Philosophy of Education*, 18, 1, pp 115–18.

Gutmann, A (1985) 'Communitarian critics of liberalism', *Philosophy and Public Affairs*, 14, 3, pp 308–22.

Gutmann, A (1987) *Democratic Education*, University Press, Princeton

Haldane, J (1985) 'Individuals and the theory of justice', *Ratio*, XXVII, pp 189–96.

Haldane, J (1991a) 'Political theory and the nature of perons: an ineliminable metaphysical presupposition', *Philosophical Papers*, XX, 2, pp 77–95.

Haldane, J (1991b) 'Identity, community and the limits of multiculture', paper presented to meeting on 'Identity, Community and Culture', Centre for Philosophy and Public Affairs, University of St Andrews, December 1991.

Halstead, J M (1986) *The Case for Muslim Voluntary-Aided Schools. Some Philosophical Reflections*, The Islamic Academy, Cambridge.

Halstead, J M (1988) *Education, Justice and Cultural Diversity: An Examination of the Honeyford Affair, 1984–85*, Falmer Press, Lewes.

Halstead, J M (1991) 'Radical feminism, Islam and the single-sex school debate', *Gender and Education*, 3, 3, pp 263–78.

Hamm, C (1982) 'Constraints on parents' rights concerning the education of their children', in Manley-Casimir M E (ed).

Hampshire, S (1983) *Morality and Conflict*, Basil Blackwell, Oxford.

Harris, J (1982) 'A paradox of multicultural societies', *Journal of Philosophy of Education*, 16, 2, pp 223–33.

Haydon, G (1986) 'Collective moral philosophy and education for pluralism', *Journal of Philosophy of Education*, 20, 1, pp 97–105.

Haydon, G (ed) (1987a) *Education for a Pluralist Society. Philosophical Perspectives on the Swann Report*, Bedford Way Papers no 30, Institute of Education, University of London.

Haydon, G (1987b) 'Towards "a Framework of Commonly Accepted Values" ', in Haydon, G (ed) (1987a).

Haworth, L (1986) *Autonomy: An Essay in Philosophical Psychology and Ethics*, Yale University Press, New Haven and London.

Henley, K (1979) 'The authority to educate', in O'Neill and Ruddick (eds).

Hirst, P H (1972) 'Christian education: a contradiction in terms?', *Learning for Living*, 11, 4, pp 6–11.

Hirst, P H (1974a) *Knowledge and the Curriculum. A collection of philosophical papers*, Routledge and Kegan Paul, London.

Hirst, P H (1974b) *Moral Education in a Secular Society*, Hodder and Stoughton, London.

Hirst, P H (1981) 'Education, catechesis and the church school', *British Journal of Religious Education*, Spring, pp 85–93, 101.

Hirst, P H (1983) 'Educational Theory', in Hirst, P H (ed) *Educational Theory and its Foundation Disciplines*, Routledge and Kegan Paul, London.

Hirst, P H (1984) 'Philosophy of education', in Sutcliffe J M (ed) *A Dictionary of Religious Education*, SCM Press, London.

Hirst, P H (1985) 'Education and diversity of belief', in Felderhof, M C (ed) *Religious Education in a Pluralistic Society*, Hodder and Stoughton, London.

Hobson, P (1984) 'Some reflections on parents' rights in the upbringing of their children', *Journal of Philosophy of Education*, 18, 1, pp 63–74.

Hull, J M (1984) *Studies in Religion and Education*, Falmer Press, Lewes.

Johnson, D (1990) *Parental Choice in Education*, Unwin Hyman, London.

Jones, M (1987) 'Prejudice', in Haydon, G (ed) (1987a).

Karjohn, L (1989) 'Annotated bibliography', in White, P (ed) *Personal and Social Education: Philosophical Perspectives*, Kogan Page, London.

Kekes, J (1988) *The Examined Life*, Associated University Presses, London.

Kekes, J (1989) *Moral Tradition and Individuality*, University Press, Princeton, New Jersey.

Kerr, F (1986) *Theology after Wittgenstein*, Basil Blackwell, Oxford.

Kymlicka, W (1989) *Liberalism, Community, and Culture*, Clarendon Press, Oxford.

Kymlicka, W (1990) *Contemporary Political Philosophy: An Introduction*, Clarendon Press, Oxford.

Lloyd, D I (1980) 'The rational curriculum: a critique', *Journal of Curriculum Studies*, 12, 4, pp 331–42.

Lloyd, I (1986) 'Confession and reason', *British Journal of Religious Education*, 8, pp 140–5.

Macedo, S (1990) *Liberal Virtues: Citizenship, Virtue, and Community in Liberal Contitutionalism*, Clarendon Press, Oxford.

McClelland, V A (ed) (1988) *Christian Education in a Pluralist Society*, Routledge, London.

MacIntyre, A (1981) *After Virtue: a Study in Moral Theory*, Duckworth, London.

MacIntyre, A (1987) 'The idea of an educated public', in Haydon, G (ed) *Education and Values: The Richard Peters Lectures*, Institute of Education, University of London, London.

MacIntyre, A (1990) *Three Rival Versions of Moral Enquiry: Encyclopaedia, Genealogy and Tradition*, Duckworth, London.

McLaughlin, T H (1984) 'Parental rights and the religious upbringing of children', *Journal of Philosophy of Education*, 18, 1 pp 75–83.

McLaughlin, T H (1985) 'Religion, upbringing and liberal values: a rejoinder to Eamonn Callan', *Journal of Philosophy of Education*, 19, 1, pp 119–27.

McLaughlin, T H (1987) ' "Education for All" and religious schools', in Haydon, G (ed) (1987a).

McLaughlin, T H (1990) 'Peter Gardner on religious upbringing and the liberal ideal of religious autonomy', *Journal of Philosophy of Education*, 24, 1, pp 107–25.

McLaughlin, T H (1991) 'Ethos, community and the school', paper presented to meeting on 'Identity, Community and Culture', Centre for Philosophy and Public Affairs, University of St Andrews, December 1991.

Manley-Casimir, M E (ed) (1982) *Family Choice in Schooling: Issues and Dilemmas*, D C Heath, Lexington, Massachusetts.

Mendus S (1989) *Toleration and the Limits of Liberalism*, Macmillan, London.

Midgley, M (1980) *Beast and Man: the Roots of Human Nature*, Methuen, London.

Mill, J S (1859) *On Liberty*, available in Pelican, Harmondsworth.

Nagel, T (1979) *Mortal Questions*, University Press, Cambridge.

Oakeshott, M (1962) *Rationalism in Politics and Other Essays*, Methuen, London.

O'Hear, A (1981) *Education, Society and Human Nature: an Introduction to the Philosophy of Education*, Routledge and Kegan Paul, London.

O'Hear, A (1985) Book Review: Charles Bailey: 'Beyond the Present and the Particular', *Journal of Philosophy of Eduction*, 9, 1, pp 146-51.

O'Hear, A (1986) 'Education and rationality', in Cooper, D E (ed).

O'Hear, A (1987) 'Taking liberties', *Times Educational Supplement*, 16 January; p 4.

O'Hear, A (1988) *The element of Fire. Science, Art and the Human World*, Routledge, London.

O'Keeffe, B (ed) (1986) *Faith, Culture and the Dual System: A Comparative Study of Church and County Schools*, Falmer Press, Lewes.

O'Keeffe, B (ed) (1988a) *Schools for Tomorrow: Building Walls or Building Bridges*, Falmer Press, Lewes.

O'Keeffe, B (1988b) 'On the margins of education: finding a demension for belief', in Green, A G, and Ball, S J (eds) *Progress and Inequality in Comprehensive Education*, Routledge, London.

O'Keeffe, B (1988c) 'The Churches and educational provision in England and Wales', in McClelland, V A (ed).

O'Neill, O and Ruddick, W (eds) (1979) *Having Children: Philosophical and Legal Reflections on Parenthood*, University Press, Oxford.

Peters, R S (1981) 'Democratic values and educational aims', in Peters, R S, *Essays on Educators*, George Allen & Unwin, London.

Phillips, D C (1975) 'The anatomy of autonomy', *Educational Philosophy and Theory*, 7, 2, pp 1-12.

Pring, R (1984) *Personal and Social Education in the Curriculum*, Hodder and Stoughton, London.

Pring, R (1985) 'In defence of TVEI', *Forum for the Discussion of New Trends in Education*, 28, 1, pp 14-17.

Quinton, A M (1971) 'Authority and autonomy in knowledge', *Proceedings of the Philosophy of Education Society of Great Britain*, 5, 2, pp 201-15.

Rasmussen, D (1990) *Universalism vs Communitarianism. Contemporary Debates in Ethics*, The MIT Press, Cambridge MA.

Rawls, J (1971) *A Theory of Justice*, University Press, Oxford.

Rawls, J (1985) 'Justice as fairness: political not metaphysical', *Philosophy and Public Affairs*, 14, 3, pp 223-51.

Rawls, J (1987) 'The idea of an overlapping consensus', *Oxford Journal of Legal Studies*, 7, 1, pp 1-25.

Rawls, J (1988) 'The priority of the right and ideas of the good', *Philosophy and Public Affairs*, 17, 4, pp 251-76.

Raz, J (1986) *The Morality of Freedom*, Clarendon Press, Oxford.

Rosenblum, N L (ed) (1989) *Liberalism and the Moral Life*, Harvard University Press, Cambridge MA.

Sacks, J (1991) *The Persistence of Faith, Religion, Morality & Society in a Secular Age*, The Reith Lectures 1990, Weidenfeld and Nicolson, London.

Sandel, M J (1982) *Liberalism and the Limits of Justice*, University Press, Cambridge.

Schools Council (1971) *Working Paper 36: Religious Education in Secondary Schools*, Evans/Methuen, London.

Scruton, R (1980a) *The Meaning of Conservatism*, Penguin, Harmondsworth.

Scruton, R (1980b) 'Emotion, practical knowledge and common culture', in Rorty, A O (ed) *Explaining Emotions*, University of California Press, Berkeley.

Scruton, R (1983) 'Freedom and custom', in Phillips Griffiths A (ed) *Of Liberty*, Royal Institute of Philosophy Lecture Series 15, University Press, Cambridge.

Sealey, J (1985) *Religious Education: Philosophical Perspectives*, George Allen & Unwin, London.

Smart, N (1968) *Secular Education and the Logic of Religion*, Faber, London.

Socialist Educational Association (1981) *The Dual System of Voluntary and County Schools*, SEA, Manchester.

Socialist Educational Association (1986) *All Faiths in All Schools: The Second Report of the Socialist Educational Association on Voluntary Schools and Religious Education*, SEA, London.

Sockett, H (1973) 'Curriculum planning: taking a means to an end', in Peters, R S (ed) *Philosophy of Education*, University Press, Oxford.

Straw, J (1989) 'Islam, women and Muslim schools', *Muslim Educational Quarterly*, 6, 4, pp 7–9.

Strike, K A (1982) *Educational Policy and the Just Society*, University of Illinois Press, Urbana.

Strike, K A (1991) 'Humanizing education: subjective and objective aspects', *Studies in Philosophy and Education*, 11, 1, pp 17–30.

Thiessen, E J (1987) 'Two concepts or two phases of liberal education?', *Journal of Philosophy of Education*, 21, 2, pp 223–34.

Walford, G (1990) *Privatization and Privilege in Education*, Routledge, London.

Wallace, R (1986) 'TVEI as liberal education', in Gibson, R (ed).

Walzer, M (1983) *Spheres of Justice: A Defence of Pluralism and Equality*, Basil Blackwell, Oxford.

Ward, K (1983) 'Is autonomy an educational ideal?', *Educational Analysis*, 5, 1, pp 47–55.

Weil, S (1952) *The Need for Roots*, Routledge & Kegan Paul, London.

White, J (1982) *The Aims of Education Re-stated*, Routledge and Kegan Paul, London.

White, J (1990) *Education and the Good Life. Beyond the National Curriculum*, Kogan Page, London.

White, J and O'Hear P (1991) *A National Curriculum for All: Laying the Foundations for Success*, Institute for Public Policy Research, London.

White, P (1983) *Beyond Domination*, Routledge and Kegan Paul, London.

White, P (1987a) 'Self-respect, self-esteem and the "management" of schools and colleges', *Journal of Philosophy of Education*, 21, 1, pp 85–92.

White, P (1987b) 'Racism, self-esteem and the school', in Haydon, G (ed) (1987a).

White, P (1988a) 'The New Right and Parental Choice', *Journal of Philosophy of Education*, 22, 2, pp 195–9.

White, P (1988b) 'The playground project; a democratic learning experience', in Lauder, H and Brown, P (eds) *Education: In Search of a Future*, Falmer Press, Lewes.

White, P (1989) 'Educating courageous citizens', in White, P (ed) *Personal and Social Education: Philosophical Perspectives*, Kogan Page, London.

White, P (1990) 'Friendship and education', *Journal of Philosophy of Education*, 24, 1, pp 81–91.

White, P (1991a) 'Humanisation, democracy and trust: the democratisation of the school ethos', *Studies in Philosophy and Education*, 11, 1, pp 11–16.

White, P (1991b) 'Hope, confidence and democracy', *Journal of Philosophy of Education*, 25, 2, pp 203–8.

White, P, (1991c) 'Parents' rights, homosexuality and education', *British Journal of Educational Studies*, XXXIX, 4, pp 398–408.

White, J and P (1986) 'Education, liberalism and human good', in Cooper, D E (ed).

Young, R (1980) 'In the interests of children and adolescents', in Aiken, W and LaFollette, H (eds).

Young, R (1986) *Personal Autonomy: Beyond Negative and Positive Liberty*, St Martin's Press, New York.

Chapter 9

Religious Schools:
Refuge or Redoubt?

Clara Connolly

Abstract

This article places the case against religious schools in the context of a discussion of the role of religion in defining the relationship between women and community, and in defining the concept of 'nation' in Britain. It argues that the principles of secularism, autonomy and equality present a more progressive way of mediating relations between community and society than a defensive retreat into 'tradition'.

Women and community

I was once rejected for a job as an Irish community worker because of my alleged 'isolation from the community'. This was in spite of my involvement in a variety of Irish women's organisations and networks reflecting a range of contacts across generations and classes which a mainstream women's group would find unusual. Many aspects of Irish community life, in this country as elsewhere, are dominated by single sex *male* organisations (sport is a particularly sound social qualification) but their *female* counterparts, unless housed in a convent, are contemptuously ignored.

Another story, with more serious consequences. A social work team refused to take an Asian teenager into care, although she had requested this to escape from a violent father. The reason? – the estimated cost to her of 'cutting herself off from her community'. In fact an Asian feminist had offered to foster her.

I want to start this article, which is primarily about the religious schools issue, by asking a question which frames the issue for me. What is the definition of 'community' that so decisively excludes not only feminists but networks of, and individual, single women?

The discourse of 'community' has a time-honoured history of managing deep conflicts in British society, by disguising widely differing perspectives on the causes of (and therefore remedies for) such conflict. It can do this because it has the critical advantage of suggesting positive values, no matter who uses the term. Even Raymond Williams, the most eloquent exponent of working-class community values, conceded on one occasion that no one cites the term negatively (Williams, 1979, pp 119–20). In a climate of deepening anxiety about 'race', it functions as a set of codewords for relations with and between various waves of settlers and their families. The word 'community' has a territorial meaning (usually, but not always, an inner-city slum) and a cultural one: for mainstream multiculturalists, it denotes a range of views (ranging from sympathetic to bewildered) towards a way of life different from 'ours'. From the inside, it defines a resistance to assimilation, and a resource against the hostility of the host society: Sivanandan's celebration of 'communities of resistance' is the best known use of the term among black writers in this country (Sivanandan, 1990, pp 24–9). What 'insider' and 'outsider' definitions share is the sense of a kinship network – families in streets – which is usually seen as natural rather than constructed, a 'given' rather than a process. It has a meaning opposed to 'nation', being at the same time smaller than the national unit (and disruptive of it) and larger, including supra-national links and structures.

If the predominant meaning of 'community' is 'kinship' networks, it follows that women are at its heart, but as mothers, wives and daughters, that is solely in relation to others within it. Women *as individuals* are excluded from community in a number of ways. First they are excluded by mainstream multiculturalism, which constructs a relationship between a homogeneous white 'society' and a series of inwardly homogeneous 'communities'. Men, women and children who 'belong' are assumed to have the same interests, whatever their class, gender or political differences. As Gita Sahgal has pointed out, this makes any challenge to an orthodox religious leadership, on behalf of women's separate interests, liable to the charge of racism (Sahgal, 1989, pp 6–7).

Second, women are excluded by patriarchal community structures – religious, political and social; that is to say, women are idealised by such organisations in their capacity as mothers, wives and daughters, within the family. The punishment for speaking out as *individuals* can be severe, as Julia Bard illustrates in her story of the orthodox Jewish woman driven out of her community for the crime of involving police and social workers in the defence of her children against sexual abuse (Bard, 1991, p 26).

This process is compounded by ourselves, when we relate to 'community' only through our relations with men and children and do not address the interests of women as a distinct category. Or, alternatively when, organised in black or ethnic minority women's groups, we make a virtue of the pain of exclusion, rather than confronting it directly, and insisting on our right to speak from within. Only thus can we contribute to the creation of a 'consenting community', containing a rich variety of political and social identities within it.

Religion, however, is one of the most powerful ways of regulating women's relation to community, and in some cases, of policing its boundaries. Religious schools can play a significant role in shaping these boundaries: this is one of the reasons why the religious schools debate is so fraught with anxiety. (My daughter said, passing the local Catholic primary school, 'I'm not Irish. If I were, I'd be going to *that* school'.)

The less rigid the boundaries, and the more fluid the notion of community, the better it is for women's opportunities for personal autonomy and control over our lives. The concept of personal autonomy, with its emphasis on individualism, is sometimes represented as a threat to communal or class solidarity. This is certainly a more sympathetic argument when the group being defended is under threat from war, or racism. But a double standard seems to operate here: the autonomy of (heterosexual) men is seldom seen as threatening the community, so why should *women's* autonomy be so represented? Is it because women are 'different', but not equal?

The rise of fundamentalism in the major world religions, which has as one of its primary concerns the redefinition of 'community' and the clarification of its boundaries, is a serious threat to women's autonomy. It was against this threat, as manifested particularly in Britain, that Women against Fundamentalism (WAF) was founded in 1989. (For a history of WAF, see Connolly, 1991, pp 68–77). Among other things, it acts as a forum for ethnic minority women (Asian, Irish, Jewish and others) who are excluded from community, by choice, accident, or 'insider' hostility. Its focus is equally 'outwards', to challenge those aspects of the British state and mainstream society that foster the growth of fundamentalism, and 'inwards', to challenge the claim of religious leaders to speak for all. I am writing here as a member of WAF, giving expression in my own voice to some of our common concerns.

Nation and religion

While, on the whole, progressives still reserve the word 'ethnic' for minority communities, the Right in recent years has learned to turn multiculturalism on its head by insisting on the rights of the majority ethnic community – that is the white population – to cultural expression. Nowhere is this more evident than in education, where it has been an increasingly successful strategy for the defence of the dominance of Christianity in the education system. The Parents Alliance for Choice in Education (PACE) has been defending a number of parents who are challenging the state system for the right to a 'Christian' education, that is untainted by the cultural or religious expression of minority school populations (see Jackson, pp 100–13).

This ability to regard the majority population as another ethnic group, without discussing the power relations that exist between majority and minorities, exposes the inherent weakness of mainstream multiculturalism, which has never been a successful method of challenging racial inequality. The right to be 'different' is not at all the same thing as the right to be 'equal', and indeed can provide a language in which alliances can be made between religious fundamentalists from majority and minority faiths. (The unsuccessful Cox Bill, however, is probably an example of the fragility of such alliances.)

The more common way to understand the values of the majority population, though, is to regard them as 'national', or 'British' values. Britain may be passing through a period of economic and political insecurity, but the resources of British (more properly *English*) nationalism – the monarchy, church and parliament, and the constitutional settlement between them – are products of long generations of history which still remain stable.

Since the Reformation, Britain has seen itself as an 'island community' defending its 'liberties' against a religiously alien European mainland. Christianity, or more properly Protestantism, is a significant thread in the weave of British historical self-definition. For the majority of the population, Christianity is now less a faith (in the strictly religious sense) than a cultural resource. Perhaps the most surprising recent exponent of this view, given her left-liberal and secular roots, is Fay Weldon's defence of Christianity against Islam (Weldon, 1990). Here, as elsewhere, the truth of

Christianity is indissolubly linked with a defiant assertion of mainstream national identity and pride.

The strength of this link, and the difficulty of conceiving a secular national identity is illustrated, in my view, by the strange lack of opposition to the 'worship' clauses of the 1988 Education Reform Act. These were, in one sense, nothing new: under the 1944 Act county schools were obliged to conduct a daily act of worship which, it was plausibly assumed, would be Christian in content. In many schools, particularly in the inner cities, this practice has been eroded, not so much by the presence of religious minorities as by the well-established indifference to religious faith of Britain's working and lower middle classes. Some teachers, particularly in secondary schools, indicated their indifference by using the 'conscience' clause to absent themselves, pupils by their restiveness at orthodox assemblies. Increasingly, assemblies were fulfilling their function as expressions of a school's ethos by drawing on multicultural or environmental themes.

The Education Reform Act (GB, Statutes, 1988) was intended to put an end to this creeping dilution of Christianity. It does seem a rather extraordinary reassertion of the centrality of faith in a country which has become increasingly secular since 1944, if its legal reforms are anything to judge by (eg homosexuality and abortion legalised in 1967).

The only explanation for this schizophrenia, and the absence of any large-scale overt opposition to it, is the widespread, inert belief that Christianity is, somewhat like the monarchy, an archaic but nevertheless potent symbol of Britishness, and a carrier of 'our cultural heritage'. It is a function of the British obsession with its past, and its inability to consider the modernisation of its social and political structures. The contrast with the USA is illuminating: there the ideology of the public education sector is secular, though a much higher proportion of the population than here is robustly Christian. To date, its secularism remains intact in spite of the growth of religious fundamentalism.

The identification of British national identity with Christianity, and its consequent predominance within the education system, helps to perpetuate a climate of national and ethnic exclusivity, and to racialise religious affiliation.

Religious schools

If the wider society – the national collectivity – is experienced as exclusive or hostile, there is a correspondingly greater temptation to withdraw into 'community', in order to exploit its emotional and cultural resources. Both before and since the Swann Report (GB, P, H of C, 1985) there is evidence to suggest that mainstream education on offer for black and other ethnic minority children is inadequate. The Burnage Report (Macdonald *et al.*, 1989) offered a sobering glimpse into the level of racism and racial harassment experienced by black children even in schools with multicultural policies in place (see also Taylor, pp 146–75).

Dissatisfaction with the mainstream fuels demand for separate schools. Many black parents are involved in unpaid forms of supplementary schooling: the dual system with its privileging of religious choice is the only state-maintained separate option available at the moment. So it is not surprising that some parents are considering this option for other than religious reasons. Commenting on *Schools of*

Faith, the Commission for Racial Equality's pamphlet (1990) setting out the arguments for and against public funding of religious schools, Mr James Shera (Chair of Rugby Racial Equality Council) said: 'What most Asians want for their children is a good education; they only look to denominational schools when they feel that the present system has failed them' (Shera, 1990).

White parents, also, use the voluntary system for a variety of reasons. In effect, it acts as a second-tier selective system, the first tier being the private sector. Fifty-six per cent of independent schools are Anglican – it is believed that their religious foundation will protect them against the onslaught of any future government (Gay, 1985, p 1). Although only five per cent of young people attend independent schools, fifty per cent of the Oxbridge intake is still drawn from there, so they play a vital role in determining the composition of the country's elite.

For parents who cannot buy into this first tier of privilege, there is the state voluntary sector. Church schools administer flexible admission policies, emphasising religious affiliation when there is a suitable local population, but using other criteria when the alternative would be closure. In this way, they can step round the rigorously non-selective policies of local education authorities (LEAs). According to some studies, at least half of parents choose Church schools because of their reputation for academic standards and discipline, rather than for strictly religious reasons (Dummett and McNeal, 1981; O'Keeffe, 1986). Other reasons have been identified also. 'White parents appear to opt for a church school because the school is all, or predominantly, white. Nine out of thirteen headteachers interviewed said race was a factor in the parents' choice.' (Dummett and McNeal, 1981). Catholic schools in particular, more exclusive denominationally than the Church of England, show an embarrassing tendency to be islands of white pupils in multiracial boroughs such as Tower Hamlets in London (Phillips, 1990). There is also some evidence to suggest that Church schools are less than enthusiastic about preparing children for a multiracial society, and are less likely than county schools to implement LEA multicultural policies (Ball and Troyna, 1987).

All in all then, religious schools, whether in the private or the public sector, are deeply implicated in the socially and racially divisive system of education in this country. Even if some minority faith schools did achieve voluntary status, it is hard to see how that in itself would effect a decisive shift in power and resources towards the black and ethnic minority communities. It would lead rather to further social and ethnic fragmentation without challenging entrenched class and race privilege.

While the present system exists however, the right of minority faith groups to establish their schools is not in question. To quote a CRE recommendation:

> No application from a minority faith school should be given less favourable treatment, either by an education authority or by the DES, than any other application. Any decision or recommendation must be made on non-racial grounds (CRE, 1990, p 22).

WAF, in its opposition to all religious schools, is more concerned to argue about the wisdom and effectiveness of this choice, especially for girls.

It has been suggested that public status for religious schools is desirable, because the national curriculum, which would then be obligatory, guarantees a minimum standard of education which is not always available in the private sector. But there are problems with this argument, which ignores the significant effect of the 'hidden curriculum' on girls' expectations of themselves. The evidence we have from Catholic schools, even where their educational standards are high, indicates a painful cost to be paid for sexual autonomy and the 'wrong' career choice (Bennett and Forgan, 1991).

It is sometimes assumed that communities with a patriarchal view of women's role – for example some Asian and Irish and Jewish – have a *negative* attitude to education for girls. But it would be more accurate to describe this attitude as one of *ambivalence*. Immigrant families as a whole are more likely to insist on high educational standards than some indigenous working-class families, who may have inherited a cynical view of educational opportunity over generations of failure. A Sheffield study, for example, has shown that black and ethnic minority pupils are significantly more likely to stay on after 16 than their white peers (Jesson, Gray and Sime, 1991). Education as a tool of social mobility may be highly regarded; for girls, however, status is won by marriage rather than by occupation, so the effects of their education on their *marriageability* may be of prime importance. Allama Nishtar, Imam of the Hanifia Jamia mosque in Bradford, expresses this ambivalence very clearly:

> mostly we think that girls should go to university, but the obstacle is that the atmosphere is not good for them. There is too much freedom for them there and boys and girls have the chance to mix freely: that is not allowed in Islam (Hinds, 1991)

My own father's attitude was somewhat similar: he encouraged his daughters to excel, but was very concerned that our resultant freedom of thought would make us unsuitable for marriage.

Sex-segregated religious schools may seem to provide a solution to such perplexing dilemmas. The cost to girls, however, in an environment which reinforces the necessity to be 'dutiful daughters', is in our view unacceptably high. Education is valuable not only for the skills and status it confers, but because it opens the door to more freedom of choice. Religious schools, with their clear agenda to reinforce community control over young people, especially young women, clash in a fundamental way with the principle of autonomy as it is understood in a democratic pluralist society. That is a dilemma for black and ethnic minority communities to resolve, according to their vision of themselves and their future in Britain. Religious fundamentalists may try to represent their view as the only, or the major, one, but it is clear that there is no uniformity of opinion on these issues. The most useful contribution that mainstream educationalists can make is to clarify how the county system – where a majority of pupils will continue to be educated, whatever the outcome of the religious schools issue – can promote an ethos which is clearly welcoming to everybody. That is, in itself, part of a larger discussion about whether a common national system of values is possible, in the sense that the Swann Committee believed it to be.

The meaning of pluralism

Swann's vision of a pluralist society is one that is 'socially cohesive and culturally diverse' (GB, P, H of C, 1985, p 6). There is here the sense of delicate balance that admirably expresses the social-democratic aspirations of the British post-war period, drawing to its close at the end of the 1970s. Alas, it was out of date even as it was being written: the Thatcher regime was busy dismantling the elements of such social cohesion as had existed. There was no attempt to implement the Report's recommendations.

The effect of recalling the antiracist left's critical response when it first appeared, in the light of the ethics of the supermarket that currently prevail in education, is a poignant reminder of the ground we have lost. But it is also a tonic, because we need reminding that the left also contributed to the abolition of the old consensus, for good as well as bad reasons. The foundations on which it was based were shaky. It is worth re-examining Swann's version of pluralism, and contrasting it with the (necessarily modest) elements of an alternative.

Swann's picture of British society was first, of a homogeneous white population (with some concessions towards regional variation), united by a confidently held common core of moral values, enshrined in a democratically endorsed legal framework. Second, it portrayed a group of (internally homogeneous) ethnic minority communities intent on maintaining their identity within the framework of a legal system that protected their rights. The relationship – mutual tolerance of difference – between majority and minorities would be mediated by respect for the law and democratic values.

1 There was no uncontested core of values then, nor is there now. Queen, church and commons notwithstanding, mainstream British society was riven by conflict, of which the miners' strike of 1984 was only the most dramatic symptom.
2 The black communities were engaged in bitter struggle against the legal framework that was supposed to protect them, in particular against the immigration laws, and the policing of inner-city areas.
3 An injunction to 'celebrate diversity' rang hollow in a climate of acute anxiety about immigration, fed by the repressive policies of successive governments.
4 (More clearly evident now in the aftermath of the Rushdie affair) the ethnic minority communities were divided between and among themselves.

A strong dose of moral exhortation was simply not enough to paper over these cracks.

Nevertheless, it is necessary to rescue the concept of pluralism from its currently debased form as a kind of cultural apartheid, which leaves the ethnic minority communities locked in an unequal relationship with mainstream society, and women locked into an unequal relationship with their communities.

An alternative version of pluralism would accept the *absence* of social cohesion as its foundation. Rather than depending on the dominant values of existing society – which justify inequality – it would attempt to forge a new consensus around the work of creating the society of the future. We do not have a blueprint for a genuinely pluralist culture: we can only attempt to create the preconditions for it. Multiculturalism cannot provide it, in so far as it evades the recognition that the privileges of one group are defined by, and in return define, the disadvantaged position of others. The first step, therefore, is not to *spread* privilege (by definition, there is not enough of it to go around) but to *dismantle* it.

In the absence of a blueprint, then, we can identify some familiar principles which could act as signposts along the way, adapting them to abolish old forms of privilege rather than creating new ones.

1 *Secularism.* Precisely because religion is such a vital cultural resource, the predominance of any one religion is an obstacle to pluralism. Christianity, as I have argued, is the privileged religion in Britain – principally through the connections of the established church with queen and parliament, through its domination of the education system, and through an outdated set of blasphemy laws. Those areas should be the target of political action, in my view, rather than the (fervent and to date ineffectual) attempts of some Muslims and others to carve out a corner of counterprivilege for themselves.

Insofar as religions – especially proselytising ones – are in competition, a secular state should offer a measure of protection against conflict in the public sphere (for example in laws concerned with the family and sexuality); and at the same time, guarantee freedom of worship and religious practice to all, without discrimination. In our view, a legal framework free of any taint of hostility to religion, but at the same time distanced from religious dogma, provides the foundation on which negotiations about the impact of moral values on the public sphere can most usefully be built.

2 *Respect for autonomy.* The separation of private and public spheres – an essential component of secularism – is one guarantee of a society of consenting members. Consent is meaningless without the right to dissent. A secular education system which respected autonomy would offer the right of variety in modes of dress and diet, and to hold collective meetings, including for the purpose of worship. It would strive to be neutral with regard to individual belief, which includes, but does not privilege, *religious* belief. Some difficulties might still arise around the issue of withdrawal from parts of the curriculum, for example sex education. In this area, too, student autonomy should be given as much recognition as parental rights. Students at secondary school level should be capable of taking decisions in their own interest, and indeed be encouraged to do so.

3 *A commitment to equality.* A free exchange of respect is possible only between individuals and groups who are in a relationship of equality to each other. Inequality breeds intolerance and fear, on both sides of the power divide. A school system, however benign, cannot realistically expect to create an island of harmony isolated from a society in conflict. But egalitarian teachers, acting with students and if necessary with organisations outside the school, can (and do) make a contribution to turning education into a site of *contest* about equal rights.

These principles – secularism, respect for autonomy, and a commitment to equality – do not provide any magic solutions to the dilemmas posed in this article about the relationship of women to community, and of communities to nation. But, in WAF's view, they present at least a workable alternative to the more oppressive, and ultimately self-defeating, strategies based on a retreat into 'tradition'.

References

Ball, W and Troyna, B (1987) 'Resistance rights and rituals', *Journal of Education Policy*, 2, 1, 15–25.
Bard, J (1991) 'The outsiders', *Guardian*, 28 August.

Bennet, J and Forgan, R (eds) (1991) *There's Something about a Convent Girl*, Virago, London.

Commission For Racial Equality (1990) *Schools of Faith*, CRE, London.

Connolly, C (1991) 'Washing our linen', *Feminist Review*, 37, Spring, 68–77.

Dummett, A and McNeal, J (1981) *Race and Church Schools*, Runnymede Trust, London.

Gay, J (1985) *The Church of England and Independent Schools*, Culham Educational Foundation, Abingdon.

Great Britain, Parliament, House of Commons, Swann Committee (1985) *Education for All*, report of the Committee of Enquiry into the Education of Children from Ethnic Minority Groups, cmnd 9453, HMSO, London.

Great Britain, Statutes (1988) Education Reform Act 1988, ch 40, HMSO, London.

Hinds, D (1991) 'Mosque opens new doors for Islamic women', *Independent*, 9 September.

Jesson, D, Gray, J and Sime, N (1991) *Participation, Progress and Performance in Post-Compulsory Education*, Department of Employment Research and Development Series no 64, Employment Department, Sheffield.

Macdonald, I, Bhavnani, R, Khan, L and John, G (1989) *Murder in the Playground* (The Burnage Report), Longsight Press, London.

O'Keeffe, B (1986) *Faith, Culture and the Dual System: a comparative study of Church and County Schools*, Falmer Press, Lewes.

Phillips, M (1990) 'A harsh lesson in conflict and claptrap', *Guardian*, 1 June.

Sahgal, G (1989) 'Fundamentalism and the peculiarities of multiculturalism', *Spare Rib*, June.

Shera, J (1990) 'Islam speaks with myriad voices', *Times Educational Supplement*, 17 August.

Sivanandan, A (1990) 'All that melts into air is solid: the hokum of New Times', *Race and Class*, 31, Jan–Mar.

Weldon, F (1990) *Sacred Cows*, Chatto Counterblast pamphlet, London.

Williams, R (1979) *Politics and Letters*, Verso, London.

Chapter 10

Learning Fairness Through Empathy: Pupils' Perspectives on Putting Policy into Practice

Monica J Taylor

Abstract

In considering ethical issues of translating multicultural antiracist policies into practice, this paper focuses on the experience of a girl of Asian origin and her peers in a virtually white secondary school. Pupil narratives as perpetrators and as a victim of racial discrimination are analysed. Pupils also voice their perspectives on curriculum strategies which they claimed had changed their attitudes and behaviour. The school's pluralist philosophy is set in the context of national educational policy; some comparisons are drawn with multiethnic schools; and the paper concludes with some core values for schools endeavouring to take an approach to multicultural antiracist education through moral education.

A crucial element in developing our aim of *Education for All* is ... to seek to identify and to remove those practices and procedures which work, directly or indirectly, and intentionally or unintentionally, against pupils from any ethnic group, and to promote, through the curriculum, an appreciation and commitment to the principles of equality and justice on the part of all pupils. (The Swann Report, GB, P, H of C, 1985, p 320)

Of the many challenges posed by ethnicity in education the learning experience of pupils should be a central ethical concern. Schools do not only have an obligation to offer a balanced and broadly based curriculum which promotes pupils' development and 'prepares such pupils for the opportunities, responsibilities and experiences of adult life'. The very processes of learning in both the formal and informal curriculum, which significantly affect pupils' achievements and life chances, are constitutive of, and carry with them, moral messages which may profoundly influence the presesnt conduct of young people and shape the future nature of society. Multicultural antiracist policies in LEAs and schools aim to orient the curriculum towards valuing and reflecting pluralism and to facilitate, through relationships and institutional structures, equality of regard and opportunity in learning for all pupils, irrespective of ethnicity. Critical to the implementation of such policies is the establishment of practices both to deal with direct discrimination in racist behaviour and to identify and challenge discriminatory beliefs, values and attitudes, which may be more recondite though no less pervasive. Education in the basic and pastoral curriculum has also to pay attention to developing an understanding of moral principles of fairness and respect for persons demonstrated in positive attitudes to others.

This chapter reviews the national context of policies on race, culture and education. It then draws upon empirical research to examine some aspects of translating these policies into practice from the largely neglected perspective of pupils in the virtually white secondary school. Starting from a group dialogue which disclosed racial harassment, the paper explores, in the voices of the young people themselves, the motivations of the perpetrators and the experiences and responses of a girl of Asian origin. In so doing, the questions of whether these pupils distinguished racial discrimination from other forms of prejudice and whether they perceived racism as unethical and morally wrong are addressed. Since the school was actively engaged in providing a democratic education which was both pluralist and antiracist, the effects of some of its curricular strategies on pupils' learning of moral principles and in changing their attitudes and behaviour are also considered. The context of the delivery of these educational experiences and of the research itself raises ethical concerns.

National policy on race, culture and education

The fundamental change that is necessary is the recognition that the problem facing the educational system is not how to educate children of ethnic minorities but how to educate all children.

Britain is a multi-racial and multi-cultural society and all pupils must be enabled to understand what this means. (GB, P, H of C, 1985, p 769)

In the mid-1980s, as the Swann Report acknowledged, the need to identify and challenge racism in stereotypes and institutional practices had only latterly been seen as a task for schools. In its view:

... much of the task in countering and overcoming racism is concerned with attitude change and with encouraging youngsters to develop positive attitudes towards the multicultural nature of society, free from the influence of inaccurate myths and stereotypes about other ethnic groups. (p 321)

Such an approach was considered to be 'even more essential in "all-white" areas and schools', but 'little progress has yet been made on this front' (p 321; see ch 5, annex C and D).

One impact of the Swann Report was to expedite the development in LEAs of multicultural and sometimes antiracist policies. At the school level these had been endorsed by Department of Education and Science guidelines on race relations, which recommended whole-school policies to promote equality of opportunity and that teachers needed support (DES, 1984). By 1988 the Commission for Racial Equality claimed that about two-thirds of LEAs had published multicultural antiracist policies. The research reported here, which was progressively focused, initially undertook a survey of 108 LEAs in 1988–9 in England, Wales and the Isles which showed that, of the 93 LEAs responding, just over three-fifths had such a policy in existence, and, in addition, almost one-fifth claimed that a policy was in preparation (Taylor, M J, 1989, 1992). In response to, or in parallel with these policies, schools had also begun to produce their own multicultural antiracist statements and, in some cases, school development plans. Research, however, challenged the assumption that the mere existence of a policy could precipitate change in school practice (Troyna and Ball, 1987) and could not show a clear relationship between a school's commitment to multicultural education and academic progress (Smith and Tomlinson, 1989).

The Education Reform Act (ERA) (GB, Statutes, 1988) has been a watershed in these developments, since its imposed agenda has, in the main, not given priority or support in practice to the implementation of a multicultural antiracist education (Taylor, M J, 1992). While its ideology has been viewed as conservative and assimilationist (eg Troyna, 1990), it can, nevertheless, at least be interpreted to underwrite multicultural education (see Leicester and Taylor, pp 15–16). The National Curriculum, moreover, in its translation of the policy of ERA into practice, has largely failed to give a clear and positive lead to the provision of a multicultural antiracist education. Thus, although it has been marketed as an entitlement curriculum, some teachers, LEA advisers and inspectors and researchers have nonetheless seen it as a 'Nationalistic Curriculum' (Taylor, M J, 1992; Troyna and Carrington, 1990). The non-publication of the report of the National Curriculum Council's working party on multicultural education and the lack of explicit guidance have also been taken to indicate that multicultural antiracist education has no status. Yet guidance on *The Whole Curriculum* (NCC, 1990a, p 2), stated that 'preparation for life in a multicultural society is relevant to all pupils' and should be a cross-curricular dimension supported by a school ethos of positive attitudes to cultural diversity:

> introducing multicultural perspectives into the curriculum is a way of enriching the education of all our pupils. It gives pupils the opportunity to view the world from different standpoints, helping them to question prejudice and develop open-mindedness. (p 3)

With the implementation of the National Curriculum, citizenship, one of five prescribed cross-curricular themes (NCC, 1990b), has ironically become the focus for delivery of a pluralistic education (see Gill, p 98). A paradox of citizenship, from an antiracist perspective, is whether it is possible to be a citizen if human rights are denied, when a person's experience is of inequality due to racial discrimination. Conversely, a duty as a citizen is to uphold the law which includes antidiscrimination laws. Racial discrimination, in whatever form, is an ethical issue because it is morally wrong. During the 1980s there has been growing concern, despite likely underreporting, about the extent of racial harassment (GB, HO, 1981; GB, P, H of C, HAC, 1986; CRE, 1987), as a result of which the Inter-Departmental Racial Attacks Group was set up to develop multiagency approaches to combatting such attacks (GB, HO, 1989, 1991). Racial harassment is likely to have a higher profile, in the light of increasing racist violence and the revival of extreme-right groups in Europe, and with immigration firmly on the political agenda in Britain in 1992 (Husbands, 1991; Runnymede Trust, 1991, 1992).

Racial harassment in Britain, while it occurs in relation to all black and other minority ethnic groups, is itself discriminatory, for it is disproportionately experienced by Asians (GB, HO, 1981; Brown, 1984). Evidence from a Community

Relations Council to the Swann Committee claimed, 'it is no exaggeration to state that for some young Asian people particularly, being racially harassed is a way of life' (GB, P, H of C, 1985, p 33). Racial incidents in schools are by no means isolated, as *Learning in Terror* (CRE, 1988) showed. An adviser in a home-counties authority recently stated that each week three or four serious racial attacks were reported; if this is reproduced across more than one hundred LEAs then the scale of the problem must be faced.

It is only relatively recently that LEAs and educational institutions have begun to respond to this cumulative evidence and to recognise the urgent need both to deal with incidents of racial harassment, through establishing and implementing codes of practice, and to address the longer-term challenge of prevention by means of antiracist education. Both the CRE report and the Elton Report on *Discipline in Schools* (GB, DES and WO, 1989) advocated that educational institutions should develop clear strategies against racism. A national survey of LEAs in 1991 confirmed the continuing development since ERA of policies on race and culture, now increasingly under an equal opportunities rubric, and also growth in specific policies on racial harassment (Taylor, M J, 1992). Such policies, following the CRE's (1989) Code of Practice, generally list various forms of overt racism (eg graffiti, name-calling, physical violence) and covert racism (eg negative images in learning materials, denial or devaluation of cultural perspectives and individual experience by virtue of membership of a minority ethnic group). They also set out principles and procedures to deal with and record racist incidents, and indicate training and support structures for teachers.[1] In some LEAs the monitoring of racial harassment is being linked with other monitoring exercises on pupils' ethnic origins, language and religious backgrounds (GB, DES, 1989), exclusions and achievement.

Despite appearances, racial harassment may particularly need to be addressed in locations and institutions with few minority ethnic people, as the Racial Attacks Group Report (GB, HO, 1989) stressed.

> . . . racial incidents do not only occur in areas where there is a large minority ethnic population. Indeed, . . . members of the ethnic minorities living in predominantly white areas may be particularly at risk. Racial harassment in such areas is likely to remain hidden. (para 32)

> The need to respond to attitudes of racial prejudice and intolerance is not restricted to schools and colleges with significant proportions of pupils or students from minority ethnic backgrounds. . . . Whatever the measures taken, we are in no doubt that racial intolerance needs to be addressed in *all* institutions. (para 145)

In many 'white highlands' LEAs and schools the 'no problem here' attitude (Gaine, 1987) is still prevalent. Such contexts may require low-key approaches (Taylor, W H, 1986; Tomlinson, 1990). Moreover, the lack of a profile on antiracist education in national *educational* policy can be used to endorse local political conservatism and policy retrenchment, which may be in those very LEAs and schools where minority ethnic pupils are most isolated and vulnerable. With the current emphasis on educational structures, few concerns focus on the interests of pupils (Taylor, M J, 1992). However, local authorities and governors have a duty under the Race

Relations Act 1976 (section 71) to eliminate unlawful discrimination and promote racial harmony (CRE, 1989).

There is, moreover, a higher imperative to combat racism which springs from moral considerations. Such an orientation, based on fundamental universalisable moral principles, is not only intrinsically ethical, but may also have greater instrumental appeal in precisely those communities and schools where 'antiracism' fails to resonate or is counterproductive. As Dummett (1986) has argued, rather than concentrating on racism we should start from 'general moral standards and arguments . . . and apply these to behaviour affecting racial inequality' (p 10). In illustration she reasons: 'It is wrong to insult anyone gratuitously. But some insults are more hurtful than others, and racial insults are especially hurtful.' This is 'because we live in a racially unequal society where such action reinforces a constant practice of cruelty or injustice'. Essentially 'race is not the determinant of a moral principle. Racial discrimination is wrong because it is a form of injustice. Justice between human beings is the principle' (p 12).

Transferring this to the educational context of the school, personal and social education (PSE), with its concern to develop in young people an understanding of concepts, such as respect for persons and fairness, and a disposition to bring these to bear in action, has a key role. Moreover, to provide an antiracist multicultural education is itself an ethical enterprise. Thus there is an *a priori* connection between PSE and an antiracist multicultural education. Since PSE is concerned with the empowerment of all pupils an antiracist multicultural perspective is integral to its rationale. Opportunities for social perspective-taking – helping students to see the viewpoint of others as *they* see it – (Selman, 1976) and developing empathy, are critical. As Lickona has noted, 'One of our tasks as moral educators is developing a generalised empathy, the kind that sees beneath differences and responds to our common humanity' (1991, p 59). Furthermore PSE, closely connected with pastoral care, links the formal and the informal curriculum and the life of pupils beyond school.

In their brochures and policies, schools purport to be moral cultures. In their practices they also have subcultures, which may be moral or immoral. For learners the informal curriculum of school life is equal to, or often more salient than, the formal curriculum. As the social context of learning it deeply influences the ability to learn and the valuing of learning and achievements. Where the school has students of different racial and ethnic origins these factors are themselves an important part of the culture of school life. As the Burnage affair confirmed (Macdonald, *et al.*, 1989; see Halstead, pp 43–5), the method and manner of multicultural antiracist policy implementation is all important. Evaluation has tended to emphasise institutional structures rather than concentrate on relations within institutions (eg Troyna and Williams, 1986). Still less has the focus fallen on the day-to-day learning experience of the pupils, whose life chances the translation of policies into practice is intended to affect. In parallel, evaluation of moral education strategies and the nature of moral development has paid little attention to the dimensions of race and ethnicity within societies (see Ward, 1991).

The research reported here, which gives due weight to pupils' perspectives, was part of a project which investigated issues in implementing multicultural antiracist policies in pastoral care and PSE in LEAs and four secondary schools of varying ethnic compositions (Taylor, M J, 1989). The approach was ethnographic and influenced by an emerging literature on understanding moral experience and development, oriented in justice and care, through narrative (Tappan and Brown, 1989; Witherell and Noddings, 1991). Thus the research strategy in our semi-structured conversations with young people aimed to embody the values of good PSE and to allow for the evolution of pupil narratives in these opportunities to reflect on their attitudes and behaviour. In so doing, we were essentially probing issues that pupils from a range of cultural and experiential backgrounds identified as moral problems, in an attempt to understand ways in which individuals are influenced by their cultural and educational experiences on matters of race and ethnicity (Witherell and Pope Edwards, 1991). This process gave credence to the pupil as author and actor. As Day (1991) has argued

> If we are to promote moral development, we must provide expanded opportunities for students to tell their own stories. How have they decided to frame and interpret the facts as they have done, how did these decisions relate to their actual conduct. . . ? (p 313)

Moreover, in attempting to provide an education which is both moral and antiracist, and which promotes a disposition to act morally, it is important to examine how the young person hears and internalises the moral voices of justice and care, in the context of social relationships and interactions, which can mediate the process of moral functioning, so as to lead to the recognition 'That's not fair!' (Tappan, 1991). How do pupils learn the language and behaviour of justice and care and come to understand that racial harassment is both unethical and unfair? This is explored through their own accounts of harassment, as perpetrators and victims, and their observations on educative experiences which changed attitudes and behaviour.

The minority ethnic pupil in the virtually white school: visible or invisible?

This chapter highlights ethical issues of multicultural antiracist education in one of the research's four case-study schools – the virtually white secondary school – which arose in two terms of observation, shadowing and interview of staff and pupils, which concentrated on two forms of Year 9 pupils. To focus here on such a school, rather than one with a more multiethnic catchment, is justified for several reasons.

1 The majority of schools in England and Wales are overwhelmingly white, although, like this school, few are without any minority ethnic pupils. In such environments their position can be that of isolation and vulnerability.
2 There is evidence that many 'white' schools have failed to address multicultural, let alone antiracist education seriously, and that this is likely to be even lower on their agenda since ERA and with the implementation of the National Curriculum (Taylor, W H, 1990; Taylor, M J, 1992).
3 Even in this case-study school – independently nominated by the LEA's inspector for its 'good and interesting practice' (see Leicester and Lovell, pp 215–16, for a definition) – where attention had been given to policy and practice in a whole-school approach, there nevertheless remain significant issues and ethical concerns.

Evaluation of this 'positive' scenario, when viewed from pupils' perspectives, and especially the experiences of one of the two students of Asian origin, is salutary, the more so since few schools – as this one did – place the affective curriculum and school ethos on a par with the academic agenda, in an attempt to link meaning, thought and action.

Such a context – with one or two minority ethnic pupils – though fairly common, is arguably the most challenging for multicultural antiracist education. In addressing cultural diversity and racism there is the risk of heightening awareness of and negative reaction to those whose interests it would most seek to serve. Yet this risk must be taken if the white majority are to be prepared to bring about and live in a culturally plural, racially just and socially harmonious society. By making a critical evaluation of aspects of this school's attempt to provide a multicultural antiracist education the intention is by no means to castigate or belittle the staff's goodwill and creative endeavours, but to illustrate how the presence of only one or two minority ethnic pupils gave rise to some particular ethical issues, not only for the staff, but also for the researchers to whom they had opened up their practice.

'An archetype perhaps of a monoethnic school in the "white highlands" of rural England' – thus was the school described in the staff handbook. The school roll was about 900 pupils, with 140 in Year 12. Its white, widespread, rural catchment abuts a growing market town in central England, which had pockets of National Front support. Its class composition was a mix of local agricultural families and incoming professional groups. The head described the norms of the locality as 'feudal' and 'in a time warp' – 'they tend to pretend the country is not multiracial'. Several staff referred to it as a 'cultural desert'. With the exception of one teacher of Eastern European origin, the teaching force was white British. Their average age was in the late twenties, and creditably, many young staff held posts of responsibility; as illustrated by the teacher with responsibility for Equal Opportunities. There was one minority ethnic governor, ostensibly recruited because of his professional connection with industry. Although the school had a mixed-ability intake, achievement in examinations was high and enrolment was increasing.

PSE was one of six faculties in the school (alongside humanities, sciences, maths, languages and design) and involved all members of staff and pupils, in addition to a year-based pastoral system. The school endeavoured to be a participative democracy, which included a school council, and a learning community for all, based on shared values and mutual respect. The head was aiming both for learning effectiveness and to build the preconditions for a just community (as in the theory and practice of Kohlberg; Power *et al*, 1989) which would be acceptable to a wide spectrum of parents. Part of the 'community of dialogue' among teachers was the production of curriculum bulletins in which they reflected on practice. Staff were often involved in LEA projects, and, at the time of the research, one deputy head was a key developer of the LEA's PSE policy. According to the head, a strength of the school's practice in incorporating multicultural antiracist perspectives in PSE was 'getting into others' shoes to understand feelings and thoughts' – the development of empathy. His goal was 'to educate children who will live lives where how they conduct themselves is the most important issue for them.'

A year or so before the research, a working party with representatives from each faculty, had engaged in a school review, in response to the Swann Report and the

LEA's multicultural antiracist education policy. This was set out under three main headings:

to develop the curriculum to reflect the needs of a pluralist society;

to ensure that education establishments' organisation and ethos are consistent with the idea of equality of opportunity for children of all races;

to meet specific language needs of children who speak English as a second language.

The school's response, as required, to the LEA policy, together with a firm position statement and its multicultural policy, were set out in the staff handbook. (Gaining governor agreement to the school policy had needed to be strategic. Discussion at a governors' meeting included remarks such as 'We haven't got any here, have we?' The policy was 'sold' by emphasing core moral values in multicultural antiracist education.)

Policy Statement

The school has a clear commitment to the concept and the reality of fairness and equality of opportunity. We lay great emphasis on values education both in PSE and in the day to day life of the school. There is no hard and fast divide between the curricular and the pastoral; therefore all staff have a joint responsibility in planning, in teaching and guiding the children. There is no one area of the school where multicultural education is specialism; it plays an integral part of resource selection, teaching against prejudice and the examination of the world in every faculty and in every year.

This policy, which was accompanied by a needs analysis and action plan,[2] agreed by staff and governors, would still serve as an example to many predominantly white schools in the process of policy development. It embodies the key values espoused by the school, such as democracy, antiracism, fairness, equality of opportunity; it sets out a broad action plan to involve every member of staff, pastorally, across the curriculum and in management; it indicates support structures and channels of consultation; and it outlines procedures for dealing with racist incidents.

How well then does the policy translate into practice? Is it mere rhetoric or does it largely correspond with the lived reality of school life? A whole-school evaluation needs to be multifaceted in terms of practice and perceptions and ongoing review. The research did in fact collect and examine perspectives of teachers, governors, administrative, catering and supervisory staff. The head, for example, suspected that a large minority of pupils were 'pretty racist', but that they concealed it from staff. But unlike most reported evaluations, this chapter allows the clients – the pupils themselves – to have the loudest voice. In so doing, it affords an opportunity to focus on the experience of one girl of Asian origin in relation to that of her Year 9 peers.

The school's response to the LEA policy ended with some particular, and revealing, comments:

Note: we have two pupils who are members of ethnic minority groups. We are aware of their needs, but feel that specific treatment or special procedures are inadvisable, since they achieve very well, are not a discipline problem, are well integrated socially and have excellent English competence.

How accurate and sensitive were these perceptions about the experience of being a girl of Asian origin in an otherwise white school? How 'aware' were staff about her needs? How 'well integrated' was she socially? More specifically, did she experience what for her counted as racial harassment or ethnic discrimination? And, if so, how did she respond? What did white pupils learn from these experiences? How were they dealt with by the school pastorally and in the academic curriculum?

Early in the research during an informal group interview, a spontaneous and dramatic episode occurred between pupils which highlighted several key issues at the interface of ethics, ethnicity and education. These disclosures were further explored in subsequent interviews with individuals and with their chosen friends. Many of these ethical concerns relating to young people's experience of ethnicity and racism in this school context paralleled those in the multiethnic case-study schools. But in this virtually white context they had heightened ethical point.

The group interview involved eight pupils, invited to participate on the basis of their interesting contributions to a morning's lessons. They represented a range of ability (including one pupil with special needs), and a gender and ethnic mix. The purpose of the discussion was to begin to get to know the young people and to explore their perceptions of school life, relationships and PSE, without their being told that race and ethnicity were of particular interest.[3] Towards the end of the hour-long session the pupils were recalling times 'when you were right on your own, with hardly anyone taking your side' (Kitwood, 1980), which focused on events leading to falling out of friendship – a preoccupation of 13–14 year olds. The conversation turned to 'picking on' people, in particular the girl of Asian origin in a drama lesson.[4]

WG1   'In Mr Z's lesson – he's the drama teacher – he says, "You don't mind do you [to the girl of Asian origin (AG), by name]?".'

AG   'Didn't have a lot of choice! . . . because some people pick on me. I got picked on in the first year.'

WB1   'That was by us [he and WB3] wasn't it?'

AG   'I know.'

WG2   'Now we sort of get to know her – now in the first year we didn't sort of know her – we know her personality.'

AG   'I know. And I picked a fight with one of the boys in the third year. Well he hit me. So I hit him back, to defend myself.'

Res1   'Why did he hit you?'

AG   'I don't know – just feeling racialist, and it gets you really mad.'

Res1   'How do you know that?'

AG   'I don't know. He just calls you names. Like you don't think about it at the time you just get really angry so you just hit him back. And then you just go to tell the teacher and he goes, "Oh, if he does it again we'll see him about it." That's all they do.'

WB2   'They didn't do anything.'

Res1   (To AG) 'So how do you feel about it, when the teacher says that to you?'

AG   'It's not very pleasing, 'cos like . . . because they don't take much notice of it 'cos there's only two of us here.'

Res1	'What would you like them to do?'
AG	'I don't want to make a big case of it like, but he could at least tell them to stop it. . . .'
WG2	'They do, they take it further than they should.'
Res1	'Did he (the teacher) actually go to that person?' (the boy who hit her)
AG	'I don't know.'
WB1	'Yes, he did, I should know.'
AG	'Why? Because *you* are one of them.'
WB1	'No.'
AG	'How do you know then?'
WB1	'[WB3] told me.' (repeated)
Res1	(to WB1) 'How do you know?'
WB1	'I think so, they usually do.'
Res1	'Do you think the teachers should?'
WB1	'Yes.'
Res1	'She said, you picked on her in the first year . . . and later you got to know her . . .'
WB1	'We all did, me, [A, another boy], etc. I only did it once.'
WB3	'Because she was a different colour and she was in our class and she was the only person in the school and you didn't really know other people.'
WB1	'We all picked on everybody.'
AG	'They were trying to degrade me.'
WG1	'People, they pick on you, try and find something to pick on you. . . . They called me "Scottie" when I first came to school.'
Res1	'What made you change your feelings about [AG]?'
WG2	'We got to know her (to AG) and we know how you react.'
AG	'That's what anyone does when they first know me.'
WB1	'I only said it, because someone told me what to say, I just said it. I didn't know what it means – I was sort of thick – now I sort of stand up for myself more.'
Res1	'So you get influenced by other people. . . . . .'
WB1	'But like after that once, 'cos she told the teacher. . . . It made me think more, 'cos I first, I didn't know what it meant 'cos I'd never heard the word before. . . .'
WG1	'What word?'
WB1	'I didn't sort of run round and torment her like going round and say . . . and run off.'

(Getting back to original subject.)

Res1	'Can you tell me about drama again?'
WG1	'We were doing picking on people and power. And me and the group we had [AG] in our group and it just so happened we were picking on [AG] and he asked [AG] whether she minded telling us the other side of the story and stuff. It's gone on from there and we're doing about power now.'
Res1	(To AG) 'How did you feel about this?'
AG	'It's embarrassing. Like I said, if you walk down the corridor. I don't really think about it unless someone points it out to me 'cos I get used to it now. . . .'

Several unethical, ethnocentric and racist disclosures were made in this dialogue, itself a dramatic episode initiated by being 'picked on' in drama. The dialogue offers a starting point, as it did in the research, for examining ethical issues of multicultural antiracist curriculum innovation, delivery and research in a situation with only one minority ethnic pupil. The dilemma of how to provide a multicultural antiracist education for all while preserving the well-being of the minority ethnic individual is highlighted.

'Picking on' people by name-calling: perpetrators' perspectives

The group discussion was the forum for acknowledgement of racial harassment and the revelation and ownership of name-calling by one of the boys in the group. (AG: 'I got picked on in the first year.' WB1: 'That was by us [he and WB3 in the group] wasn't it?' AG: 'I know.') In this lively situation such a disclosure seemed almost matter of fact, but coming two years after the event it could also be seen as a catharsis for those involved. Although he was quick to admit to what was later confirmed as racist name-calling, WB1 claimed both that it was a one-off event for him (WB1: 'I only did it once') and that, being ignorant, he was influenced by others ('I only said it, because someone told me what to say' . . . 'I didn't know what it means' . . . 'I'd never heard the word before . . .').

Subsequently, individual interview with WB1 provided an opportunity to explore further why and how this incident took place and WB1's perceptions of current race relations in the school.

WB1   'Everyone takes them [AG and her sister] for granted, they don't take them as different people, 'cos probably been here from the start. If we got some new people, new coloured people in, everyone would take a bit of notice more. Normally don't notice they're a different colour, only when someone brings it up, but take them as normal people really, which they are. Thing is, I don't like people who are racist because I don't think that's fair at all.'

WB1 immediately interprets 'different' in terms of 'colour'. This, rather than 'black', was the more usual referrent by pupils in this school, especially if talking about black people in Britain, compared with those in South Africa (see p 167). Like some other pupils in the school, WB1 appeared to experience some cognitive dissonance in thinking about black people in general, as distinct from those – the two pupils of Asian origin – with whom he had a *personal* relationship. Though he had acquired some knowledge about the achievements of black people, he had yet to appreciate as a reality black self-esteem and pride.

Reminding him of when in group interview, he had admitted to name-calling,

Res1   'Do you think name-calling matters?'
WB1   'Yes, I think it does, 'cos people call me names like, not because I'm coloured . . . I've put up with a lot of name-calling and I haven't told at all . . . In senior schools, when there's older people, like fifth formers bullying younger pupils . . . That's just stupid, because they don't think what it would be to be in their position. . . . If you change it around, "How would you feel in a black school?" I don't know, because everyone thinks white is best

	anyway, whether you're in the black school or not.'
Res1	'Do you think black people think that?'
WB1	'Dunno, because people think they think differently and they're a different type of humans just because of their skin colour. They might have different ways and things, but they're still human, still feel and think and that and probably some of the best athletes, scientists and things like that are coloured. They're probably one of the strongest people.'
Res1	'So when you called [AG] names, was that just because you didn't really know her, or was it a sort of testing out thing, or was it because you were a bit led by other people you were with?'
WB1	'What it was, I think it must have been right at the start of the first year and [WB3] obviously knew what it meant. And he told me to say this word, "Nigger", and I didn't know what it meant, because I'd never heard that word before. So I just said it. And she must have told. Mr [Y] talked to us. He was the head of the first year and asked me why I said it and that and I said, "Because I didn't know what it meant." And he didn't believe me. And he doesn't believe many people, he's one of those people. . . . I know what words mean now, but then I just came out of primary school, I didn't know much at all. . . . I wouldn't say anything like that at all now. If someone started bringing it up, like [B] does sometimes, everyone tells him not to. And . . . if you call coloured people names you get disliked . . .'

There are several lessons to be learnt here. First this pupil's testimony, and that of others – both the perpetrators and the victims of racial harassment – and in the multiethnic case-study schools, clearly demonstrated that there was a need for antiracist education to start earlier, in the primary school. Minority ethnic pupils in these 'good practice' secondary schools repeatedly claimed that their experience of racial harassment by other pupils was worse in their primary schools and, incidentally, in other secondary schools attended (Troyna and Hatcher, 1992). Many students, like AG, even reported 'you get used to it'. But can habituation to such injustice be right? Second, and conversely, as WB1 shows, it does not pay to be ignorant about race as he was easily led by others. Ignorance can be no justification for racist behaviour, though it could be a motivation for reform (Straughan, 1982). Third, however, even if the pupil turns out to be morally culpable, in investigating incidents and implementing the code of practice teachers need to act fairly and initially to suspend judgement and 'believe' the perpetrator. Justice needs to be tempered with care. This is also important for the pupil in terms of building trust with the teacher if there is to be an educational engagement in changing beliefs, attitudes and values (see p 164). Indeed, the ignorance of WB1 seemed quite possible; staff recognised that a major constraint on multicultural antiracist education in the school was pupils' lack of exposure to other cultures – when faced with multicultural materials they would say 'What's this name?'. (This might also have been related to the fact that AG had Westernised and abbreviated her first name.) Ignorance was also diagnosed by WG3:

> 'This school's very unknowledgeable about what it's like to be Indian because there's no Indian people, we've got two and that's it. And there's very ignorant people who take the mickey out of them. I totally disagree with that.'

In the initial group discussion of racist name-calling, WB3, who, according to WB1, had told him what to say, remained uncharacteristically quiet, making only one explanatory contribution ('Because she was a different colour and she was in our class . . . and you didn't really know other [coloured] people . . .'). There seemed to be a link between her physical appearance and the strangeness of her ethnic group – fear of the unknown. Alone, he confirmed that in the first year of secondary school 'a lot of people' harassed AG ''cos they don't know the people really. Don't give them a chance to see what they're like, just take the mick out of them.' WB4 also explained:

> '. . . just coming from primary school and I reckon you'd probably just heard adults before saying about black people and probably thought "Oh, I'm going to say that as well or something . . .", . . . when I was in a gang I did, but when I'm on my own I wouldn't. . . . When you're in a gang with other people it just changes all your . . . might like them to think you're hard when you call someone it . . .'

In the group WG2 had also asserted 'Now we sort of get to know her, in the first year we didn't sort of know her – we know her personality,' and repeated this later. Others in the multiethnic schools confirmed the importance of this process. Indeed, most pupils in these schools *liked* a multiethnic environment, which they saw as important for getting to know each other as persons and unique individuals with characteristics influenced by ethnicity. Important though ethnic mixing is in terms of providing opportunities for enhancing knowledge, and even understanding through personal relationship, developing tolerance of or friendship with individuals from other ethnic backgrounds does not necessarily give rise to the lessening of group stereotyping (see Bagley, p 182). WB1 suggested that 'If we got some . . . new coloured people in, everyone would take a bit of notice more.' But also that 'I don't like people who are racist because I don't think that's fair at all.' Just as there are gaps between belief and action, so there are gaps in universalisability from realising through personal experience that if racism is unfair for some it is unfair for all. As WG4 noted:

> 'There's been the odd joke that I heard, but nobody says anything to her . . . if they were talking about coloured people . . ., oh, just the usual racist jokes about chocolate and dirt and things.'

As the group discussion revealed, 'picking on' people was a pervasive strand of school subculture (WB1: 'We all picked on everybody.' WG1: 'People, they pick on you, try and find something to pick on you . . .'). 'Picking on' people is an act of differentiation and distancing by identifying some difference which is (usually) negatively valued. 'If somebody's going to be picked on they'll find anything wrong with you.' In school this can take many forms, and, from pupils' perspectives, between teachers and pupils, as well as among pupils themselves. Central to denigrating discrimination is unfairness and lack of consideration for others. 'Picking on' which is racially motivated, either intentionally or by collusion, is at least partly based on unchangeable attributes, like skin colour, and is an expression of deeply held attitudes entrenched in the institutions and structures of society. In this it is not unlike discrimination on grounds of gender or disability. But an additional factor is that discrimination against individuals from minority ethnic backgrounds reinforces discrimination against their family and the group as a whole. As the Swann Report noted:

> We believe the essential difference between racist name-calling and other forms of name-calling is that whereas the latter may be related only to the individual characteristics of a child, the former is a reference not only to the child but also by extension to their family and indeed more broadly their ethnic community as a whole. (GB, P, H of C, 1985, p 35)

A key question, which the research sought to address, is whether pupils see racial discrimination as different in kind from other forms of discrimination. Name-calling is a prevalent aspect of 'picking on' pupils, and, in all the case-study schools, was the predominant form of pupil–pupil harassment, though fights also occurred. These white pupils found it easy to recall discrimination they themselves had experienced, and that it had mattered to them, for example:

> 'I've got three brothers. Everyone says that's a lot. When you see a family of six you think that's a lot but when you're in it it's not.' (WB1)

> 'They called me names like "bitch" and it affected me.' (WG5)

> 'I think that it does matter a lot because it humiliates you, because I have been called names . . . in the second year I used to get teased a lot about being flat-chested. Boys used to call me horrible names, like "fried egg" and "doormat", and that really upset me . . .' (WG4)

> 'People used to take the mickey out of me, used to say to me "Popeye" and things like that because I've got big eyes. It really used to get to me.' (WB5)

> 'I have a problem of speaking. I can't say some words. And they take the mickey out of me about that. I say it back to them and things like that, make up my own names to call them.' (WB4)

Ethnic and racist name-calling also occurred, in relation to white pupils in the 'white' school:

> 'They called me "Scottie" when I first came to school.' (WG1)

> 'I have been called "Paki", things like that, just because I have a bit of a tan. It's stupid. I felt hurt. It's really not nice for anyone.' (WB5)

'Paki', in particular, seemed to be a universal term of racial abuse. WG3 had avowed that she 'totally disagreed' with her peers who engaged in racist name-calling – 'they just don't think of her as a person'. She considered people from minority ethnic groups, like AG, 'as a normal person, because there's nothing wrong with them'. Yet she admitted using the word 'Paki' out of habit, though not with the intention to denigrate racially or to cause hurt, and acknowledged her own inconsistency, 'I'm too ignorant to change it. I really should, because I should do as I preach.'

WB1 was said to 'make up some names, totally different, just for a laugh.' But name-calling, especially racist name-calling, is different from having a nickname. For example, in the case-study school with 70 per cent minority ethnic pupils, all the students in one form had nicknames. One popular boy of Afro-Caribbean background was nicknamed 'duck' and occasionally called 'quack, quack' as a joke, which he accepted. He introduced himself positively as 'I'm . . . [first name and surname] and I'm black'. But reference to him as 'black duck' was clearly perceived by him and his peers as racist abuse. Being called 'whitey', for instance, did not have the same salience for white pupils in the minority there.

Pupils in the 'white' school seemed ambivalent about whether 'picking on' others because of race was qualitatively different from other forms of personal discrimination. Clearly white individuals disliked being 'picked on' on account of some difference from the supposed norm and viewed this as hurtful. On reflection, they were able to extend their cognitive perspectives to appreciate that others, including AG, felt similarly. They could, by analogy, see that 'picking on' people was unfair, even though this did not always stop them doing it. They also said they thought racial discrimination was unfair. But could they, additionally, make an emotional leap to empathise with AG? Were their own experiences of being 'picked on' enough to develop the moral imagination and insight necessary to 'climb out of our own skin into another's' to feel the pain of others? As WG3 claimed:

> 'Having talked to [AG] about it [racism] I can't put myself in her shoes, but I can grasp an idea of what it must be like. Because I wear glasses I got called names and things.'

WB3 and WG2 thought racial discrimination was 'just the same really' as 'picking on' people if they are fat. And there was also a feeling, confirmed as much by intonation as the words used, against anything that might be interpreted as positive discrimination: 'I think you should treat them the same. I don't see why they should be no different from anyone else.' (WG2). Pupils seemed to see black and other minority ethnic people as persons with thoughts and feelings, and, in AG's case 'just the colour of her skin is different, nothing else'. But it took particular pastoral and curricular experiences to bring home to them personally that it was wrong to call racist names and, if only temporarily, to have a sense of being black.

Being 'picked on': the victim's view

'That's what anyone does when they first know me.' As the group discussion accidentally revealed, and subsequent interviews confirmed, this girl of Asian origin was subject to what she herself clearly perceived as racial harassment – despite what the staff handbook affirmed. Indeed, she, too, would have preferred to 'ignore' the fact that sometimes her peers were 'feeling racialist' and were 'trying to degrade me'. The following exegesis of her school experience – the episodes, explanations and effects – is only one chapter in a narrative of her life story. Despite claims to the contrary, black and other minority ethnic pupils *are* subject to racial discrimination where they comprise an insignificant proportion of the school roll, and even in schools which they, too, attest to be 'good'. This analysis is offered in the hope that the hidden curriculum of these pupils' biographies will be more closely examined and reflected upon to improve the quality of their learning experience.

Interviews disclosed several episodes of racial harassment in non-curriculum time, such as in the corridor between lessons, at lunch time and at the end of the school day. With the possible exception of 'the dinner ladies', 'who tend to pick on you a lot' 'they pick on me anyway' (AG), racial discrimination in this school was always between pupils. (The head himself noted that kitchen staff would willingly help pupils with disabilities, but would make racist comments.) The first year of secondary school (Year 7) seemed particularly eventful. In addition to the encounter uncovered in the group discussion, AG recalled a fight as a result of a disagreement between friends.

> 'We were going out to the mobile, I think the last day, and [C, a girl] slapped me round the face, and then you [WG1] held me back and I was sent to the office. Mr X made us make friends. I hate it when they do that.'

Year 8 brought a more persistent episode:

> 'I always used to get called names, . . . just by one boy it was. I used to get picked on – he'd call names down the corridor. I just ignored him, and then a teacher heard, but they just took me out of the lesson and said, "Is it OK?" and I go "Yes". But they still told him. But they didn't do a lot.'

By halfway through Year 9, as a result of name-calling and being hit by a boy, AG had retaliated ('he hit me, so I hit him back, to defend myself'). It is not possible to be sure whether this was a spontaneous act of self-defence ('like you don't think about it at the time, you just get really angry so you just hit him back') or, as her earlier remark ('and I picked a fight . . .') suggests, whether it was more deliberate. In the three multiethnic schools studied, retaliation of this kind by black pupils was usually after a cumulative series of events. Compared with other descriptions of racial harassment of pupils (eg in CRE, 1988), those revealed by AG may seem few and minor. But the fact that they happen at all should be a matter of ethical concern. Where minority ethnic pupils lack the actual, if not the moral, support of numbers they may be particularly vulnerable and immediate reassurance and support should be given by staff. When the victim of sustained verbal and physical racial harassment responds in kind how should this be regarded in relation to a school's policy of non-violence?

AG interpreted these episodes, but not all her experiences of being 'picked on', as racist in intent, 'just because I was black and they'd think they were really hard'. She was sometimes also 'picked on' by peers because of her academic endeavours, when they perceived her primarily as a rival learner, 'I was trying to finish off my work and they were calling me "swot" because I was writing and I just write fast anyway.' For the most part, her reaction and her response to racial harassment, her feelings and her behaviour, were differentiated. She had an affective reaction, which was often internalised ('it gets you really mad' and 'you just get really angry').

> 'I think only once I really went mad, because [C], she slapped me round the face, and it didn't hurt, but I felt so angry that I just started crying, but I felt really angry.'

She admitted that 'it did actually get to me in the first year', but 'you get used to it'. Yet her retaliation in Year 9 suggests that the anger had accumulated to such a degree, or was so intense on that particular occasion that 'you don't think about it . . . you just hit him back.' Her standard response was 'I just ignore them.' But attempts to deny the effect of racism were also challenged: 'if you walk down the corridor, I don't really think about it unless someone points it out to me. . .'. Here AG may be referring both to having got used to being only one of two pupils of Asian origin in school *and* to having got used to racial harassment, except when she suddenly becomes the focus of attention. Her habit of running down the corridor when changing lessons appeared to be an attempt to deny the perceived difference which was most forcefully brought home to her in the school corridors and seemed to indicate a desire for invisibility. When racial harassment occurred in the company of friends, AG felt both a sensitivity for them and a renewed concern for herself:

> 'Say if I was walking down the corridor with my friends and someone just called out to me. I just carry on talking, and they would feel more embarrassed and wouldn't know what to say.'

In fact AG identified her 'nicest' friend as WG4 'because she knows, she doesn't feel embarrassed.'

AG as a unique individual and a pupil had certain personal characteristics, of which ethnicity was one. She was perceived to be intelligent by staff and peers. She saw herself, and was seen by a friend, as 'quite shy'. Yet the retaliatory episodes indicate that she could be assertive, at least when provoked, and she was quite forthcoming, even talkative, in interviews. Drawing on issues she identified, illustrates how the interaction of *all* these characteristics *and* the fact of being only one of two minority ethnic pupils in the school affected her perceptions of the learning culture: in aspects of teaching style, the formal curriculum, pupil subculture, the pastoral curriculum and in her aspirations for the future. Such observations raise questions for the learning experiences of other isolated minority ethnic pupils.

Teachers – who were generally felt by students to have high expectations – could hardly fail to be aware of AG's presence as the only black pupil in a class. Indeed, for individual differentiation in learning teachers should be attuned to her particular needs and interests. She was attentive and often seemed to know the answers to questions, but was reluctant to draw attention to herself by volunteering a contribution: 'If you get it wrong everyone looks at you.' WG4 perceptively recognised that some teachers experienced tension and uncertainty about gaining AG's active participation in lessons and whether they should discipline her as they would other pupils:

> 'I don't think she is really treated any way differently but sometimes there's teachers who don't know how to react to her and they'll put on her a bit or ask her lots of questions in class or how to do things. I think maybe they don't really know how to react to her and they don't know whether they should tell her off or not because she might feel they were being racist, but she doesn't. I think she sometimes gets a bit annoyed if they treat her differently.'

AG was also aware of different teaching styles and the differentiated responses these required. Yet *her* increased visibility and potential vulnerability in a participatory learning culture was not always acknowledged.

Implementing a multicultural curriculum also raised her profile, as WG6 observed: 'like if we read in English about a black person, she feels, I think she feels embarrassed.' Specialist PSE lessons, which AG liked, included the study of family types, nuclear and extended, with reference to minority ethnic lifestyles in Britain. But such occasions made her self-conscious, 'everyone would turn round and look at you and I'd get embarrassed.' General PSE with the form tutor offered opportunities to discuss school life and share perspectives, but this also threatened to be too personal.

AG perceived little understanding of ethnicity in pupil subculture. When called ' "Paki" and things like that' she made no attempt to explain that this was incorrect, 'Well there's no point because they probably wouldn't understand anyway.' She would also want to distance herself from any incoming pupils of Asian origin in school: 'I don't think I'd like to go and talk to them.' AG derived close support from her older sister and one particular friend. By contrast, minority ethnic pupils in multiethnic schools were more likely to challenge the misapplication of 'Paki', to offer support to new pupils from the same ethnic group, and to have a wide supportive network.

Similarly, AG was sceptical about the pastoral support offered by a code of practice against racial harassment. She knew the school had a policy from year 7 PSE, but did not easily resort to asking for help from teachers, 'I don't want to make a big case of it like. . .'. She preferred to 'sort it out for myself', but this was difficult 'because they tend to be older'. AG placed little faith in teachers' ability to deal meaningfully with her abusers in a way that would last. There was 'no point' in complaining 'because there's only like two of us' and 'most of the people who do it don't really care whether they get told off or not'. Yet, if other pupils' testimonies are *also* to be believed, this sometimes had more effect than she realised.

AG placed little value on her bicultural background and, in a white school, her access to biculturalism remained unsupported. On entering the culture of the school she denied her few remaining bicultural ties: 'I say I'm British when I come to school, but if I was like with my family or relations it would be Sikh.' Yet she and her sister had not wanted to learn Punjabi, and were 'detached from the relations, but we don't mind.' AG acknowledged:

> 'I change if I go out to see my family or relations and that. If I went to the temple, I enjoy it, because its peaceful, it's somewhere you can go, but then I don't understand it.'

In her education she aimed to 'get good grades 'cos whatever you do will still be behind you'. Her fear for the future was not of institutionalised discrimination – of which some minority ethnic pupils elsewhere were aware – but of personal harassment, 'probably I would be called names and that'. She was more used to, and was opting for, a white Western culture, 'as I've been brought up like white people in that community, so I think I'd rather stay there'. The irony is that, no matter how Westernised, how academically successful and how 'well integrated socially' she becomes, she remains liable to the personal and structural discrimination of a society which has not yet fully accepted and valued its multiethnic diversity.

Changing attitudes and behaviour

Since racial prejudice and discrimination did exist, what steps was the school taking to change attitudes and behaviour? Here, through the pupils' own voices, consideration is given to some pastoral and complementary cross-curricular strategies, which they identified as formative learning experiences of fairness, equality and empathy: through teacher dialogue and peer pressure; drama lessons; and a module on South Africa, including an active learning experience, Apartheid Day.

Pastoral learning: complementary influences of teachers and pupils

Unlike many students in the multiethnic schools studied, most of the 16 Year 9 pupils, interviewed in depth at least twice, were unsure whether the school did in fact have a multicultural antiracist policy. Yet pupils were aware that staff did not tolerate racial harassment, as WB1 said, 'I know that if it's bad they don't put up with it', incidentally suggesting that it was a matter of degree. Students in the group discussion were divided about what was done (AG: 'the teacher . . . goes "Oh, if he does it again we'll see him about it." That's all they do.' WB2: 'They didn't do anything.' WG2: 'They do, they take it further than they should.') and whether it was effective. WB1 had learnt through dialogue with a teacher ('It made me think more . . .'). The quality of teacher–pupil relationships is critical to pastoral encounters. From the pupil's perspective several conditions are necessary, including: trust, care, taking time, listening, not jumping to conclusions, believing the pupil, checking out the evidence, explaining the procedure being followed, being fair and consistent. Exploring allegations of unfairness and racism requires seriousness and sensitivity, including a detailed knowledge of the biographies of all involved. Both what is done and how it is done will spring from and reveal value positions.

Since it is often the form tutor who is initially or most closely involved, from the pupil's viewpoint it is especially important that she or he is someone to be trusted and with whom interaction is meaningful:

WB3   'He always tries to help you out. . . . He cares about all the kids so you can always go to him . . . he's like your father . . .'

WB1   'He doesn't have it in for me. He doesn't really have it in for anyone. He sort of, he disciplines people rightly and he takes what you've got to say. If he thinks you've done something to someone he takes you into his office and talks to you about it. And if you've given him a different story he believes you. He doesn't sort of think "Oh, he's lying", he doesn't sort of tell you he thinks you're lying.'

'. . . if someone's annoying me you could go up to him and tell him and he'd do something about it . . . straightaway. He doesn't forget it the next day. He carries on until it's dealt with.'

It was, WB1 claimed, through dialogue with a respected teacher ('Talking is learning sometimes') that he had changed his actions, including racist behaviour, and acquired self-discipline:

'The best thing to do is them ask why you've been stupid and that instead of them telling you. Because that makes you realise, rather than the teacher telling you what you've done. . . . I didn't do it again because I thought talking was enough . . .'

By comparison, WB3 averred that making a complaint about racial harassment would not be taken seriously, 'they would just make you apologise'. For him that was inadequate. What would count? 'Giving you a detention or a black person calling you names in class and saying "We don't like taking the mickey out of you, why do you take the mickey out of us?" – try to make you feel guilty.' WG4 described how peer pressure on racist name-callers could work:

> 'There was the odd time when people picked on her [AG] but if she didn't stand up for herself then we'd stand up for her 'cos we couldn't stand anyone picking on her . . . it sometimes just helps to . . . shout at that person and make them feel bad or we'll shout at them so they have to look [AG] in the eye so that they're not just saying it to someone else they have to say it to her.'

Thus young people could act ethically against discrimination on grounds of race and ethnicity. Their ethical intervention seemed to depend on a constellation of several factors, including: the degree of injustice felt on behalf of the other, ego-strength, individual or group power to act in a particular context and, often, most tellingly, a personal relationship with the oppressed.

WB3, however, claimed to have stopped racist name-calling 'in case you get done even more'. But the impression that he was more bothered by punishment than because he genuinely thought it was morally wrong to call racist names might have been erroneous. The significance of knowing the pupil's biography was underscored when further discussion revealed that he had three black cousins whom he had visited in Southern USA. It was this personal relationship – 'because of cousins really' – that had changed *his* behaviour' ''cos if I see somebody picking on a black person, then I do shout out or whatever'.

Cross-curricular learning: cognitive and affective

Drama is a powerful vehicle for the exploration of ideas and emotions and in this school was often skilfully used to develop empathy. In Year 9 drama was linked with PSE, which included a module on prejudice. The drama teacher (who had previously taught in multiracial schools) was developing a drama resource pack on prejudice for the LEA, based on materials on trial in the school. These contained the significant rubric: *'It is important that you explain that the racist attitudes are acceptable only within the drama and that the racist behaviour is not acceptable otherwise.'* But a prior ethical question is whether it is indeed acceptable to express racist attitudes or behaviour, even in drama, because of the possible dangers of condoning or reinforcing racism by permitting its expression (see also Carrington and Short, pp 206 and 212).

WG4 described an occasion in drama when cultural prejudice was clearly displayed:

> 'there were only a few of us defending coloured people and there were quite a few people just keeping quiet and there were a few people that were being really racist. They said really terrible things, like there's a lot of coloured people in [U, the nearby town] and . . . how they shouldn't live in [U] and if they're not going to adopt our culture then they should go back to live in their own country . . . it's really hard to speak to someone like that . . . because they won't listen, they won't change their point of view, they'll just shout you down and tell you what they think. And if you ask them a question

and they don't know what to say they'll just back down with a silly answer like "it's just different".'

The ethical tension regarding such drama is between offsetting potential disadvantage to the pupil(s) in the ethnic minority in consequence of raising the temperature on racial and cultural diversity, especially when the school situation of power and authority mirrors that of society at large, against the possible learning experience for the white majority – 'getting pupils to understand their values by putting them in other people's shoes'. On the one hand, what number of minority ethnic pupils is likely to generate ethnic solidarity and outweigh the risk of discrimination against individuals? On the other, students from years 8, 9 and 12 claimed that, especially by taking the role of a black person bearing the brunt of racist criticism, their awareness had increased. One year 12 student had played the part of a racist whose son was going out with a black girl in a drama *'showing different attitudes'*, which another saw as helping some to engage with the process of attitudinal change:

Yr12   'You're bound to hear a certain amount about this from kids who are racist
WM1   – emotive words, like "They're lazy" or "They're violent". So I found it easy
        to do, but I didn't like doing it because I've always been opposed to racism.'
Res1   'Do you think people learn anything from doing that kind of thing?'
Yr12   'Usually the people who are racist when they go to things like that . . . you
WM2   do see a slight change in attitudes, even if it's only tiny, you can still see that
        change. I don't know whether it will be long term, but in the short term they
        might change their minds for a while.'

This certainly suggests a need for multicultural antiracist education, but that changing attitudes and behaviour is as much a matter of how it's done as what is done – process *and* content. A cross-curricular module on South Africa showed how affective and cognitive learning could be mutually reinforcing.

The South Africa module – topical at the time – was delivered mainly through History and Geography. Study included the country's history, discrimination, Steve Biko's death, a visit from a South African refugee, a video 'Girl's Apart', the film 'Cry Freedom' and an in-school, active-learning experience – Apartheid Day. The aim, through these cognitive and affective experiences, was positively to influence pupils' conation with respect to race and ethnicity.

At the cognitive level the module had clearly succeeded in providing information and raising awareness which some, even self-confessed name-callers, claimed had changed their views.

'I think the way we are learning about South Africa in History and Geography is good because you are learning about how bad the situation is and it makes you like the black people and makes you think they should have justice.' (WG4)

'After we done this South Africa thing it's just like a jigsaw puzzle and I can see how it fits together now. We didn't, I personally didn't know what it was like over there. I didn't know how bad it was. Now I know how it is I changed my mind now.' (WB4)

'Cry Freedom' was widely felt to have had an emotional impact on beliefs and values. For example, WB1 reported:

> 'When we watched the film "Cry Freedom" I thought it was really bad how the whites treated the blacks and I felt as though I wanted to do it the other way round, so the blacks could do it to the whites, to see how they liked it.'

The impression made by the film seems to have enabled WB1 to develop perspective-taking and to have the concept of reversibility. But undoubtedly for white pupils the most educative experience, which attempted to enhance an understanding of the concepts of fairness, justice and equality through empathy, was that of Apartheid Day. This complex and controversial cross-curricular experience, whose evaluation in itself raises several pedagogical and ethical issues, can only be lightly sketched. Essentially, it involved Year 9 pupils being divided into two groups, according to hair colour (the fair-haired becoming 'whites', those with dark hair 'blacks'), who then participated in the timetabled curriculum in role under simulated conditions of apartheid. This allowed privileges to the 'whites' and severe restrictions on the 'blacks', who, being more numerous in the school situation, sought means of retaliation. The aims of the exercise, according to the head of Humanities in a debrief with pupils, were that:

> 'We wanted you to feel the same sort of thing which perhaps is felt in South Africa, between blacks and whites, a feeling of anger, a feeling of hatred . . . Obviously what we were trying to create is a system that was not fair, which we weren't used to and you weren't used to either, because most of what we do in schools is to try to create fairness, rather than blatantly try to create unfairness.'

This active-learning strategy engaged pupils' hearts and minds as they felt personally involved and found themselves 'learning about feelings', for, as WB1 put it, 'when it's actually happening to you you can remember it more'. For many white pupils Apartheid Day seems to have been a powerful learning experience, which complemented the informational input into the foundation curriculum. Through cognitive dissonance, perspective-taking and being put in others' shoes they learnt concepts of fairness and equality and came to feel empathy. For example, WB3 found the experience as a 'black' valuable and 'learnt how they treated you was really wrong. I reckon it should be the other way round really. Should be equal.' WB4 claimed 'I think a lot of people now realise what it's like to be black and they probably don't like being called names now.'

Yet Apartheid Day again raises particular concerns for AG. For her it has additional layers of meaning and risk. Moreover, her narrative of the experience is at odds with that of her peers, and even her close friends misperceive her reaction, as reported to the researchers. For instance, WG4 stated: 'I think that she just took it the same way as we did, but I think that she always feels uncomfortable about it, probably feels she's the only one.' In contrast to her peers, who, even if they found some aspects 'funny', claimed to have learned from the serious explicit and implicit messages of the event, AG chose to distance herself and interpret it as a 'joke'. She thought 'Everyone took it as a joke, not seriously, because they knew what it was about', from the previous Year 9. The researcher of Asian origin explored this.

Res2   'Did you feel they should have put you in the "white group"?'
AG   'I did, no, because I have black hair and they did it on the colour of the hair.'

The dialogue reveals AG's ambivalence as she has to reverse her real-life knowledge of discrimination as a black person. In the simulation exercise she is still a black, but for once in a majority, who, albeit disadvantaged, have at least the power of hostility. It is, as she recognises, one occasion when to be a 'white' is to be in a disliked minority and 'you get picked on even more then'. Interestingly, WG5 who had been 'picked on' after 'falling out' with other girls, and who was a 'white' as she had fair hair, found that role 'uncomfortable' and would have preferred to be black, 'because there were more'.

> 'I thought it was a good idea and it showed you how bad blacks are treated, but the pupils that were black took it really bad, they were being really bitchy and took it too seriously. . . . It showed you how unfair it was, it was unbelievable, I couldn't get over how people could be treated so differently.'

The experiment attempted to create conditions similar to those in South Africa in the school, but did pupils' perceptions of the evils and injustice of racism remain safely distanced and 'out there'? To what extent were they enabled and able to transfer their learning to the UK and their own situation in the school? Pupils acknowledged the existence of racism in Britain, and contrasted it with the apartheid system in South Africa; WG4: 'I think there is racism in this country, but I think nothing so bad happens in England' and WB4: 'Some of it happens round here, like in the riots in Tottenham and that. The police were racist to them or something. . . . It does happen in England, like black people punished for no good reason.' Despite this learning, there remains a concern that they may have continued largely ignorant of the subtle institutionalised racism in the UK. Since it may be more difficult to teach about racism in its covert, but no less insidious forms, there is a need to reinforce and increase the salience of powerful but distant learning experiences. The relevance of national information on racial harassment and discrimination in socioeconomic life could be brought home by, for example, enabling white rural pupils to participate in shared learning experiences in multiethnic urban schools.

Moreover, though these young people had extended their cognitive and empathetic skills, had their conation also been developed? Had these experiences challenged their disposition, will and determination (Wilson, 1990) to alter their attitudes and behaviour with respect to racism? There is evidence of change by some in relation to their contemporary, AG, on account of this whole-school approach to multicultural antiracist education. Whether pupils' learning about racism and the acquisition of principles of fairness, respect and consideration for persons will endure, and can be generalised in their attitudes and behaviour towards black and other minority ethnic people outside the school, also depends on the extent to which such principles are upheld in the culture and conduct of parents, significant others and society as a whole. There is therefore, as ERA implies, an additional obligation on the education system to support parental and lifelong education.

Being 'picked on' in drama and research: ethical notes for the teacher and researcher

Ending the group dialogue WG1 explained: 'We were doing picking on people and power . . . and it just so happened we were picking on [AG] and he [the teacher] asked [AG] whether she minded telling us the other side of the story. . .'. However, a drama group exploring the behaviour and central concept of racism – 'picking on people and power' – above all when AG is being picked on, oversteps an ethical boundary. The racially skewed situation of this school demanded an approach which was less personal for AG. The drama must be credible and relevant to the lives of young people, *but without invading her personal space* or necessarily precisely reproducing real-life experience of racism.

By contrast, in another drama class small groups of year 9 pupils were exploring self-chosen incidents, involving a teacher–pupil relationship, through the medium of a diary entry. Three boys performed an episode about a boy seeing his friends vandalise a Pakistani shop and whether or not he should tell his teacher. The moral issues were debated keenly by the group as a whole. In this scenario the victim of racist violence was not personalised yet the crime generated a conflict of loyalty to friends against bringing the perpetrators to justice – essentially the dilemma faced by pupils witnessing racial harassment in schools.

The encounter in drama proved the catalyst for discussing 'picking on' AG in the research dialogue. As in drama, the research is interested in exploring AG's experience; but whereas in the drama AG is being *deliberately* 'picked on' in order to reproduce racism and consider the nature of 'power', in the group discussion the recollected experiences of racial harassment, and the perpetrators' admissions are *spontaneous* outcomes of the dialogue. Nevertheless in the research also the only Asian pupil is given a higher personal, and thereby ethnic profile, which *might* expose her to renewed racial discrimination.

It was an hypothesis and an integral part of the research design that the proportion of minority ethnic pupils in the school would affect the translation of policy into practice and the conduct of the research. The ethical issue in *this* school context was should the only minority ethnic pupil in Year 9 have been actively involved in the research process at all? If so, should she have been included in the initial group interview, in the final interview with a friend, or only in the individual interview? Refusal to participate and to speak were options for AG, as in drama, though for a girl with her character traits difficult to exercise because of the imbalance in authority between teacher and pupil, which is largely reproduced with the researcher. It therefore behoves teachers and researchers to take special care not to put such a pupil in a position where she might be further disempowered both as a pupil and as a 'black' pupil.

An irony of antiracist teaching and research which is committed to improving educational practice, and hence the learning experience of all pupils, is the danger of increasing the minority ethnic pupil's personal vulnerability through the process of exposing racism. Yet, in this school climate, with these dialogical conditions and the sociability of the group, AG's allegation of being 'picked on' made for admissions on the part of two white boys and provided an opportunity for others to re-examine their own attitudes and behaviour. Thus, the research itself may offer learning encounters, generating greater awareness of ethical issues which may help teachers and researchers to develop methods which are less unethical.

Core values

In conclusion some general remarks may be made about the core values underlying provision of a multicultural antiracist education in addressing the needs and interests of pupils, teachers and schools. A postscript updates pupil involvement, school and LEA change since the case-study research.

Pupils' interests

It was a premise of the research and this paper that greater attention and value should be given to pupils' perceptions of and learning from their experience of school life if the quality, coherence and meaningfulness of their learning environments and relationships are both to complement and enhance opportunities for academic achievement in the formal curriculum and enlarge their social and personal horizons.

As this research illustrates, there is a need to take more account of pupils' biographies, including their ethnicity, in the learning contexts of the formal and pastoral curricula; but this must be acutely sensitive to young people's privacy and their individual learning profiles. Teachers should support students, if they wish, by providing opportunities for pupils to tell their own moral stories so as to learn from their experiences. As Tappan (1991) has argued,

> By representing the cognitive, affective and conative dimensions of their moral experience through narrative, students will therefore be encouraged to reflect on their experience from the standpoint of their own moral perspective. This will lead not only to an increased sense of authority and authorisation on behalf of that perspective, but also an increased sense of responsibility for action. (p 252)

Such occasions can be used to challenge negative attitudes and behaviour and reinforce other-considering conduct.

Furthermore, if schools are to have a serious role in preparing young people for citizenship in a pluralist society, then school life needs to lay the foundations for active participation (NCC, 1990b). Thus pupils require opportunities to engage in genuine decision-making, both by taking part in the processes of school organisation and having a say in curriculum content and learning methods. School councils may facilitate democratic participation if their procedures and recommendations are accorded due consideration and weight by staff and governors. There is an ethical obligation to regularly publicise the school's racial harassment policy and incident code through reminders in assemblies, explanations in tutor periods and display in the form room. Pupils, like teachers, need to be educated about policy rationale and be included in making and revising codes of practice (see, e.g. GB, HO, 1991, annex 5D). This process would be a direct engagement with concepts, issues and experience.

Teachers' needs

Many teachers feel understandably anxious about providing an antiracist multicultural education, though it would be seen as integral to a good education. In the current educational climate, in which schools are embroiled in implementing the national core and foundation curriculum, there is a need to assert the importance of cross-curricular dimensions if teachers are not to be left with the impression that these are of less than equal value. If the National Curriculum *is* to be an entitlement curriculum for all then due attention has to be paid to the underlying prior conditions for learning, the aims of education and its contribution to the nature of the society to which we aspire. If governmental statements (e.g. GB, HO, 1990, p 2) about a participative, pluralist, just and equal society are not mere rhetoric, then teachers, other staff and governors in educational institutions have a moral responsibility, which should be reinforced through their conditions of service, appraisal and career prospects, both to uphold the law on racial discrimination and to promote racial justice by putting into practice their LEA's and school's multicultural antiracist policy.

Just as the process of policy development is a significant learning experience, in order to operate by these principles and procedures, teachers require much more support, in initial and in-service training, and in opportunities for reflection on the life of the school as a whole. Since most teachers have pastoral responsibilities, in the course of which they address core values, these offer a common starting point for reviewing antiracist practice. One challenge of implementing antiracist codes of practice, especially if a teacher is implicated, is that the sanctity of power relationships, in which teachers are usually seen as both an authority and in authority, is called into question. If pupils are to be empowered to invoke the policy, to make and justify complaints, then they need the support of a school culture that expects them to stand up for fairness and what is morally right for others and themselves, as well as taking responsibility for their own actions. Another central difficulty glossed over in policies, but critical to their implementation, is: on what criteria is an incident to be judged as racially or culturally discriminatory? In practice incidents and the telling of them are rarely as unambiguous as guidelines suggest. The boundaries of unfairness, and whether it has a racist dimension are often, from a pupil perspective at least, fluid, contextualised and located in a history of powerlessness and to some extent denial of personhood and moral agency. Teachers need clear and detailed guidance on the precise procedures to be followed and the manner in which to investigate allegations. These actions should in themselves seek to endorse the core values of fairness and respect for persons.

Schools: a way forward?

In addition to, and even prior to, a multicultural antiracist policy, a school should have a statement of the values by which it intends to be guided and which it aims to promote. This will form the ethical basis for a good pluralist education. Arriving at such a statement offers a challenge to consult with pupils and their parents as well as the wider communities in which the school is located (endorsed by CCW, 1991; SCCC, 1991). Such a process, involving conversations between representatives of diverse cultures, would be a local attempt at seeking a common framework of values in which the school's practices should be grounded (see Leicester, pp 36–7). The values statement should be made public and presented in a handbook for parents and pupils which should also include the school's multicultural antiracist policy.

In the case of the school featured in this paper, the pupil perspectives uncovered in dialogues suggested an experience, which, while not wholly commensurate with the school's policy, nevertheless largely endorsed it, and testified to the school's ability to have an influence on their beliefs, attitudes and behaviour. The school's practice was commendable in that it made education for pluralism which embraced values issues and ethnic diversity a fundamental orientation, and in its involvement in the research demonstrated that it was keen to reflect on its approaches. Yet the presence of even one minority ethnic pupil should always affect planning, preparation, execution and debrief of curriculum strategies and thinking about the organisation and ethos of the school, if learning for all is not to be at her or his expense.

Attempts at school change and providing a multicultural antiracist education, have to be in dynamic with the prevailing local culture. 'White' cultures of the community beyond the school – for example, regional, rural, working-class and some evangelical Christian cultures – may remain at a deeper unarticulated level and may embody values different from those of the school. Multicultural antiracist education in the almost white school is distanced from the felt realism and authenticating ethos of a multiethnic school community. The virtually white school has to be at the leading edge in directing its efforts towards raising cultural and racial awareness and preparation for encountering black and other ethnic minorities largely *outside* the boundaries of the school, while being attuned to the needs and interests of the small, but significant minority *within*. It is charged with just such a moral responsibility if it is to provide a good education which is fair to all pupils in preparing them for the 'opportunities, responsibilities and experiences of adult life' in a multiethnic and pluralist society. In this school, from most pupils' perspectives, putting the policy into practice *had* meant learning about racism, changing their attitudes, and, in some cases, behaviour.

> 'They try to bring us ideas of why people are racist, what it is. . . . I think it is important to do that, even though we don't have many people who are coloured. I think it is important that you should know that for when you go out and start a job and there is more coloured people, because there will be.' (WG3)

Postscript

Since the research in this school AG achieved ten GCSE Grade I passes and a few pupils of Muslim Asian background have entered the school. The LEA is engaged in revising its racial harassment policy, which failed to gain wide recognition, resulting in underreporting of racial incidents. According to the inspector with responsibility for multicultural education, this was due to lack of understanding of what a racist incident is, with a tendency to see it as just a behavioural and discipline issue, plus fear that reporting incidents would show schools in a bad light and that they might be labelled 'racist'. A group of heads is reviewing the policy and working out comprehensive guidance which will be disseminated in induction and in-service training for teachers and governors.

Acknowledgements

The data reported in this paper formed part of a research project, 'Multicultural/ antiracist policies: pastoral care/personal and social education issues', sponsored by the Economic and Social Research Council. I should like to thank: the LEA advisers, staff and students, especially those who are the focus of this paper; my research colleague, Rani Dayaramani; and our project secretary, Jocelyn Simmons; for sharing in the experience of this research.

Notes

1 See, for example, Hampshire County Council (1991) *Combatting Racial Harassment: County Guidelines For Schools, Colleges and Other Educational Establishments*; Manchester City Council Education Committee (1991) *Equal Opportunities in Education: Antiracist Policy Statement.*
2 Extract from Needs Analysis

   1.10   Specific policies on combatting racism and developing positive images of black people to be included in whole school policy. (Hidden curriculum/pastoral/ PSE.)

   (For further information and access to materials please see [teacher with responsibility for multicultural education].)

   1.10.1   Any overt prejudice shown by a pupil must be treated as a serious matter. We have few black children in school and no personal offence may be caused. Nevertheless, it is important to challenge the illogic and the potential for offence in any action or statement.

   1.10.2   An act of racist name-calling should be referred to the year head for action, and a log kept by [a deputy head], with the action taken.

   1.10.3   An act of violence with any racist connotation should be similarly dealt with, and the punishment should include reference to the parents of the offender.

   1.10.4   Any material in the school which would cause offence to an ethnic group, whether it has been brought into the school or produced by a pupil, should be confiscated, handed to [the teacher with MCE responsibility], who will act on the matter in consultation with the year head and log the matter with [a deputy head].

   1.10.5   The school as a democratic institution will not allow itself to be used for any undemocratic or racist purpose; no pupil may wear such badges or symbols, or openly advocate such ideas without being challenged. No such organisation will be allowed to use the school's facilities or address the school.

3 A methodological issue was that of 'informed consent'; namely, whether from the start to tell the pupils of an interest in race and ethnicity as one factor in the research. The problem is that by altering subjects to a concern with controversial issues there is a greater likelihood that the researcher will be told what they think she or he wants to hear.

   At the time of the introductory group interview we wished to see whether 'race' would arise spontaneously – as indeed it did. Thus at this stage pupils could not give their informed consent to discuss race and ethnicity. Interestingly, their form tutor reported that at afternoon registration, after the pupils had been invited to interview, but before it had taken place, the first person they mentioned as being in the group was AG.
4 To safeguard anonymity in the transcripts and to enable pupil narratives to be traced

through the paper, codes have been used as follows: WG1 = first Year 9 white girl to speak, similarly for boys, WB1 etc.; AG = girl of Asian origin; Res 1 = researcher (MJT); Res 2 = researcher (Rani Dayaramani); Yr12WM1 = Year 12, first white male to speak.

References

Brown, C (1984) *Black and White Britain*, Policy Studies Institute, London.

Commission for Racial Equality (1987) *Racial Attacks: A Survey in Eight Areas in Britain*, CRE, London.

Commission For Racial Equality (1988) *Learning in Terror. A Survey of Racial Harassment in Schools and Colleges*, CRE, London.

Commission For Racial Equality (1989) *A Code of Practice for the Elimination of Racial Discrimination in Education*, CRE, London.

Curriculum Council for Wales (1991) *The Whole Curriculum, 5–16 in Wales*, CCW, Cardiff.

Day, J (1991) 'Role-taking reconsidered: narrative and cognitive-developmental interpretations of moral growth', *Journal of Moral Education*, 20, 3, pp 305–15.

Dummett, A (1986) 'Race, culture and moral education', *Journal of Moral Education*, 15, 1, pp 10–15.

Gaine, C (1987) *No Problem Here: A Practical Approach to Education and 'Race' in White Schools*, Hutchinson, London.

Great Britain, Department of Education and Science (1984) *Race Relations in Schools. A Summary of Discussions at Meetings in Five Local Education Authorities*, DES, London.

Great Britain, Department of Education and Science (1989) *Ethnically-based Statistics on School Pupils*, Circular 16/89, DES, London.

Great Britain, Department of Education and Science and Welsh Office (1989) *Discipline in Schools*, Report of the Committee of Enquiry chaired by Lord Elton, HMSO, London.

Great Britain, Home Office (1981) *Racial Attacks: A Report of a Home Office Study*, HO, London.

Great Britain, Home Office (1989) *The Response to Racial Attack and Harassment: Guidance for Statutory Agencies*, the report of the Inter-Departmental Racial Attacks Group, HO, London.

Great Britain, Home Office (1990) *Section 11 Ethnic Minority Grants. Grant Administration: Policy and Guidelines*, HO, London.

Great Britain, Home Office (1991) *The Response to Racial Attacks: Sustaining The Momentum*, the second report of the Inter-Departmental Racial Attacks Group, HO, London.

Great Britain, Parliament, House of Commons (1985) *Education for All*, the Report of the Committee of Inquiry into the Education of Children from Ethnic Minority Groups (Swann Report) cmnd 9453, HMSO, London.

Great Britain, Parliament, House of Commons, Home Affairs Committee (1986) *Racial Attacks and Harassment*, HC409, HMSO, London.

Great Britain, Statutes (1988) *Education Reform Act 1988*, ch 40, HMSO, London.

Husbands, C (1991) 'The extreme right – a brief European overview', *Race and Immigration*, 247, pp 5–14.

Kitwood, T (1980) *Disclosures to a Stranger. Adolescent Values in an Advanced Industrial Society*, Routledge and Kegan Paul, London.

Lickona, T (1991) *Educating For Character. How Our Schools Can Teach Respect and Responsibility*, Bantam, New York.

Macdonald, I, Bhavnani, R, Khan, L and John, G (1989) *Murder in the Playground. The Report of the Macdonald Inquiry into Racism and Racial Violence in Manchester Schools*, Longsight Press, London.

National Curriculum Council (1990a) *The Whole Curriculum*, Curriculum Guidance 3, NCC, York.

National Curriculum Council (1990b), *Education for Citizenship*, Curriculum Guidance 8, NCC, York.

Power, F C, Higgins, A and Kohlberg, L (1989) *Lawrence Kohlberg's Approach to Moral Education*, Columbia University Press, New York.

Runnymede Trust (1991) 'Europe round-up', *Race and Immigration*, 250, pp 1-2.

Runnymede Trust (1992) *Runnymede Bulletin*, 252 (whole issue).

Scottish Consultative Council on the Curriculum (1991) *Values in Education*, An SCCC Paper for Discussion and Development, SCCC, Dundee.

Selman, R L (1976) 'Social-cognitive understanding, a guide to educational and clinical practice', in Lickona, T (ed) *Moral Development and Behavior. Theory, Research and Social Issues*, Holt, Rinehart and Winston, New York.

Smith, D J and Tomlinson, S (1989) *The School Effect. A Study of Multi-racial Comprehensives*, Policy Studies Institute, London.

Straughan, R (1982) *I Ought to, But . . ..: A Philosophical Approach to the Problem of Weakness of Will in Education*, NFER–Nelson, Windsor.

Tappan, M B (1991) 'Narrative, language and moral experience', *Journal of Moral Education*, 20, 3, pp 243-56.

Tappan, M B and Brown, L M (1989) 'Stories told and lessons learned: toward a narrative approach to moral development and moral education', *Harvard Educational Review*, 59, 2, pp 182-205.

Taylor, M J (1989) A Good Education For All. An Investigation of Issues in Implementing Multicultural/Antiracist Policies in Pastoral Care and Personal and Social Education in Secondary Schools. Unpublished Report for Economic and Social Research Council.

Taylor, M J (1992) *Multicultural Antiracist Education After ERA: Concerns, Constraints and Challenges*, NFER, Slough.

Taylor, W H (1986) 'Antiracist education in non-contact areas, the need for a gentle approach', *New Community*, 13, 2, pp 177-84.

Taylor, W H (1990) 'Multi-cultural education in the "white highlands" after the 1988 Education Reform Act', *New Community*, 16, 3, pp 369-78.

Tomlinson, S (1990) *Multicultural Education in White Schools*, Batsford, London.

Troyna, B (1990) 'Reform or deform? The 1988 Education Reform Act and racial equality in Britain', *New Community*, 16, 3, pp 403-16.

Troyna, B and Ball, W (1987) *Views from the Chalk Face: School Responses to an LEA's Policy on Multicultural Education*, Centre for Research in Ethnic Relations, Policy Paper 1, University of Warwick.

Troyna, B and Carrington, B (1990) *Education, Racism and Reform*, Routledge, London.

Troyna, B and Hatcher, R (1992) *Racism in Children's Lives. A Study of Mainly-white Primary Schools*, Routledge, London.

Troyna, B and Williams, J (1986) *Racism, Education and the State: The Racialisation of Education Policy*, Croom Helm, London.

Ward, J V (1991) ' "Eyes in the back of your head": moral themes in African American narratives of racial conflict', *Journal of Moral Education*, 20, 3, pp 267-81.

Wilson, J (1990) *A New Introduction to Moral Education*, Cassell, London.

Witherell, C S and Noddings, N (eds) (1991) *Stories Lives Tell: Narrative and Dialogue in Education*, Teachers College Press, New York.

Witherell, C S and Pope Edwards, C (1991) 'Moral versus social-conventional reasoning: a narrative and cultural critique', *Journal of Moral Education*, 20, 3, pp 293-304.

Chapter 11
A 'Life History' of White Racism

Carl A Bagley

Abstract

This chapter explores the use of 'life history' as a strategy for gaining access to and understanding the possible ambiguities, inconsistencies and ambivalences in teachers' values, beliefs and attitudes on 'race' and education. Analysis focuses upon a senior teacher, Walter White, and the complex process by which his personal and professional self came to be constructed. The chapter concludes by examining the possible use of the cognitive dissonance between an individual's perspectives on issues related to 'race', class and gender for facilitating antiracist change.

Introduction

> 'Certainly, some of the negative attitudes held by white people are justified. . . .
> It is a fact that the majority of Pakistani people do lie as a matter of course. That
> isn't just prejudice, that's cold facts.' (Walter White)

As Walter White is a senior teacher in a multiethnic school, with a significant degree of power, authority and influence over the delivery of education and the welfare of pupils, I take such a perspective to be highly unethical and racist. Yet Walter White is simply stating what he perceives as the 'cold facts'. How Walter White comes to hold and justify such views and how they shape his professional practice is the question this paper attempts to explore.

Rattansi (1991) contends that proponents of both multicultural and antiracist education in presenting their analysis and prescriptions for change have paid insufficient attention to the complexity of racist ideologies and individuals. He argues that multicultural and antiracist approaches have neglected the contradictions in both discourses and practices associated with 'race'. Individuals are assumed to hold prejudiced perspectives 'consistently and express them and act in accordance with them in a consistent, uncontradictory manner' (Rattansi, 1991, p 24). In effect they have tended to essentialise the values, attitudes, beliefs and behaviour of 'the prejudiced individual'. Rattansi does not suggest that multicultural or antiracist protagonists abandon their respective approaches, rather they should 'acknowledge and analyse its limitations in the light of a more complex understanding of the nature of racism and develop forms of educational engagement more likely to open up racist subjectivities to alternative discourses' (Rattansi, 1991, p 36).

It was in reflecting upon the need for the development of an approach which might enable a more sophisticated understanding of the nature of racism that I came to consider the life history. The value of life histories in the study of education is well established and has been considered in the context of schooling (Goodson, 1980), teacher knowledge (Woods, 1987), the relationship between the personal and institutional domains (Benynon, 1985), and teachers' professional self-development (Woods and Sikes, 1987). It is also in the tradition of racist deconstruction such as the work of van Dijk (1984).

In attempting a life-history approach as a means to opening up racist subjectivities to alternative discourses the speculative nature of this framework is apparent; in this case it is based on only one teacher and covers a vast field, some parts of which are inevitably sketched over lightly. The purpose is not to present a comprehensive model or an exhaustive biographical account, but more simply to raise some issues in this hitherto relatively unexplored area of life-history methodology. I should like to emphasise that I am not claiming the values and beliefs of Walter White are in any way typical either of teachers in his school, other schools or in society as a whole. However, from conducting a series of teacher life histories, one might be able to identify certain common themes which would then contribute to the construction of a more general theory of 'race' and education (Goodson, 1980), and I should like to offer this chapter as a contribution to any such development. While I in no way excuse, condone or defend the values and beliefs of Walter White I am not interested in personality castigating him, and for this reason I have anonymised the text to protect his right to privacy.

The selection and interview process

For two years I had been working as a university researcher on a different project[1] in the school where Walter White was a senior teacher. (He has since retired.) In discussion with the headteacher he had referred to Walter White as:

> 'Giving true meaning to the expression red neck. I literally saw his neck change colour with anger and frustration during an in-service day we had on multicultural education.'

In my discussions with black pupils he was frequently cited as the 'most racist teacher in the school'. I therefore decided that, given his senior position in the school and his allegedly racist disposition, he might prove an interesting subject for a life-history interview. I explained the nature of the life-history method to Walter White: that it would entail him talking in detail about his personal and professional background and the way in which he believed his perspectives had developed, in particular on the question of 'race' and education.

Walter was willing, even keen to participate in the interviews, stating that he 'could go on for years' and 'write books' about 'race' and education. He considered himself 'used to public speaking' and 'a bit more verbose than the rest of the staff'. Moreover, he believed that he would not be simply stating his own values and beliefs but he had 'the ability to put into words what most of them (the rest of the staff) are thinking anyway'. It is certainly not my contention that the values and beliefs expressed by Walter White were in any way representative. Nevertheless, the fact that he perceived them as such gave for him his expression of those values and beliefs an added sense of legitimacy and authority.

Three interviews of 90 minutes each were conducted. The interviews were tape recorded and assurances of confidentiality were given. They were conducted in private and took place in Walter's office. In order to develop the trust and confidence of Walter White, I found it necessary to make professional judgements, within the boundaries of 'informed consent' (Bulmer, 1982), concerning if, when, in what ways and to what degree I should disclose my own antiracist perspective on 'race' and education. As Woods (1986) states 'It is not necessary to lay all your cards on the table at one time . . . the possibility of controversy at too early a stage may awaken fears and close off avenues of access' (p 30).

In conducting these interviews I was aware of the ethical dilemma associated with a process whereby I would be primarily engaging in non-conflictual dialogue with this individual in order to elicit his perspectives. In adopting such a posture I may have appeared to be condoning, if not encouraging, the very beliefs and practices that the approach was intended to help deconstruct (Troyna and Carrington, 1989). Consequently, I found myself having constantly to weigh the potential benefits of access to information against the dangers of reinforcement, and the principle of antiracist disclosure against reactivity and restricted access. On balance I decided that in this case engagement with the complex construction of racist attitudes and beliefs and its potential for the development of antiracist strategies outweighed any dangers of reinforcement since Walter White's attitudes and beliefs were so entrenched.

Walter White's family structure

Walter was a white 57 year old, of average height and medium build. He had married at the age of 21 and had two children: one son of 20, who was adopted, and one daughter of 19. After marrying, he and his wife had 'lived with some regret' for the first five years with the in-laws but 'by going without' they eventually managed to buy a house. After eight years of marriage, they decided to have a family but found they were unable. However, Walter eventually found a Harley Street specialist who could supply children for adoption. Walter stated:

> 'He produced a boy for us. Now that boy is a bit on the dusky side, again where he comes from I don't know and I am not concerned . . . but when people accuse me of racism . . . they don't always know the rest of the story and what you've actually done in your life and what you believe in.'

Researcher   'Are you saying that your adopted son is black?'
Walter   'He got called "Paki" round here.'
Researcher   'The manner in which you expressed the term "Paki" implied that you may not consider it derogatory.'
Walter   'Ah, "Paki" is an interesting word. I imagine in the context others used it towards him it was meant in a fairly derogatory way. I have at times

used the word with a child when, for instance, they say, "he called me 'Paki'" and I say, "Well you are a 'Paki' aren't you?" and there's nothing wrong with that, any more than if they called me "Brit" when I am a "Brit".'

Researcher   'Did his experiences in any way shape your attitude on issues of racism and education?'

Walter   'No, I don't think it was material to it. I don't think any experience that you have in life doesn't contribute to one's attitude to some degree, it might even confirm it, but I would think, I'm absolutely certain, my attitude towards mankind as an egalitarian was fairly well developed by then.'

The contradictions and inconsistencies in Walter's values, beliefs and behaviour are immediately apparent. For example, Walter and his wife have been willing to adopt a black child whom he then describes as 'dusky'. Moreover, he offers the information about his son's 'dusky' appearance in the context of a defence against accusations of his being a racist. He states that his detractors might be misguided precisely because they don't have such an insight into his personal life history. Walter recognises that his son suffered racist abuse in being called a 'Paki' and then admits to using the same term in the classroom with pupils – practice which he perceives as legitimate and presumably in keeping with his values as an 'egalitarian'. While disclaiming that his son's experiences of racism shaped his own 'egalitarian' views on racism and education, he acknowledges the significance of life experience in shaping and confirming his attitudes.

Walter White's career development

At the time of the final interview, Walter's teaching career had spanned 33 years and had consisted of three years in a secondary modern school, one year in a grammar school, 14 years in a comprehensive school and, finally, 15 years at his present school. Although he had a professional background in Physical Education, Mathematics and Craft, for the last 25 years he had taken a pastoral role, culminating in his present position as a senior teacher.

Walter was originally from London's East End docklands. His grandfather was an unskilled dock labourer and his father was a toolmaker. His working-class background was very important to him, and, from the outset, he stressed the fact that he considered himself to be 'decidedly working class'. In terms of his education, he initially went to a secondary modern school but was transferred to a grammar school one year later. Following his time at the grammar school, Walter went into the army as 'a somewhat unwilling National Serviceman' and was posted to Egypt as a clerk. He recalled:

'Some of the officers who were with me were ex-Indian army rubbish of mixed race ... with high degrees of incompetence, great immorality ... you were asked to look after their children whilst they engaged in their wife swapping. There was a terrible lot of that. There were some officers I respected, they tended to be the ones who had come up through the ranks and subsequently got commissions.

'You were reasonably aware of some of the not too good things that the British had done in their colonial attitudes. The rightness in our being in Egypt when they had had a basin full and were fairly poor in their standard of living . . . but there I was commanded to go and kill people. Now that is a fairly hefty thing. They may well command you but nevertheless if you pull the trigger I believe you bear the moral responsibility.'

Interestingly, in this example he implicitly links the issues of class, 'race' and sexual morality. He condemns the 'wife-swapping' officers who are 'mixed race . . . ex-Indian army rubbish' but 'respects' the officers who 'have come up through the ranks' and he also questions the 'colonial attitudes' towards the 'fairly poor' Egyptians. (The cognitive dissonance in his perceptions on 'race' and class are returned to later in the paper.)

In order to remove the 'moral responsibility' of having to shoot somebody, Walter applied for a commission which he knew would entail the Army sending him back to England. On 'deliberately' failing the exam, 'I gave a little lecture on the value of coeducation and a small dose of socialism which I knew would make them not select me', he obtained a local posting. At the end of his National Service, in keeping with the family background, he obtained a job as a draughtsman and began studying engineering. Nevertheless, his 'interest in education and trying to do something more positive for society was still there'. Furthermore, as his elder brother had gone to college this provided him with the incentive to do likewise. As Walter observed:

'At that time coming from a working-class background nobody had ever been to university or college and you just didn't know about these things, these were the things that rich people or fortunate people did.'

He attended college for two years, taking PE and Mathematics, and then started his teaching career in a secondary modern school where he first began to get involved in 'teachers' unions and things like that'. (This interest had continued as at the time of the interview he was a union official.) After three years, he returned to training college and did a year in Craft because 'I thought I might get on a little better if I did Craft rather than general subject teaching.' He then took up a post at a local grammar school. Walter eventually found that the elitist academic ethos of the school was not in accord with his commitment towards comprehensive education and 'beliefs about helping people who weren't very capable. I couldn't change the situation so I handed in my resignation.' On leaving the grammar school, Walter joined a purpose-built comprehensive school under a headteacher who 'exploited all the best things he'd learnt about public schools with socialist aspirations for comprehensive schools'.

After 14 years at the comprehensive, with the departure of the headteacher, he decided it was time for a career move. Walter stated he joined his present school when it had the reputation of being one of the worst schools in the LEA. He was appointed to deal with the discipline problems in the school and to establish an effective pastoral system.

Walter White's perspectives on 'race' and education

The school catered for 680 pupils of whom approximately 30 per cent were black; the majority of pupils were of Pakistani origin, and the remainder of Afro–Caribbean origin. Walter's attitude towards educational provision for black pupils within the school was assimilationist. He believed:

> 'Having chosen to come here they must accept what this country wants to do for the majority of its indigenous people. . . . Take the instance of a non-English speaking child, I don't think it is right to adjudge disproportionate resources to get that child to learn English when there's plenty of other kids going short of teachers. It would be very nice if it were possible without taking funds away from somebody else but in fact it isn't possible. . . . In any case Pakistanis nearly all intend to go back taking their riches or their skill and live the good life when they go back. So most Pakistanis . . . are only using the facility of the school and this country. They don't really consider themselves British. They haven't thrown their lot in with this country at all.'

Walter White frames his values and beliefs on 'race' and education in terms of resources; if the educational demands by blacks are accommodated, then some groups of whites stand to lose. Subsequently, Walter attempts to ground his beliefs in what he perceived as real and material conditions. As Wellman (1977) observed:

> In crucial ways they are ideological defences of the interests and privileges that stem from white people's position in a structure based in part on racial inequality. (p 37)

Subsequently, his argument becomes linked to a nationalist theme. The education system becomes 'our' system, just as this is 'our' country and, if 'they' want to come here, 'they' must abide by that system. If 'they' receive special educational privileges, then 'they' will be receiving unequal treatment. As Billig et al (1988) state:

> This type of complaint provides a justificatory reason for prejudice by claiming simultaneously to defend nationalism and equality. (p 120)

Moreover, according to Walter's perspective, instead of the school failing the educational needs of black pupils, it is 'they' who are exploiting the existing system. Consequently, far from viewing society as at present systematically providing economic, political and social advantages for whites at the expense of blacks, for Walter White it is the black groups who having 'not thrown their lot in with this country' are attempting to obtain a 'disproportionate share of the resources'. Non-compliance with this country's present educational practices is translated into a demand for privileges. As Barker (1981) has suggested, the new racism involves a redefinition of prejudice:

> You are racially prejudiced if you refuse to adopt the characteristic lifestyle of the country in which you have chosen to live.

Subsequently, when Walter was asked whether he believed in dealing with the prevailing racist attitudes among white pupils in the school, he stated:

> 'Well you would have to define what their attitude is before you decide whether

you need to change it. You need to work with other people in order to find out what they are really like. For instance, my parents were working class from the East End and I had received wisdom about the Jews ... it's particularly important not to end up with one definition or concept of what all people of that particular type are like. I think that's the biggest failing.'

I then asked whether white youngsters coming into the school may have received similar negative or stereotypical views about black people from their parents, and whether he therefore thought the school had a part to play in countering these views. He remarked:

'. . . some of the negative attitudes held by white people are justified. I can talk to you about all sorts of people I've had at Court. Five people went to prison or was it six? All but one were our ex-West Indian cons. All villains, liars, cheats and pedlars. The same is true of the Pakistani community. It is a fact that the majority of Pakistani people do lie as a matter of course. That isn't just prejudice, that's cold facts.'

Walter emphasises how important it is not to 'end up with one definition or concept of what all people are like'. Then virtually in the next sentence informs me that the 'majority of Pakistani people do lie as a matter of course'. In an attempt to point out this contradiction, I asked Walter White how he could justify the statement that all Pakistanis are liars? He replied:

'Well, I didn't actually say that, I didn't say they were all. I said there was a racial disposition towards getting yourself out of trouble by telling lies and I believe that. . . . They do, Pakistanis, life is tough for them, their country's based on corruption, so to survive you don't do as well for your family or for yourself unless you engage in that sort of conduct. And that's what they do here. For instance, I heard two Asian girls talking about how they use false names so they don't pay prescription charges. It is my experience that they lie automatically and when you find out that the parents lie automatically, you know you have to be careful.

'This is just a fact. Fathers will plead poverty, can't do this, can't do that and the same man came in, his son was on the wag, couldn't find him anywhere. The police picked him up entering a house. What house was he entering? It turned out he was entering a second house his father owned and was renting to someone else. Now that's sheer realism.'

Van Dijk (1984) noted that many of his respondents who expressed negative attitudes towards immigrants justified their opinions by relating them to events in their personal lives. He believed that in this way individuals attempted to convey the image of reasonableness, the personal account implying that the expressed belief was based upon 'factual' happenings rather than any personal prejudice. Similarly, the majority of Walter White's racist beliefs are supported by reference to personal and professional instances which he uses to validate his case. Furthermore, he attempts to give them added legitimacy by reference to their historical and cultural background.

Issues raised through in-service training are also dismissed when they are contrary to his personal and professional life experiences. For example, in reference to the 'red neck' incident described earlier by the headteacher, Walter was asked for his opinion about the antiracist, in-service training day he had recently attended. He replied:

'A load of rubbish. When some loquacious person who has not had the problem of having to teach comes and tells me about what's going on and how to do it and when he comes down with inaccurate facts like there is nobody else coming into this country, immigration has stopped, he is a liar, either that or he's extremely ignorant. I know of no child in this school who has married anybody other than someone from the Asian continent.

'Now it's a fact they go through an engagement, which in their eyes is as good as a marriage, because it is binding, by avoiding official marriage in England you are officially unmarried so you can import another one can't you. . . . Now this is where the resentment goes on, this is where the increase of the population is a drain on the supplies and resources in this country. . . . The number of illegal immigrants here is legion.'

The external body of information upon which the in-service facilitator was drawing is countered by the contrary personalised knowledge base of the recipient, Walter White. In formulating and expressing his values and beliefs, he makes frequent reference to personal and professional life experiences. Moreover, they shape and guide his professional conduct and make his commitment to the validity of his values and beliefs self-assured and extremely difficult to change.

Developing antiracist strategies for change

The final section considers how information derived from the use of a life-history approach might be used to penetrate resistance to change.

Woods (1987), in considering the ways in which to change teacher values and attitudes, postulated:

There is a danger that a confrontational approach here – impressing on them the sexism and racism in their thought and practice – may only achieve opposition and resentment and drive the stanchions of those dispositions further into their belief systems. This is because 'we are what we are' – the product of a lifetime's socialisation and adaptation. Coming to terms with teaching is a complex matter, such that adaptations for many are protected by boundaries and counter-armament in the event of threat. Demands for change, that go to the root of one's construction of self are very difficult to meet without some examination of how that self has come to be constructed. (pp 19)

Consequently if strategies are to negotiate teacher resistance to change, then it may be crucial that one understands how that teacher's self has come to be constructed and precisely what his or her values and beliefs on 'race' and education are. As I have shown in the case of Walter White, the life-history approach might provide the curriculum developer with such an opportunity. Furthermore, the information gleaned from a life history grounded in teacher knowledge might facilitate the development and refinement of antiracist strategies grounded in and utilising the subjective reality of the teachers themselves. Strategies might be developed which, rather than being based on distant prescriptive educational theory, accommodate and utilise the existing values and beliefs of teachers.

In considering approaches to overcoming teacher resistance to antiracist education, Carrington and Short (1989) stressed the importance of the 'psychological processes associated with attitude formation and change' (p 234). They contended that, as a large percentage of teachers do not support an antiracist perspective (Troyna and Ball, 1985), tactically antiracist facilitators of change need 'to ensure a closer correspondence between their own ideas and those they hope to change' (p 235). To support this approach, Carrington and Short (1989) cited the theory of cognitive dissonance (Festinger, 1957) which states that 'individuals are unable to tolerate contradictory cognitions, ie thoughts, attitudes and beliefs that are inconsistent with one another' (Carrington and Short, 1989, p 236).

I would contend that, as in the case of Walter White, teachers might hold ambiguous, ambivalent and apparently contradictory values and beliefs on a range of issues, yet not perceive them as such. 'Race', gender and class may for some individuals be related but for others the issues remain diverse and totally unconnected.

For example, as in the case of Walter White, some teachers might be reluctant to address the question of racial inequality, while being strongly opposed to a policy of selective education on the grounds of class inequality. Equally, some women teachers might express concern over gender inequality in education but not perceive any link with racial equality in education.

The most common view of teachers towards addressing racism may indeed be assimilationist (Carrington and Short, 1989) but that does not necessarily preclude the possibility that the same teachers may hold more radical teaching perspectives in terms of gender-related and/or class-related issues. It may be at the level of these apparent contradictions of an individual's values and beliefs about education and society that the opportunity lies for enabling attitudinal change to occur. Instead of conceptually altering the approach to make it multicultural rather than antiracist in an attempt to make it more congruent with the existing perspectives of teachers and supposedly therefore more acceptable, as Carrington and Short (1989) suggest, in the strategy I propose the antiracist perspective might remain explicit.

In this case the curriculum developer should attempt to identify the values and beliefs of teachers on issues of gender and class which may then be related to the issue of racism. It might therefore be possible for a programme to be developed which, by operating at the level of these 'self-contradictions', links the issues of racism, sexism and class and enables the individual to formulate a more consistent perspective. In terms of in-service programmes the teacher would be not only practically, but also ideologically and personally involved since the exercise would relate to the subjective reality of the participant.

The viability of interrelating an individual's differing value positions on issues, if not to facilitate his or her personal commitment to antiracist change then at least to minimise or neutralise his or her resistance to antiracist change within an institution might also be considered. For example, in the case of Walter White, his contrasting value positions on 'race' as a teacher and class as a trade union official might have been used to advantage by a curriculum development team to confront his cognitive dissonance. At the final interview I decided to introduce into discussions the antiracist whole-school policy guidelines provided by the union for which he was an official. I began by asking for his views on the need for a whole-school policy on 'race' and education. He replied:

Walter	'A waste of time . . . I don't think writing a policy is going to change a bigot from being a bigot . . . you've got to have . . . one or two people prepared to go and tell them (the black pupils) in a fairly straight way you think that it's unfair or unpleasant.'
Researcher	'This union antiracist policy statement, it's your union, you're an official from this union, do you stand by this document?'
Walter	'Largely, but it is a plea for resources really as most things from teachers' unions are.'
Researcher	'So if I were to come along and say "Okay Mr White, as the union official we'll take this code of practice and adopt it as the school's code of practice", would you feel comfortable with that?'
Walter	'Well, that's a council for perfection, the state of affairs we would like to have in society but we are not quite at that level of society, are we?'
Researcher	'But the school could adopt this policy and move towards improving the situation now.'
Walter	'What good would it do?'
Researcher	'Well, for example, it could provide guidelines and a framework from which the school may begin to respond to racist behaviour and stop racial discrimination.'
Walter	'I know the job and how to do it. God knows I've been doing it long enough and a damn sight longer than these people with any guidelines.'
Researcher	'So why is this document produced by your union then?'
Walter	'Because they were probably asked to produce it.'
Researcher	'By your members, who apparently thought they needed it.'
Walter	'The reality of the situation is that unions have hardly any effect these days in a government which is anti-union – but we don't want to go into the politics of it now. I am a member of a pressure group called . . ., which is a group of people largely consumers of education who would like to feel that things could be improved. It tries to get local and central government to value education and put the necessary resources into it. It's non-political. It certainly has a racial mix. One of my good friends is a Pakistani for instance. And I must get membership forms to two other West Indian friends of mine.'

As his perspectives were constructed from experience, so the enactment of those beliefs in terms of his professional practice did not require any external guidelines or policies. Walter recognises the need to change people's opinions and bigotry, not through policy but through personal example and discussion – professional responsibility which he sees himself as already fulfilling. However, he conceives the opinions and bigotry that need changing to be those of black students. In defending his stance Walter once again frames the question not as being about values but about limited resources. However, in this case the plea for resources is being made by the teaching union of which he is an official.

Consequently, when he is questioned further about the union's antiracist policy Walter chooses not to evoke the nationalist no 'special provision for any one group' argument he used previously. Moreover, he is faced with the dilemma of one value position, trade unionism, of which he is strongly in favour, being used to argue for another value position, antiracism, to which he is strongly opposed. Subsequently, when pressed on the matter he goes on the defensive, attempting to avoid further direct discussion on the matter, introducing black friends to show that he has no personal prejudice (Billig *et al*, 1988).

The juxtapositioning of Walter's values on 'race' and class through my introduction of reference to his union's whole-school policy on antiracist education may not have changed his perspective on it. Nevertheless, it might have been possible for a curriculum development team to minimise the resistance of a senior teacher, Walter White, by basing its antiracist recommendations on the union's policy for which he was an official. A curriculum development team able to conduct life-history interviews with key members of staff might be able to use the information to complement other antiracist strategies.

In more general terms it might be possible for a range of life-history interviews conducted with a sample of teachers to be used for in-service training purposes. Suitably anonymised transcript copies of these life histories might then be used in group work sessions as the basis for discussions on racism and education. The presupposition is that the teachers on the course could learn from some of the ambiguities and inconsistencies demonstrated in the life histories since these dissonances are likely to be part of their own thinking. Unfortunately until such approaches can be tested in practice the possible strategic utilisation of information extracted from life histories must remain speculative.[2]

The portrait I have offered of Walter White provides a clear example of the way he, as a white person, attempts to minimise, neutralise and deny the existence and significance of racism and the numerous ways he attempts to marginalise any response to it. In revealing the interrelated construction of his personal and professional self and the concomitant ambiguities, contradictions and ambivalence of his values and beliefs, one might begin to comprehend the magnitude of the task of deconstruction. Nevertheless, it might be by beginning to understand and engage with these complexities that successful strategies for antiracist change can be assembled.

Notes

1 This was a two-year local education authority project on multicultural education. The project, a response to the Swann Report (GB, P, H of C, 1985) was located in two secondary schools: one a multiethnic, coeducational, inner-city school and the other an all white, coeducational rural school. The project was undertaken by a curriculum development team of four teachers and I acted as an independent evaluator.
2 Sikes and Troyna (1991) have piloted the use of the life-history method in initial teacher education programmes in which students share their perspectives on education and teaching.

References

Barker, M (1981) *The New Racism*, Junction Books, London.

Benynon, J (1985) 'Institutional change and career histories in a comprehensive school' in Ball, S J and Goodson, I F (eds) *Teachers' Lives and Careers*, Falmer Press, Lewes.

Billig, M, Condor, S, Edwards, D, Gane, M, Middleton, D and Radley, A (1988) *Ideological Dilemmas, a Social Psychology of Everyday Thinking*, Sage, London.

Bulmer, M (ed) (1982) *Social Research Ethics*, Macmillan, London.

Carrington, B and Short, G (1989) 'Policy or presentation? the psychology of anti-racist education', *New Community*, 15, 2, pp 227–40.

Festinger, L (1957) *A Theory of Cognitive Dissonance*, Stanford University Press, Stanford, California.

Great Britain, Parliament, House of Commons (1985) *Education for All*, report of the Committee of Inquiry into the Education of Children from Ethnic Minority Groups, (Swann Report) cmnd 9453, HMSO, London.

Goodson, I (1980) 'Life histories and the study of schooling', *Interchange*, 11, 4, pp 62–76.

Rattansi, A (1991) 'Race', *Education and Society*, Course ED 356, Unpublished Draft, The Open University, Milton Keynes.

Sikes, P J and Troyna, B (1991) 'True stories: a case study in the use of life history in initial teacher education', *Educational Review*, 43, 1, pp 3–16.

Troyna, B and Ball, W (1985) *Views from the Chalk Face: School Responses to an LEA's Multicultural Education Policy*, Policy Papers in Ethnic Relations no 1, Centre for Research in Ethnic Relations, University of Warwick, Coventry.

Troyna, B and Carrington, B (1989) 'Whose side are we on? Ethical dilemmas in research on "Race" and education', in Burgess, R (ed) *The Ethics of Educational Research*, Falmer Press, Lewes.

van Dijk, T A (1984) *Prejudice and Discourse: An Analysis of Ethnic Prejudice in Cognition and Conversation*, Benjamins, Amsterdam.

Wellman, D T (1977) *Portraits of White Racism*, Cambridge University Press, London.

Woods, P (1986) *Inside Schools: Ethnography in Educational Research*, Routledge, London.

Woods, P (1987) 'Life-histories and teacher knowledge' in Smyth, W J (ed) *Educating Teachers: Changing the Nature of Professional Knowledge*, Falmer Press, Lewes.

Woods, P and Sikes, P J (1987) 'The use of teacher biographies in professional development' in Todd, F (ed) *Planning Continuing Professional Development*, Croom Helm, London, pp 161–80.

Chapter 12

Unasked Questions, Impossible Answers, The Ethical Problems of Researching Race and Education

Harbhajan Singh Brar

Abstract

This chapter examines the 'theoretical' ethical problems that arise out of researching race and education and specifically addresses some of the ethical dilemmas that arise out of ethnographic research in education. It explores the nature of 'race' research and attempts to address four fundamental questions. Why are we carrying out research? Who should and should not be carrying out research? What are we researching? How is the research actually being carried out? The main thrust of the paper argues that 'neutral' or 'value free' research is not possible and that links between the individual, political and academic worlds are inseparable. Finally, the chapter argues, using illustrations from my own research, that the 'state' is neither neutral nor benevolent, for academic research has too often simply helped the state to reinforce and reproduce racism.

Introduction

In academic research the issues of ethics are rarely considered. Commonly, ethical concerns appear as an afterthought, quickly dismissed as marginal. When researchers do manage to convince themselves of the importance of 'ethics', they normally do it in a simplistic manner, often finding the easiest and most facile answers. I believe that there are a number of important questions that have to be faced at the onset of any research project, rather than at the end. In particular, I am going to argue in this chapter that:

1 neutral or value free research is not possible;
2 the links between the individual, political and academic worlds are inseparable; and
3 the state is neither neutral nor benevolent. Too often research has simply helped the state to reproduce racism.

Over the past 30 years we have seen a vast increase in the output of empirically based research in the area of race and education. This research has emanated from many differing schools of thought and has had a significant impact on policy directions with regard to race and education at the local as well as at a national and international level. Because of this quantity of work, what is clear from the outset is the enormity and impossibility of the task of drawing up, in a single chapter, a set of ethical research guidelines that are universally applicable. Instead, by looking at these ethical issues in the context of a number of case studies, this chapter will simply be raising important questions which too often are not even asked by the researcher. It must, however, be stressed that there are no easy answers to these questions, but to fail to ask them is often simply to condone racism.

The unasked questions

The four most important ethical questions that must be asked by all researchers are:

1 *Why* and for what purpose are we carrying out research?
2 *Who* should and should not be carrying out academic research? For example, are there areas within 'race and education' research, where a black researcher would be more suited than a white researcher?
3 *What* then are we studying? Are there unacceptable, as well as acceptable and legitimate areas of study? For example, in the case of race and education should we be studying 'racism' or should we be looking at exotic black cultures?
4 *How* then is this particular piece of research undertaken? What accountability and responsibility does the researcher accept when undertaking a research project?

It is very clear that whenever attempts are made to try and find answers to these questions, the answers are often influenced by the 'politics' of the individual researcher and in the parameters set by the funding agencies who often dictate the direction and findings of such research. It is therefore imperative that the individual comes to terms with these questions from the outset of any research project, and is clear with himself or herself about the boundaries that shape the findings of the research.

While trying to find some of the answers to the questions above, this chapter will undoubtedly revive some of the old, sensitive and often uncomfortable debates that surround the issue of research ethics which have never been fully addressed in academic literature. It will try to provide an insight into ethical aspects of these complex issues, and address some of the above questions through a number of case studies. The main thrust will be geared towards qualitative research, though many of the issues that will be raised will also apply to quantitative work. The reason for this is, as Mac an Ghaill (1989) states, 'Qualitative research enables us to go beyond the distorted, de-racialised, de-genderised, white male world of much academic work.'

Racism is not an object that can be scrutinised out of social context. It is a set of practices which implicate the observer. There is a clear need to go deeper than some of the crude sociological and biological explanations of racism that are commonly held, for, as Sivanandan pointed out as early as 1983, 'Racism does not stay still: it changes shape, size, purpose, and function.'

What is needed is a more complex understanding of the fact that there is no singular 'racism', but as Hall *et al* (1978) pointed out, there is a 'multiplicity of racisms'. Unless this task is undertaken and the definition of 'racism' addressed explicitly, the ethical research position that any researcher takes will inevitably be flawed.

The ethics of 'why' we carry out research

The basic questions that need to be asked are, why are we carrying out a particular piece of research and what is the actual value of the research? Can and should research be scientific, 'pure' and objective, notionally value free, and should research then be handed to policy makers in some pure clinical form for them to do as they wish, as many academics would argue (eg Finch, 1986)? Alternatively, can research then be used as a tool to change society through a process of social engineering (Webb, 1956); is 'political' research as a research style ethically acceptable or is 'political' research simply a process of propaganda generation?

Within the academic literature (see Finch, 1986), there is basically a view that researchers can take one of four possible stances: they can act as providers of critical enlightenment, as advisers, as advocates on behalf of the researched, or they can be directly engaged with policy. Such models of research start from the notion of 'pure research' which is supposedly objective across the spectrum to a 'radical and critical' social science – which some Weberian academics have simply dismissed as political propaganda – where the researcher's own views have totally guided the direction of the research. Other academics have simply dismissed this style of research as being crude, simplistic and journalistic rather than academic, a criticism that is often hurled at 'good' qualitative research.

In the first instance there is the idea of research as somehow being *'objective'* and *'value free'*, where the researcher is acting as a provider of some notional 'critical enlightenment', where extra insights to a particular research problem are given, but not specific answers on how to act on them as that would then fall into the realms of policy making. There have been numerous discussions about the ideal of 'value free' and 'objective' research in the social sciences, for many researchers have strongly argued that even when simple numerical statistics are given, they are by their very nature value laden. One simply has to examine the sorts of questions that were asked in order to access the numbers and ask what sorts of questions were omitted and why, and here value judgement would have to come into play. If, for example, we look at the Policy Studies Institute (PSI) statistics (Brown, 1984) supposedly 'objective and value free', different researchers have clearly read different meaning into these numbers. This idea of the research somehow producing clinical numbers simply puts the researcher in to a role of a 'non-thinking technician' which is blatantly false (Finch, 1986).

Often what the researcher wants to see and not see is determined by the researcher's own hidden agenda. Lord Rothschild in a paper to the Social Sciences Research Council (SSRC, 1982) (quoted in Finch, 1986) said that certain areas of research can be 'more value free than others', but there are

> other parts of social science [that] cannot be value free without distorting the aim, for example the sociological effects of studying the effects of housing on a given population. Value judgements will be implicit in noting some of the effects, good and bad.

Within this debate about value free research, discussions have taken place on whether you can actually have a 'value free science of sociology' and what form this value free science takes. The basic idea is that the scientist may study evaluation, without actually carrying out an evaluation of the process, and for Freud this Weberian position is 'completely free from bigotry'. Gouldner (1961) then takes this position even further for he argues that this 'value free doctrine' has significantly contributed to the growth of sociology, by helping it break free from traditional morality, embedded in sociological research.

Others, primarily from non-Weberian perspectives, have argued that such an approach to research creates a 'safe option' behind which academics hide from the whole debate that surrounds the area of ethics. This approach, it is argued, was initially raised in order to safeguard the peace of the 'academic house', where there was a need to restrain so-called 'political passions'. Today, however, the debate has become 'trivial' and 'idealised' simply in order to sustain a guise of professionalism and the professional respectability of academia. This then gives the academics a 'professionalism veil' to hide behind, from critical external evaluation. What is rarely considered is that the very decision of someone claiming that they are taking a non-political stance is surely a political decision in itself. To hide behind the notion of, *to know all is to measure all*, is simply an escape from the real world, for no researcher can know all, so 'all' can never be measured.

This whole debate around the notion of a 'pure science' clashes with the basic ideals of 'critical intellectualism' in which the idea and notion of 'truth' is seen as much more contentious. Claiming to be *truthful* is surely to accept the idea that you can conceal values.

There is a school of thought that claims that science is by its very nature political; some argue (eg Rein, 1976) that a researcher can't keep out of decision making, for no researcher can be above ideological disagreement.

> Whatever the academic arguments in favour of doing a specific piece of research, it is politically naive and potentially dangerous to see research as autonomous from its contextual political environment ... governments and other interested bodies necessarily take a strong role and have a stake in academic research about so-called deviant groups in society. (Solomos (1989))

This school of thought argues convincingly that in research you have basically to question what the information or research is for, and taking a partisan approach is then at least being honest with oneself, and the researched. 'Political' in this instance does not, however, mean a total slide into relativism. Myrdal (1970) spells this out, when he states,

> the existence of a body of scientific knowledge acquired independently of all valuations, I soon found to be naive empiricism. Facts do not organise themselves into theories just by being looked at. . . . The specification of value premises should overcome the inhibitions against drawing practical and political conclusions . . . and would consequently render practical social science research a much more powerful instrument for guiding rational policy formation.

The second model of research is the *technician* or *social engineering* approach to research. The idea here is that research can and should be used to change society. Entwined within this, however, is the notion of remaining a 'professional' and 'academic' first and at the same time holding specific political values which then allow the academic and political to go together in some form of an 'unholy alliance'. This is where the researcher takes on the role of an adviser and puts in an active input into policy, what Greer *et al* (1985) call a 'hand maiden to policy'. (See also the work of Beatrice Webb and the Fabian society (1956).) This model, like the 'value free science' also allows the academic to hide behind the ideal of academic respectability and professionalism, where the might of the so-called 'objective institution' is used to convince the policy makers of academic neutrality for 'the ethos of social science is the search for objective truth'.

The problem with this model is that a form of social engineering is again somehow seen as unproblematic, as though facts, produced through this approach, can be 'ideologically and academically neutral', with the academic somehow acting as the 'honest' broker. In this vein, Gouldner (1975) strongly argues that moral involvement does not distract from scientific objectivity, as though scientific objectivity was the sole goal, rather than the 'ideological good' emanating out of the research.

This then leads onto the third model, that of a *political researcher*, where the researcher sets out with a set of specific 'political' aims, in the broader sense, and embarks on a 'mission' to find research evidence to prove them. For instance in his work Gutzmore (1983) has pointed to the tradition of research that looks at black youth as a problem, where,

> The criminalisation process . . . depends in a very real sense for its validity on the work of a number of sociologists, not only of the Right, but self-claimed radicals

With this third model, the 'political' is the most important element, for the 'politics' guide the parameters of the research. In the past, the political parameters of much of the research produced have not been able to go beyond the development of simple, crude, racist pathologies. There is therefore a strong need to shift the focus away from such pathologies to where the researcher can be used positively to help dismantle and deconstruct 'popular common-sense racist myths'; though it has to be said that in many instances, such research can in fact simply reinforce and create myths, such as the false idea of black children being caught between two cultures. These myths then become harder to overcome as they are seen as 'truths' arising out of the respectability of the house of academia.

With this particular model of research, the researcher can take on the role of an advocate acting on behalf of the research subjects and notionally in some cases become the voice of the powerless by empowering them (see Mac an Ghaill, 1989). This then begs the questions, can the powerless really be represented? Telling *their* story is fine in theory but can it be told correctly and what are the consequences of the telling? There are all sorts of assumptions tied up within such a project. It presumes that the researched can't somehow tell their own story, which in most cases in patronising and that the story told will be the correct one, which in most cases is not true.

It is not true in the sense that 'telling the story' can only be done if persons researched have the full right to veto the story being told if they are unhappy with the results, and also if all of them are fully consulted over the findings. One has to ask, in how many so-called 'enlightened' research instances does this actually happen? Telling a group's story does not mean talking to a select number of people and putting their views over as being a representative voice of that group or community. Often researchers get caught up in their own 'liberal' traps of convincing themselves that their research is somehow empowering. An example of this is the interesting and illuminating work of Mac an Ghaill (1988) in *Young, Gifted and Black*. The researcher makes a claim to empower the 'researched', but at times the work slips into the dangerous area of pathologising the pupils; in reproducing Rasta Heads and (Sikh) Warriors as names of racialised groups, he perpetuates the myth commonly held in many schools, that all Rastas and Sikh youth gangs equate with problems within schools. In the context of empowerment the question that also has to be asked is: What if the researched are 'racists', do you and should you also empower them?

The political researcher can also directly engage with policy, which is the fourth and the most active model that a researcher can take, where he or she enters the arena of public debate. This is where the research is widely publicised and disseminated, including publishing in non-academic journals, and where it then becomes the accepted wisdom of the social scientist. This type of research then breaks down the 'ivory tower' view of academics and academia, where the academics become actively involved in 'practical' and political struggle. This is the model that should guide any research in the field of race and education, where the goal of antiracist education is the bench-mark.

The question that still remains unanswered is how much impact can such research have, for while it can take the form of 'passive enlightenment' all the way to 'direct engagement', there is little measure of impact. This then means asking the question 'Whose side are we on?' for, as Becker (1961) states, we can't avoid taking sides, 'we must always look at the matter from someone's viewpoint'.

Other ethical questions relating to why we carry out a particular piece of research can be crude and often are simplistic but are no less significant in the day-to-day politics of carrying out research. In contemporary academic settings a commonly held rhetorical defence position is that, 'if I don't carry out a particular piece of work then someone less "ethical" than me will carry out the research'. Alternatively in the current fiscal climate where success is judged by money raised, 'it's better that I have the research monies than someone else having them'. These arguments then look very tempting when research monies are required simply to sustain employment. Are such self-centred views acceptable when carrying out research in the field of racism; where economics then plays a crucial and fundamental factor, where research is seen simply in business terms, above any ideological commitment to the antiracist bench-mark outlined above? All this links to the issue of the funders then dictating the nature of the research and findings, where the researcher, in order to ensure further monies, writes what is expected rather than what is needed, often by not fully spelling out 'good' antiracist research.

The ethics of 'who' should carry out research

If research in race is about dealing with 'political' issues, then the question has to be raised as to who is best able to carry out this research and why. One of the most important debates in the field of researching race and education has been the role that both black and white researchers play. Most of the 'politically aware' left academics talk of using race and education research to bring about some form of 'positive' social change. If this is the goal of research, then does the 'colour' of the researcher make any difference to the research and its outcomes? I would strongly argue that it does for all forms of academic research. If a white researcher is carrying out research on black communities it is legitimate to question whether this white researcher can really collect meaningful data. There are clear power differences in the relationship between the researcher and the research subjects compounded by the fact that there are no common shared experiences of racism. Bhikku Parekh (1981) spells this out plainly for he argues,

> White people don't understand what it is like to be black and therefore can't understand the complex structures and behaviours of the black community.

On the other hand, John Rex (1983), a prominent sociologist of race, entwines Weberian notions in the idea of political research and clearly states that,

> Good research in the social sciences does not ultimately depend on the position of the researcher in a class and power structure and still less on the colour of his skin.

Indeed when he was asked at a conference on researching race[1] about what perspective guided his research, he simply stated that he 'was not doing white, green or black research, but simply research'.

This whole question as to who should study what is open and forms a part of an ongoing debate. In crude simplistic terms, the formula that should be applied to researching race and education is that basically white antiracist researchers should be looking at racism within white structures and institutions, to which black people have little or no access, where they can expose and tackle racism directly, and black researchers should be looking at the communities with whom they have a greater understanding and which they are less likely to stereotype and pathologise. What is at stake is not an absolute rule (there is no suggestion that white people can *never* carry out effective research on black communities) only that such deployment normally represents the most effective use of research resources. Research using such a formula is likely to yield more valuable, accurate and useful findings, as it is primarily based on a greater understanding and empathy with the research subject.

This position is not an 'elitist' position or one of exclusivity, for as a black teacher in my research explained to me,

> the expertise, knowledge and skills of black teachers are appropriated to glorify the public relations attempts of prospective heads, inspectors, white MSS teachers. White teachers placed in Southall become instant experts and can include on their curriculum vita that they have experience of working with the black community. (Minhas, Holland, Senn and Brar, 1988)

This formula relating to the types of research undertaken by black and white researchers is in no way a 'cut and dry' formula, and will inevitably anger and provoke unease in many researchers, but will at the same time hopefully stimulate healthy debates and exchanges that are much needed over this issue. There are also inherent dangers with such simplistic equations if they are taken too far, for they can very easily lead to a marginalisation of 'black' research, where it is given less importance and even less funding.

At the same time it must also be clearly stated that it does not mean that all black researchers researching black communities will themselves automatically carry out more ethical research. Often black researchers become caught up in the everyday models of research that stereotype and pathologise, which are inevitably developed by white researchers. It is said that if you tell a story enough times, an element of it begins to take on a life of its own and inevitably takes on some semblance of dangerous 'truth'. If, for example, we look at the only academic textbook in the field of 'race and pastoral care' which is written by a black headmaster, we can see he too falls into the same pathology trap for in his book he talks of,

> Their [black pupils] natural exuberance, friendliness and sometimes exhibition-ist attitude together with their physical appearance (they are often bigger than their peers) are often misunderstood and have earned them such labels as disruptive, antisocial, aggressive . . .

He goes on to say,

> During bad weather, such as very cold days and periods of snow, black children frequently find being sent out doors exceptionally uncomfortable. Every effort is made, no expense spared, whatever their financial circumstances, to keep their house warm. Without experience of living in colder homes they find it less easy to adapt to the extreme cold outside. Treating them all alike in this regard is not as equal as it seems (Duncan, 1988).

If black authors, such as Carlton Duncan, have reproduced such stereotyped black pathologies, one has to question where their 'black perspective' lies, especially if they make claims that their research is guided by their understanding of, 'what it's like to be black'?

Notwithstanding such examples, black researchers will be able to bring to the research the lived experiences of racism, a qualitative contribution to producing good academic 'race' research. For many white researchers in the field, researching and confronting racism is simply an academic exercise, which they can leave at their ivory towers when they close their front doors at the end of the day, while for black people it is a lived daily experience that is carried with them throughout their lives. The black researchers, like the black communities being researched, cannot escape back to academic ivory towers, and often cannot counter the influential 'expertise' that emanates from them.

Moreover, the 'Ivory Tower' itself is not free of racism. It can be argued that often black researchers, simply in order to gain employment, or sustain their career chances have themselves reproduced the 'common-sense racist' pathologies that have become readily accepted. They are often reminded that they should be grateful for the job and therefore should not 'upset the academic apple cart'. There are many instances within academic research where white senior researchers have employed junior black researchers simply in order to get around the issue of access to the black community. Syd Jeffers (1991) has described this as being *parachuted in* to the community. These researchers are then often both exploited for their ease of access and are at the same time held up as examples of positive-action equal opportunities policies, while in reality their skills are simply 'appropriated' to further the career chances of senior researchers. Academia is no different from any world of work, for the different power relationships of race and gender are simply mirrored in a much more closed 'old boy' setting.

The ethics of 'what' we research

It was not black people who should be examined, but white society: it was not a question of educating blacks and whites for integration, but of fighting institutional racism: it was not race relations that was the field of study, but racism (Bourne, 1980).

A researcher researching race and education in the first instance needs to question what it is that is being examined: is the research looking at racism or is it, as in many cases, simply looking at culture? Researchers have to ask themselves, what are 'we' really looking at: are we as researchers looking at the structural subordination of black people (ie institutional racism) or are we simply developing a cultural 'encyclopaedia of ethnicities', which records a clinical sociology of one community after another for academic reference, with little analysis or understanding of the racism(s) and communities' struggles as they occur at the chalk face?

There is an argument among researchers, such as Lawrence (1981) and Bourne (1980) that such cultural research on the black communities simply provides the state with data on black people to maintain black communities in a subordinate position. This leads back to the earlier question of whether white researchers should be examining black people as mere research objects. Robin Jenkins's (1971) position on this matter is quite simple: he warned blacks not to submit themselves to the scrutiny of white researchers, who in effect act as spies for the government. They should, he said, be told to 'fuck off'.

Lawrence, like Bourne, argues that racism and not race relations should be studied, for race relations mainly studies the pathology of the black community, which then leads to the development of 'common-sense' popular racisms, based around, for example the notions of black underachievement, the 'black mugger', which allows passing references to the black 'penchant for violence' (Cashmore and Troyna, 1982) to develop and the crude, simplistic and often derogative stereotypes of the extended Asian family.

Due to such crude forms of analysis, Lawrence (1981) in an article entitled 'White Sociology, Black Struggle' concluded that race relations sociologists have themselves become a part of the problem of researching race. Often, under the guise of 'professionalism' and 'good research dissemination', researchers put themselves forward as instant 'experts' on the black community, readily available to the mass media. For example, at Warwick University, white researchers researching the Muslim communities have often talked of 'my Muslims' in a patronising and non-problematic manner, having studied them for only one or two years. Often with little real understanding, they exert influence on policy directions, and in such instances, the commonly used saying 'a little knowledge is a dangerous thing' aptly applies.

In a reply to Lawrence's article, Cashmore and Troyna (1981) in almost a 'knee jerk' defensive action, argued in an article 'Just for White Boys? Elitism, Racism and

Research' that the research that they carry out as sociologists was by its very nature looking at white racism and claimed that Lawrence's stance is an 'elitist one'.

The fundamental question that has then to be asked is whether there can be an agreed ethical and principled stance about what research should and should not be undertaken. I want to argue that there cannot. Research must be antiracist but no absolute principles can be drawn up, no universal antiracist research contract is possible, because, as I shall show below, the answer to these questions ultimately depends on the research context.

The ethics of 'how' we carry out research

Having attempted to try and raise the questions around, who, why and what we research, we now come to the last and the most difficult question to answer, which is: How is the research to be undertaken? As I have said earlier, this chapter mainly addresses issues of qualitative research, for, as Mac an Ghaill (1989) states,

> Qualitative research enabled me to see the education system as a part of a wider system of constraints which, often unwittingly, helps to maintain black people in a position of structural subordination. The major problem in the schooling of black youth lies not with their culture, but with racism.

In the first instance the type of qualitative research method that is going to be used has to be established. One of the most frequent methods used in qualitative research which is ethnographic in its approach is that of participant observation and the use and development of friendship. The remainder of the chapter will primarily focus on this, often using data from my research project on pastoral care in schools (Brar, forthcoming).

This chapter aims to stimulate debate and asks the researcher to think a little deeper and always to question the ethics of methodologies being used in any research project. In focusing on the specific problems of ethnography the last section of the paper raises many general ethical questions, few, if any, of which can be answered in a single paper.

The role of friendships in qualitative research

The use and development of friendships in research can confuse and confound the notions of research objectivity, for in order to gain ethnographic research data there is an essential need to develop at least rapport if not a full friendship. Within traditional anthropology we are, however, told that the researcher should not change the life of the person(s) being researched. Yet this is problematic, for simply being there in the research setting changes the research environment. In the area of researching race and education this can lead to a number of additional problems, which the last section of this chapter will seek to address.

Basically, according to Aristotle (1926 edn) there are three different types of friendships: utility based, pleasure based and virtue and goodness based.

With the development of rapport which is basically 'utility based' there is little need for actual liking of the research subject, for all that is required is just a process of trust without hurting. This form of rapport essentially meets the needs of the researcher, rather than addressing the needs of the researched. Then there is the ethical issue of how this rapport is to be established in order to gain access to research data. The researcher can try to look like the study group, adapt to their language, and play the group's 'cultural' games and conform to the group's cultural rules. (See Pettigrew's study of the Sikhs, 1975.)

One of the main ethical problems however with this type of research is that when you are researching the 'controversial' area of race and education you may be directly faced with racist behaviour. The question that all researchers then have to address is, do they challenge it or do they play along with it, for the researcher has to reconcile the short-term goals, of preventing, for example, a racist incident against the long-term goal of the anticipated final outcomes of the research project. The purpose of developing rapport in research is, primarily, distance-reducing, anxiety-quietening and trust-building. The question that has to be addressed is, is this honest 'research'? If, for example, you are carrying out research on the police, is it ethical to accept in the short term the racist 'bar-room culture' that occurs and to play along with it, simply in order to gain research material, which may or may not have long-term benefits in tackling racism; or is the issue of tackling racism so paramount in any research project, that the researcher should challenge the racism where it occurs, irrespective of the consequences to the research project? With such dilemmas there are no clear-cut prescribed answers which can be applied to all instances, for in most cases it is dependent on the actual group being researched, and on the researcher's ability to draw a balance between the long- and short-term goals (see Keith, 1991).

In the whole area of qualitative research, trust and the maintenance and betrayal of this trust is one of the most crucial factors. If the process of trust develops into a closer friendship, it then poses a different set of ethical problems for the researchers. If the researcher is carrying out 'objective', 'value free' research, then the development of friendships is warned against, as there are dangers that the development of such trust may blur the researcher's objectivity.

There is, for example, a tendency for the researcher to go to the people in the research context who are seen as politically alike and sympathetic. These are the type of people that the researcher would choose as friends in a non-research context, who would give support and encouragement and would probably see the 'political' goal of the research in the same light as the researcher. While this may give the researcher pleasure in the research task, it may also distort the data, as the friendships can influence the overall direction that the research takes. An example of this is my qualitative research on pastoral care. The staff in the school are crudely divided into four main sociopolitical groups, the old disciplinarians, the liberals, the new realists, and the independents (Brar, PhD research, based on Mac an Ghaill, 1988) and for me there was a natural draw in the school to the 'liberals' as their views and politics fitted most closely with my own. There was then a danger of my research being guided by the views and ideas of this group, which would and could have easily closed off access to research information and reduced the objective 'academic' validity of the research findings in the eyes of the other groups within the school. In such a situation the researcher has to develop the skills of not alienating any one group in order to access the full information required.

The problem with the development of friendships in research is that being friends with one group naturally prevents access to others, especially if the others see you associated with one particular faction. You can, however, get a different set of insights if you develop friendships in research as against promoting just a process of rapport, but then the additional problems of trust and confidentiality arise (King, 1974). There is also the danger that often a process of rapport can be mistaken for friendship by another and this may then close particular doors.

With the development of friendships, what role does intentional deception play: is it unethical to mislead people simply in order to gain access to research data? Where does the crucial issue of informed consent fit in to this model of research? Is the friendship falsified to 'spy' on the researched? In such research contexts, can and should the researcher adopt an 'end justifies the means' position? Is this position unethical or is it acceptable in certain circumstances? For example, with research that was carried out in Ealing (Minhas *et al*, 1988), documents that were kept hidden had to be surreptitiously removed, even when the researchers had been told that they would have full access to all data required. In this situation (though not always) adopting an 'end justifies the means' approach is surely ethical, for in the long term the research clearly helped to expose the racist attitudes and practices of certain officers within the institution, but in the short term ethical rules of acceptable behaviour were broken.

There is also a whole area of research which can be aptly titled false research, where the researcher claims to be looking at one thing while in reality is really studying another. In participant observation do you, for instance, lie about your own 'political' position. If informants find out you are a committed antiracist, will they work to hide racism even further? As Gans (1968) in his research on political participation discovered, 'if people found out I was a Democrat, my future chance of obtaining data from Republicans was nil'.

Another ethical dilemma that many researchers face is, can they ever be off duty or do they record everything? An example of this was in my research in schools, when teachers made so-called off-the-record comments. I often put them down in my own handwritten records and have used the data without ever naming the teacher, as it was pertinent in uncovering racist practices. Is this unethical? Have I broken or betrayed promises? Or does the value of the research outweigh such assurances?

There is a school of thought that argues that good research should by its very nature involve the researched group. After all,

> Interviewers define the role of interviewees as subordinates; extracting information is more valued than yielding it; the convention of the interviewer–interviewee hierarchy is a rationalisation of inequality: what is good for interviewers is not necessarily good for interviewees. (Roberts, 1981)

Stenhouse (1985) gave the data that he had gathered back to the respondents to corroborate its accuracy. In his research this led to the respondents spotting mistakes they made and then claiming that it was not representative of what was said, which then invalidated the findings of the research.

Thus the involvement of the researched is not so straightforward, for such an enlightened project can have a number of serious flaws. What form does involvement take? Is it simply offering some form of feedback at the end of the project, and is there the danger that the respondent might be easily identifiable from the feedback data within a wider context? Would this jeopardise any promise of confidentiality? In an educational setting is there not a danger that such feedback may, for instance, be used for teacher appraisal, especially if teachers can easily be identified? The question has also to be asked, who is this feedback being offered to, and at what point in the research is it to take place? The researcher must also ask why this offer is being made. Is it simply to ease some 'liberal' guilt about disempowering the researched or is it about some form of genuine empowerment? All these questions can only be answered in particular contexts at specific times.

Often there are ethical issues that arise when particular research findings are published and about how they are published. In Burgess's (1989) research on education, which was written when certain teachers had left the school being studied, Burgess found that he had angered the head, who felt that he had not been informed earlier about the problems found in his school. The head felt that the problems could have been sorted out if he had been informed earlier. The problem that faced Burgess was that the research could have affected the career chances of the teachers, and the ethical question that he had to face was, should he have told the head the findings earlier for the sake of the pupils? Here one has to ask, is the research really emancipatory, as is often claimed, and in this instance for whom? Often the researcher, in order to regain access to the research environment and to sustain employment, sacrifices many of the ethical principles outlined above.

In many research settings, social laws and legal rules are broken by information as well, which leaves the researcher in a difficult situation. What should the role of the researcher be, if, for example, this rule-breaking is perceived to be harmful. Should the researcher 'turn a blind eye' in order to carry on gaining material and at what level does 'turning a blind eye' become no longer acceptable? (See Patrick, 1973.)

In another situation, while carrying out research in a secondary school, I witnessed a member of staff physically assaulting pupils on a number of different occasions. The ethical question that arose was what do I do in this situation as a participant observer carrying out qualitative research in the school? Should I 'jeopardise' the possibility of being able to gather further research evidence by confronting the teacher with the evidence of the assaults or should I simply consider the assaults as a part of the data collection exercise? In this instance the answer was simple, for the pupils, who were the primary focus of research, had asked me to address the issue by supporting their complaints to the head. The problem is, what would I have done if the pupils had not presented me with such an avenue for escape by asking me to talk to the head on their behalf. I had to ask myself what harm it would have done to the development of my friendship with the pupils if I had not confronted the issue of teacher violence, and even more importantly, what harm it would have done to the pupils, for they would have seen my silence in this situation as collusion with the adult violence being perpetrated on them.

How far does a researcher then go in order to maintain a position of trust with the research subjects? During my research on pastoral care, a colleague and I witnessed a violent fight occurring outside the school gates, which involved the police being called. My colleague, in order to help the police, identified the hiding places of pupils involved in the fight without taking into any account the local history of hostility between the police and young black communities. A number of the pupils turned on both of us and said that we had 'grassed on their friends'. This seriously affected my working relationship with the pupils, and it took a great deal of time to convince them that I was not involved in 'grassing' on their friends. I had to redevelop the trust lost. The easiest way would have been simply to identify the individual who had informed on them. This would, however, have made his position in the school unworkable.

In any research project on education and race, it is clear that there are a huge number of ethical problems that may arise, for there are all the dangers of such research being used to pathologise the pupils. Often in such research the researcher can simply see the teachers as unproblematic, due to the power relations in schools, where he or she simply believes the adults. It is necessary to question the views and motives of the teachers as well as the pupils from the outset, and to delve into the stereotypes/typifications of black pupils that are used by teachers in school. Too often teachers are overlooked as peripheral to the perpetuation of racism.

Answered question! Conclusion

It is abundantly clear that many researchers are not willing to address the issue of research ethics, due to the fact that it would, and often does raise uncomfortable questions that they feel unable to address satisfactorily. Ethics for many researchers are an inconvenient distraction from the research task. Ethics are often seen as a problem, for the issues of deception, propriety of intervention, harm to the participants, contract obligations, informed consent, social wrongs and rights will never go away for researchers.

This tempts one to ask whether the whole debate on research ethics is fruitless, for do research 'ethics' actually exist and what are they? Can they be developed into antiracist ethical guidelines, for example in the form of an 'ethnographer's contract', or is discussion on this whole area of ethics a complete waste of time?

I believe that issues surrounding research ethics must always be raised, for the answers can often influence behaviour. But it is clear that it is the importance of the questions and the necessity to ask them that counts, not the dogma of the answers.

Acknowledgement

I want to thank Michael Keith and Kamaljeet Jandu for their help, ideas and criticisms on the earlier drafts of this chapter.

Note

1 Conference at the Centre for Research in Ethnic Relations, for postgraduate students researching race issues, organised by the Graduate School of Ethnic Relations, University of Warwick.

References

Aristotle (1926 edn) *The Nicomachean Ethics*, G P Putnam's Sons, New York.
Becker, H S (*et al*) (1961) *Boys in White*, Chicago University Press, Chicago.
Bourne, J (1980) 'Cheerleaders and ombudsmen: race relations sociology in Britain', *Race and Class*, 21.
Brown, C (1984) *Black and White Britain: The Third PSI Survey*, Heinemann, London.

Burgess, R (ed) (1989) *The Ethics of Educational Research*, Falmer Press, Lewes.

Cashmore, E and Troyna, B (1981) 'Just for white boys? Elitism, racism and research', *Multi-Racial Education*, 10, 1.

Cashmore, E and Troyna, B (eds) (1982) *Black Youth in Crisis*, Allen and Unwin, London.

Duncan, C (1988) *Pastoral Care: An Antiracist/Multicultural Perspective*, Blackwell, Oxford.

Finch, J (1986) *Research and Policy: The Uses of Qualitative Methods in Social Sciences*, Falmer Press, Lewes.

Gans, H J (1968) 'The participant observer as a human being: observations on the personal aspects of fieldwork', in Becker, H S *et al* (eds) *Institutions and the Person*, Aldine, Chicago.

Gouldner, A (1961) *Anti-Minotaur: The Myth of Value Free Sociology*, Penguin, Harmondsworth.

Gouldner, A (1975) *For Sociology: Renewal and Critique in Sociology*, Penguin, Harmondsworth.

Greer, C, Gartner, A, Reissman, F (1985) *The Assault on Equality*, Harper and Row, New York.

Gutzmore, C (1983) 'Capital, black youth and crime', *Race and Class*, 25.

Hall, S, Critcher, C, Jefferson, T, Clark, J and Roberts, B (1978) *Policing the Crisis: Mugging, the State and Law and Order*, Macmillan, London.

Jeffers, S (1991) 'Is race a sign of the times or is post-modernism only skin deep?' in Cross, M and Keith, M (eds) *Racism, The City and the State*, Routledge, London.

Jenkins, R (1971) 'The production of knowledge in the Institute of Race Relations', Paper to the British Sociological Association conference, 1971.

Keith, M (1991) *Lore and Disorder*, Cambridge University Press, Cambridge.

King, A (1974) *Science and Policy*, Oxford University Press, Oxford.

Lawrence, E (1981) 'White Sociology, Black Struggle', *Multi-Racial Education*, 9, 3.

Mac an Ghaill, M (1988) *Young, Gifted and Black*, Open University Press, Milton Keynes.

Mac an Ghaill, M (1989) 'Beyond the white norm: the use of qualitative methods in the study of black youth's schooling in Britain', *Qualitative Studies in Education*, 2, 3.

Minhas, R, Holland, P, Senn, S and Brar, H (1988) 'Ealing's Dilemma: Implementing Race Equality in Education: Report of the Independent Enquiry into the Recruitment and Promotion of Ethnic Minority Teachers in Ealing', London Borough of Ealing.

Myrdal, G (1970) *Objectivity in Social Research*, Pantheon Books, New York.

Parekh, B (1981) 'Britain's step citizens' *New Statesman*, August.

Patrick, J A (1973) *Glasgow Gang Observed*, Methuen, London.

Pettigrew, J (1975) *Robber Noblemen*, Routledge and Kegan Paul, London.

Rein, M (1976) *Social Science and Public Policy*, Penguin Education, Harmondsworth.

Rex, J (1983) 'Doctors of the revolution', *New Society*, 13, 1.

Roberts, H (1981) *Doing Feminist Research*, Routledge, London.

Sivanandan, A (1983) 'Challenging racism: strategies for the 80s', *Race and Class*, 25, 2.

Solomos, J (1989) *Race Relations Research and Social Policy*, ESRC, Swindon.

Stenhouse, D (1985) *Active Philosophy in Education and Science*, Allen and Unwin, London.

Webb, B (1956) *Beatrice Webb Diaries 1924-1932*, Longman Green and Co, London.

Chapter 13

Researching 'Race' in the 'All-White' Primary School: The Ethics of Curriculum Development

Bruce Carrington and Geoffrey Short

Abstract

This chapter is concerned with the ethical dimension of antiracist research in the 'all-white' primary school. While particular attention is paid to the unwitting reinforcement of stereotypes and the unnecessary infliction of pain, other issues, such as the role of procedural neutrality, are also considered. Following a brief but illustrative review of the literature, we discuss our own approach to dealing with these issues in the context of three studies recently carried out in different parts of England.

Introduction

Over recent years we have undertaken a number of studies in the area of young children and 'race'. In the present chapter we reflect on this research and particularly on some of the ethical issues underpinning it. As will become clear, our major concern has been to avoid two of the more serious accusations levelled against earlier studies; namely, their tendency to reinforce pejorative stereotypes of minorities and inflict unnecessary pain. To illustrate the nature and form of these malign practices, as well as their persistence, we begin by looking briefly at examplars stretching back more than half a century.

Extant research

It is not surprising that the earliest reported investigations of children's racial attitudes come from the USA. In one of the first, Horowitz (1936) required his subjects (white boys aged between 3 and 14) to choose from a selection of photographs of black and white children those they would want as companions in various imaginary contexts. For many of the children this task may well have seemed meaningless as there were no rational grounds upon which to base a decision. To make sense of it they might have assumed that the experimenter was really testing their knowledge of cultural norms. In other words, Horowitz was asking who they should choose in order to comply with social convention. If a significant proportion of the children did indeed construe the task in this way, the results of the study are as disturbing as they are misleading. For such children are likely to have inferred that they not only had to respond in accordance with convention but that the conventional view was the correct one. Horowitz' failure to provide the children with the option of expressing no preference for either the black or white figure strengthens this suspicion. Along with numerous later studies utilising a restricted 'forced choice' approach, this piece of research may simply have reinforced prevailing stereotypes of black people.

There have been similar cases in Britain. For example, Brown and Johnson (1971) asked a sample of 3 to 11 year olds to ascribe positive and negative behavioural characteristics to drawings of black and white children. The subjects were presented with eight 'stories' and were then asked to indicate whether each one referred to the black or the white character. The stories included the following:

- One of these boys is very good and goes to the shop for his mummy. Which do you think is the good boy?
- One of the girls is a bully and hits the other. Which do you think is the bad girl?

As in Horowitz' study, the children have not only been presented with a fatuous task demand, but with one that will either have reinforced negative stereotypes of ethnic minorities or introduced such stereotypes to children who were previously unaware of them.

A better-known and more recent British study is similarly flawed. Davey (1983) worked with 7 to 10 year olds drawn from multiethnic schools in London and Yorkshire. In the course of the investigation, he presented his subjects with statements such as, 'these are clever people' and 'these people make trouble'. The children were then told to 'post' the statements into one of four boxes. Three of the boxes were identified by photographs of adult couples representing either whites, Afro-Caribbeans or south Asians; the remaining box was simply labelled 'Nobody'. Now in so far as this activity allowed the children an opportunity to eschew racial stereotyping it was clearly an advance on much previous research. Nevertheless, for those children who had already internalised the popular conception of Afro-Caribbeans as 'trouble makers', this test once again could be perceived as validating their existing 'knowledge'. An equally serious ethical problem concerns the way in which the statements were worded, for any remark that begins 'these people . . .' encourages children to think about individuals in terms of their group membership rather than their personal qualities.

Our concern with the infliction of unnecessary pain has its origins in the classic American study by Clark and Clark (1947). The subjects of this investigation were black children aged between 3 and 7. When they were shown black and white dolls and asked to make self-identifications, 'some of (them) who were free and relaxed at the beginning of the experiment, broke down and cried' (p 611). Now while the absence of a precedent may partially exonerate the Clarks from responsibility for this state of affairs, replicating the study under similar circumstances is clearly reprehensible. This said, moral considerations do not seem to have prevented its replication on numerous occasions in different parts of the world, including Britain (eg Milner, 1973).

In research on children and 'race', ethical guidelines surrounding the infliction of pain are not, of course, restricted in their application to black children. They need to be taken every bit as seriously in studies such as our own conducted in 'all-white' settings. Thus in carrying out our research we abided, wherever possible, by the following principles:

1 all participants were to be volunteers;
2 they were to be encouraged to abstain from answering any questions they found embarrassing; and
3 they were to feel free to withdraw their cooperation, without explanation, at any time of their choosing.

Researching children's knowledge of 'race' in the 'all-white' school

Fieldwork for the first of our three studies was carried out in 1987 (Carrington and Short, 1989). The children taking part were aged between 6 and 12 and came from two 'all-white' schools in south east England. The research, which formed part of a wider study of the development of children's understanding of unfair discrimination (Short, 1989), aimed to provide teachers in such settings with data upon which to base curricular initiatives to combat racial and other forms of structural inequality.

Foremost among our concerns in devising the methodology was that nothing we said to the children could be interpreted as reinforcing racist imagery. Thus, rather than using dolls or pictures representing different racial groups and then asking leading (as well as fatuous) questions of the 'Which is the nice doll/picture?' variety, we presented the children with a set of three pictures that formed the basis of a story. The pictures showed a white girl and boy preventing a black boy from taking part in their ball game. The children were then required to explain what they thought was happening. Those who recognised the rejection but attributed it to a factor other than racism were asked if they could think of an alternative explanation. If they were unable to do so, they were not pressed – for fear of upsetting them – and the interview was terminated. The vast majority, however, regardless of age, not only commented on the rejection but referred to racism in some form as the reason. Having thus broached the issue of racism in a meaningful context, we were then able to probe the children's understanding of it in ways that made sense to them but without reinforcing, or introducing them to, racial stereotypes. The children were asked various questions such as, 'What are the best/worst things about being a black/white child/adult?' and 'If, as a child/adult, you could choose to be black or white which would you prefer or are you not bothered?'

In order to avoid the charge of indoctrination, various strategies were employed during the interviews to ensure that we did not put ideas into the children's heads. Among other things, we deliberately abstained from taking issue with any contentious remark that was made and sought only clarification and elaboration of the children's responses. The technique is illustrated in the following conversation (cited Carrington and Short, 1989, p 67) with Simon (aged 8:11; ie, 8 years, 11 months). He was explaining why, as an adult, he would rather be white.

Simon   '(Black people) are mostly unemployed.'
GS   'Why's that?'
Simon   'It's their colour.'

GS   'What do you mean?'
Simon   'Most (whites) only want their own colour.'

From an ethical standpoint, the decision to rely exclusively on clarification and elaboration is not entirely unproblematic. For at the same time as it offers researchers protection against accusations of indoctrination, it renders them vulnerable to the charge of reinforcing reprehensible attitudes by default. In other words, a failure on the researcher's part to challenge a blatantly racist remark is effectively to condone it. (We return to this point later when we consider the limitations of the 'neutral chair' approach to prejudice reduction.) But in confronting an unacceptable remark the researcher runs the risk of aborting the interview or, at least, of distorting its trajectory. For if children are led to believe that they have violated a 'party line', there is a danger of them ceasing to respond honestly and a possibility of them ceasing to respond at all.

We considered two possible solutions to this dilemma. The first was for the researcher to say nothing during the course of the interviews but to challenge all misconceptions when the investigation was complete. The problem here, however, was that in the course of the debriefing the children might feel they were being 'got at'. If this was the case, then, in the light of Brehm's (1966) notion of reactance, there would be a real danger of their attitudes hardening. (Reactance refers to the motivational state aroused whenever individuals believe their freedom to have been infringed. Invariably, people respond to such threatening situations by taking steps to regain some sense of personal control. As far as children who make racist remarks are concerned, they may well, when faced with a rebuttal of their views, adapt a stance *contrary* to that being advanced by the researcher.) The second (and preferred) solution has its theoretical roots in Piaget's work on the development of moral autonomy. In his book, *The Moral Judgment of the Child*, Piaget (1932) claimed that children are more likely to take issue with a peer than with an adult and for this reason we interviewed our respondents in pairs. It was our hope that if one member of a pair articulated a myth or half-truth about ethnic minorities, the other would challenge it. As illustrated in the vignette below, there were occasions when our optimism was borne out.

GS   'If you're born one colour, can you change?'
David (7:2)   'Yes, if it's very hot and you sunbathe, your brown skin might come off and you'll be all white.'
Steven (6:11)   'No it can't.'
David   'It can.'
Steven   'Can't.'
David   'It can peel off.'
Steven   'Yes, but when you have a new skin, it will be brown.'
David   'No it won't.'
Steven   'It will.'

A further illustration of the potential of this technique for promoting debate is provided in the following transcript. It comes from a recent investigation of anti-Semitism (Short and Carrington, 1991a) which not only focused on the perceptions of primary school children but on those of young adolescents as well. The conversation is between the researcher and two 13 year olds.

Andrew   'They worship Allah.'
Dominic   'The Jews?'
Andrew   'Yeah.'
Dominic   'Allah!'
Andrew   'Yeah.'
Dominic   'No they don't. They worship God.'
Andrew   'Yeah. That's their name for God.'
Dominic   'Is it?'
GS   'I'm not going to tell you.'
Dominic   'No it's not. It's God. They worship God.'

More often, however, we encountered the situation where one child's misconceptions or prejudices were either ignored by the other or elaborated upon. Presumably, such situations arose because both children thought along the same or similar lines or did not feel sufficiently strongly about the differences between them to engage with one another. Whatever the reason, as researchers we were faced with a dilemma. Having decided not to intervene during the interview, for fear of losing (or invalidating) the data, we could either intervene at the end (or ask the teachers to do so on our behalf) and risk counterproductive consequences or remain silent and thereby reinforce racist or anti-Semitic attitudes. In the event we opted for silence as the lesser of the two evils. We did so because we were not well acquainted with the children and thus did not feel in a position to judge the likelihood of a counterproductive reaction. This was a major consideration for us because, in the event of such a reaction, we, as researchers, would not be around long enough to 'pick up the pieces'. The class teachers expressed no interest in intervening on our behalf, and not knowing the situation they would face, we did not think it right to ask for their assistance.

Teaching about racism in the 'all-white' primary school

Our approach to confronting racist remarks was very different in the next piece of research we consider (Short and Carrington, 1987). This was a class project undertaken with 10 and 11 year olds at Oldtown primary in the North of England. At the time, one of us (Geoffrey Short) was the class teacher and the other (Bruce Carrington) a frequent visitor who had got to know the children well. It was this degree of familiarity that gave us the confidence to challenge the comments of individual members of the class without fear of inducing a negative reaction. In other words we felt able to reject at a practical as well as a theoretical level support for the principle of 'procedural neutrality'. The origins of this principle are to be found in the Humanities Curriculum Project (Stenhouse, 1970). In contrast to the Education Act (1986) which calls on teachers to ensure 'a balanced presentation of opposing views', advocates of neutrality (eg Jeffcoate, 1979; Ruddock and Plaskow, 1985) insist that teachers do no more than promote 'open, rigorous and coherent enquiry'. On no account are they to express a point of view when handling controversial issues such as racism in class discussion. Thus while children articulating racist sentiments may encounter opposition from other pupils in the course of debate, teachers committed to procedural neutrality must keep their own beliefs firmly under wraps and refrain from openly censuring contrary opinion. We objected to this pedagogic strategy because of the danger of condoning racism by default. But in contrast to the previous study, we felt able on this occasion to act in accordance with our view that racist beliefs are so morally abhorrent and at variance with democratic principles as to warrant an unequivocal challenge.

The actual intervention sought to help schools in 'non-contract' areas devise their own curricular programmes to teach about racism and other human rights violations. Because the children concerned had little or no first-hand knowledge of other ethnic groups, our immediate problem was to find an ethically acceptable way of raising the issue of racism. Specifically, we needed to broach the issue but in such a way that the children would not learn in the process to respond to people principally in terms of their racial or ethnic identity. We were therefore keen to diminish the salience of 'race'. In the investigation already discussed, we achieved this by sandwiching the pictures and questions on 'race' between those pertaining to gender and social class. In the present study we did it by adopting a holistic perspective. That is, we incorporated our teaching about racial inequality and discrimination in a broad project dealing with change in popular culture and lifestyle in Britain since World War II. One of the topics focused upon in the early part of the programme was the acute labour shortage facing the country in the immediate post-war years. The children, working in small collaborative groups, were set the task of solving the shortage. This problem not only permitted the issues of 'race' and immigration to arise spontaneously, but provided an appropriate context for the children to question the *post hoc ergo propter hoc* reasoning characteristic of racist myths about black people as the cause of unemployment and other social problems (see Cohen, 1988). (In this respect it is interesting to note that prior to any discussion of the issue, one boy had publicly stated, 'My dad thinks it is all the blacks here that causes unemployment.' The remark was promptly contested by BC.)

A number of studies have suggested that racist name-calling, jokes and mimicry, together with forms of physical abuse, may be far from uncommon in primary schools with few ethnic minority pupils (eg Commission for Racial Equality, 1988; Akhtar and Stronach, 1986). For this reason, we decided to provide the children with an opportunity to explore this particular facet of contemporary racism. To stimulate discussion, the children were invited to say how they would have responded in the following situation.

'You are playing in the street where you live when a pantechnicon draws up. Mr Taylor, a lorry driver from Birmingham, gets out. He says he's got a couple of twins and wants advice about this school. What will you tell him?'

(The class was also informed, almost as an afterthought, that 'the family are black, from the West Indies'.) In the ensuing discussion, the children initially eschewed any mention of 'race' or racism. Unwilling to shape the direction of the debate (fearing, once again, the accusation of improperly influencing children's minds) we did not intervene or prompt them in any way. Eventually our patience was rewarded; John's remark seeming to act as a catalyst.

John	'I wouldn't count on anyone liking your kids.'
GS	'What do you mean?'
John	'They'll be black and everyone else in the school's got a different colour skin and won't mix with them.'
Everybody	'The lads and lasses will skit them (poke fun at them) all the time.'
Patsy	'I think the teachers will ignore them as well as the other children.'
GS	'Why do you think that?'
Patsy	'I don't think the teachers would like them or get on with them.'
GS	'Do you think the teachers would see the black children as different from the white children in some way?'
Patsy	'Yes, they might think they're going to start trouble.'
Samantha	'I don't think it's fair how they get picked on because the whites think they're different in all ways. But it's just the colour that's different, not the personality.'
Terry	'You cannot judge people by their skin. It's the way they act (that's important).'
Peter	'I'd be friendly with them 'cos they've as much right as white people to be in this school even though they're coloured.'
Derek	'I don't think they should be picked on because they're human beings just like us. It doesn't matter what colour they are.'

Arguably, the most significant feature of this extract is the absence of any hostile comment about ethnic minorities. The reason for the absence is not known, but fear of the teacher's likely reaction must be a strong possibility. If this speculation is correct it is to be regretted. For while we believed it imperative to challenge the children's racist views, we also believed that they had a right to express their views openly and honestly. Not wishing to inhibit the exercise of this right, various steps were taken to democratise the classroom. These included restrictions on the role of didactic pedagogy. It was also determined at the outset that should we have occasion to confront a child's racism, it would be done in such a way as to cause the child the minimum of embarrassment. An opportunity to act on this principle arose from an activity that was planned to expose the myth of immigration as a cause of unemployment. Following a discussion of London Transport's recruitment drive in the Caribbean in the 1950s, the children were asked to design their own posters inviting workers to come to Britain. Here we describe one child's interpretation of this task together with our deliberately low-key response.

Kathy, appreciating the need to offer potential migrants a range of incentives, referred in her poster to the prospect of better accommodation in Britain. She then proceeded to contrast mud huts with brick built houses. The unwitting racism of her picture was privately pointed out to her and, in a later session, the class discussed the role of the media and of comics in particular, in transmitting unflattering images of the Third World. (Short and Carrington, 1987, p 226)

In this case study every child in the class was white. There can be no doubt that our approach would have been very different had some members of the class been black or Asian. For in that event our principal concern would have been to ensure that such children did not suffer any form of distress. One means of achieving this end would have been to consider the issue of personal racism indirectly, that is, by examining manifestations of prejudice unrelated to 'race'.

The primary school where we undertook a controlled experiment to assess the effectiveness of another teaching programme did include a small ethnic minority population (Short and Carrington, 1991b). On this occasion, however, it was not possible to respond to the sensitivities of the few black and Asian children by adopting the indirect approach suggested above. For as will become clear, the experiment required us to refer directly to discrimination on grounds of 'race'. Consequently, we had to consider an alternative means of protecting the feelings of the ethnic minority children. As we go on to point out, when discussing the design and implementation of the programme, it was the LEA who proposed the alternative.

The intervention aimed to teach some of the defining principles of unfair discrimination to a group of children drawn from two classes, one Year 3 (comprising 7 and 8 year olds), the other Year 5 (comprising 10 and 11 year olds). Approximately half the sample received the teaching programme (as members of the experimental group) with the remainder acting as controls. Two of the principles are set out below:

● People should be rewarded or made to suffer on the basis of their known individual qualities, not those stereotypically associated with any group to which they 'belong' by accident of birth.
● An entire group should be punished only if every member of the group has engaged in an antisocial activity.

It is evident from these principles that we were not just concerned in this study to diminish the salience of 'race', but of all characteristics irrelevant to forming judgements of other people. Hence the teaching programme deliberately eschewed any reference to socially defined groups. For example, the programme was introduced by inviting the children to describe the personality of a variety of individuals depicted in a photograph. The children's descriptions were subsequently challenged by the researcher so as to leave them in no doubt about the unreliability of judgements based on appearance alone. We had no compunction about intervening in this way as there could be no suggestion of insidiously corrupting immature minds. The researcher was concerned solely with promoting the development of rational thought, that is, teaching young people to recognise the need for evidence in support of an opinion.

In order to drive home the second principle, we read and discussed with the children a number of stories. Each of them made use of animals or individual people to illustrate the principle. There were no references to individuals *qua* members of a social group in any story as can be seen in this example.

> They had been caught. Two children from the local school had been caught in the park. It was the park keeper himself who had seen them pulling up flowers and then throwing sticks at conker trees. There was a rule which said you would get into trouble for doing these sort of things. You could read the rule on notice boards around the park.
>
> The two children had been caught and told off by the park keeper. He then went round to the children's school and saw their headteacher. The park keeper told the head exactly what had happened and because the two children had

broken the rule, the park keeper decided that *all* the children from that school would be banned from playing in the park for two months. When the rest of the school heard the news they were upset and angry. It was nearly the summer holidays and they had been looking forward to going back to the park to play games, to go fishing and to have a picnic. Now they wouldn't be able to.

The follow-up question for group discussion was, 'Do you think the park keeper was right to ban *all* the children from going in the park?' It should be noted that in this story, as in others, we were intent on not reinforcing *any* social stereotype. Hence the children's gender was not mentioned (in order to avoid associating boys with trouble) nor was that of the headteacher (to avoid associating men with positions of power and prestige).

We tested the various principles we set out to teach by presenting the children with moral dilemmas relating to gender, 'race' and social class. The two dilemmas on 'race' were as follows:

'A long time ago in London you could be walking down the street when you would see a notice in a shop window which said, "We won't serve black people in this shop." Do you think that was fair?'

'One day two people went for a job at a factory; one was black the other was white. The person who owned the factory said, "I'll give the job to whoever has the same colour skin as me." Was that fair?'

The evaluation showed that none of the 10 and 11 year olds responded to the dilemma of the notice in the shop window by condemning the owner for punishing an entire (racial) group. Whether this was because the children had failed to grasp the principle or were simply unable to apply it was not known. To help resolve the ambiguity, the younger age group were presented with a dilemma embodying the same principle but in a context assumed to be more familiar.

'One day a black and a white child went into a shop and one of them started messing around. The shopkeeper said to the naughty one, "Right, from now on, I'm not going to let you or anyone who is the same colour as you come into the shop." Do you think the shopkeeper was fair?'

In presenting the dilemmas, we were as concerned as when reading the stories, not to reinforce existing stereotypes. Thus, there was no allusion to either the 'race' or sex of the factory owner or to that of the 'naughty child'.

As pointed out earlier, a very small proportion of the sample was of ethnic minority origin. In discussing the nature of the proposed research with the LEA's adviser for multicultural education, we were told none of the racial content (ie the dilemmas above) could be presented to black or Asian children. Because of our commitment to the avoidance of unnecessary suffering, we were happy to go along with this restriction. The minority children therefore were only questioned on the dilemmas relating to gender and social class.

In this study, as in the other two, we were faced with the problem of knowing how best to handle the articulation of unacceptable attitudes. On one occasion, for example, a ten-year-old boy responded to the factory dilemma by saying: 'This is our country. They wouldn't like it if all of us went over there.' Once again we were faced with a dilemma; to intervene and risk a hostile response or say nothing and effectively endorse unacceptable attitudes. In contrast to the first study we discussed, the class teachers involved in this initiative had taken an active interest in it from the beginning. We therefore had no hesitation in asking for their help. They agreed to take responsibility for challenging the derogatory views children expressed on 'race', gender and social class after consultation with the researcher on possible strategies for avoiding an adverse reaction. In particular, the teachers were warned about the dangers of reactance. It was suggested that, as far as possible, they refrain from expressing their own views and aim instead to achieve the same result by encouraging the children to debate with one another.

Conclusion

In this chapter we have explored some of the ethical issues that arise in researching young children and 'race'. Focusing on the principles that underpinned our own work in 'all-white' schools, we have appraised various techniques which allow children's taken-for-granted beliefs and assumptions about 'race' to be probed, and if necessary challenged, in a sensitive manner. Throughout the chapter we have underlined the importance of a research design which avoids the unwitting reinforcement of racial stereotypes and myths. We have also emphasised the importance of playing down the centrality of 'race' both in formal experiments and in action research. In our assessment of strategies for handling controversial issues in the classroom, we have not only drawn attention to the limitations of the 'neutral chair' but have highlighted some of the problems associated with alternative approaches. We have noted that while, in principle, researchers (or teachers) should respond unequivocally to any racist comment made by children, in practice there may be difficulties; not just over the form and timing of any challenge, but over whether the challenge can be mounted without evoking a hostile and counterproductive response.

References

Akhtar, S and Stronach, L (1986) 'They call me blacky', *Times Educational Supplement*, 19 September, p 23.

Brehm, J (1966) *A Theory of Psychological Reactance*, Academic Press, New York.

Brown, G and Johnson, S (1971) 'The attribution of behavioural connotations to shaded and white figures by Caucasian children', *British Journal of Social and Clinical Psychology*, 10, pp 306–12.

Carrington, B and Short, G (1989) *'Race' and the Primary School: Theory into Practice*, NFER-Nelson, Windsor.

Clark, K and Clark, M (1947) 'Racial identification and preference in Negro children', in Newcomb, T M and Hartley, E L (eds) *Readings in Social Psychology*, Holt, Rinehart and Winston, New York.

Cohen, P (1988) 'The perversions of inheritance: studies in the making of multi-racist Britain', in Cohen, P and Bains, H (eds) *Multi-racist Britain*, Macmillan, London.

Commission for Racial Equality (1988) *Learning in Terror: A Survey of Racial Harassment in Schools and Colleges*, CRE, London.

Davey, A (1983) *Learning to be Prejudiced*, Edward Arnold, London.

Horowitz, E L (1936) 'Development of attitudes towards Negroes', in Proschansky, H and Seidenberg, B (eds) (1965) *Basic Studies in Social Psychology*, Holt, Rinehart and Winston, New York.

Jeffcoate R (1979) *Positive Image: Towards a Multiracial Curriculum*. Writers and Readers Publishing Cooperative (in association with Chameleon Books), London.

Milner, D (1973) 'Racial identification and preference in black British children', *European Journal of Social Psychology*, 3, 3, pp 281–95.

Piaget, J (1932) *The Moral Judgment of the Child*, Routledge and Kegan Paul, London.

Ruddock, J and Plaskow, M (1985) 'Bring back the neutral chairman', *Times Educational Supplement*, 21 June.

Short, G (1989) 'Unfair discrimination: age-related differences in children's understanding of "race", gender and social class', unpublished PhD thesis, University of Newcastle-upon-Tyne.

Short, G and Carrington, B (1987) 'Towards an anti-racist initiative in the "all-white" primary school', in Pollard, A (ed) *Children and their Primary Schools: A New Perspective*, Falmer Press, Lewes.

Short, G and Carrington, B (1991a) 'The development of children's understanding of Jewish identity and culture', paper presented to the XIV ISPA Colloquium, University of Minho, Braga, Portugal.

Short, G and Carrington, B (1991b) 'Unfair discrimination: teaching the principles to children of primary school age', *Journal of Moral Education*, 20, 2, pp 157–76.

Stenhouse, L (1970) *The Humanities Curriculum Project: An Introduction*, Heinemann, London.

Chapter 14

Antiracist University Education: Positive Discrimination as Good Practice

Mal Leicester and Tessa Lovell

Abstract

This chapter is informed by a University Funding Council (UFC) research project looking at university provision and ethnicity. It discusses the important post-school issue of access to higher education. Distinguishing between 'positive action' and the ethically more controversial notion of 'positive discrimination', a case is made that, should positive action prove insufficient to ensure fair access for all ethnic groups, resort to some form of positive discrimination may be justified. The chapter begins by exploring the ethical notion of good practice in education and draws on the UFC project data to illustrate good department practice in relation to antiracism.

Introduction: the survey

The 1985 Swann Report, *Education for All* (GB, P, H of C, 1985), encouraged schools in their development of antiracist multicultural education and, to date, the main focus for institutional and curriculum development and of related writing and research has been the school rather than the post-school sector. Such literature as there is about university education suggests that there are barriers to access for black people, and an ethnocentric culture and curriculum within institutions (eg, see Brandt *et al*, 1987 and Williams *et al*, 1989). Perhaps the more elitist the educational level the more resistance to democratic change one might expect to find. University education could be called – *Education for Few*.

Since we believe that racism influences both access to the universities, and what is on offer within them, in 1991 we undertook a survey of a range of departments in all UK universities to find out what they were doing to counter racial discrimination (including barriers to access) and to provide an antiracist multicultural curriculum.[1] Our findings confirmed existing evidence. For example, few departments reported having black academic full-time staff and many respondents were unfamiliar with the notion of ethnocentricity. The general picture that emerged was that departmental good practice is patchy, arising from the commitment of individuals rather than from departmental policy. We found isolated initiatives which have not yet been widely built into structures and routines (Leicester and Lovell, 1992).

Our survey was based on a number of ethical assumptions:

1 that university departments should develop organisational structures to eliminate racial discrimination;
2 that higher education (HE) should provide a non-ethnocentric, pluralist curriculum;
3 that it is worthwhile to identify current practices conducive to achieving such antiracist organisation and curricula in order to disseminate these to other well-intentioned academics. We share a belief that research about ethnicity and education ought to have antiracist outcomes, that is, outcomes that promote racial justice (see Brar, pp 188–202). In order to meet the responsibility implicit in this third assumption, we have used a variety of means to disseminate the good practice we identified.

While our survey was underpinned by ethical assumptions, and though we recognise a moral responsibility to disseminate the good practice we found, the focus of this present paper is not directly on the survey itself, but upon two conceptual ethical issues related to it. First, the notion of 'good practice' was central to our investigation. What were we looking for and how did respondents pick these practices out? In other words, what is understood by this widely used term and what does it mean in relation to antiracist education? We provide a brief analysis of the concept and illustrative examples drawn from our data.

Second, several respondents drew a distinction between positive discrimination, which they regarded as unfair, a reverse discrimination in fact – and positive action, which they see as legitimate. We investigate the hypothesis of an ethical difference between positive discrimination and positive action and illustrate our own position on this by reference to the issue of access to HE. Since access is a crucial issue for the universities, it is not surprising that this aspect of the survey generated most response. Questions sought information about students coming from access courses, the provision of access courses targeted at minority ethnic groups and steps taken to increase the number of black students coming into other courses. We will argue that access to HE itself raises ethical issues and that, in relation to black access to the universities, positive discrimination is justified.

The notion of good practice

In discourse about education the notion of 'good educational practice' is frequently invoked, though often undefined. Presumably practice would be 'good' education-ally in so far as it is effective in meeting educational aims and objectives. Since educational aims are conceived to be of value, 'good' carries, in this context, an ethical as well as a pragmatic connotation. In other words, good practice must be effective *educationally* and, thus, simultaneously, in some sense ethical.

By 'good practice' in the context of our survey we primarily mean practices that have been developed (usually, but not necessarily, deliberately) to counter racism, that is to say, racial discrimination in organisational structures and through curriculum bias. When good practice is designed to counter a racially or culturally biased curriculum this is an instance of the good educational practice described above, because it is about meeting antiracist *educational* aims. (Our own conception of education is such that *educational* aims will necessarily be antiracist. For example, through their development of critical skills students will more readily recognise prejudiced assumptions and ethnocentric bias.) When good practice is designed to counter racial discrimination in organisational structures, then the practice is not directly about the educational process (good educational practice) but about constructing an education *system* which is racially just. (Nevertheless this practice, as 'good practice', will need to be consonant with educational aims.)

To sum up, good practice in relation to antiracism in education will:

- promote racial justice, either through structures that eliminate racial discrimination or through an ethnically unbiased curriculum;
- in addition to meeting this primary aim, practices will not count as 'good' if they are unethical, for example, in being unfair;
- nor will they count as 'good' if they are ineffective;
- nor will they count as 'good' if they are anti-educational, for example, in being indoctrinatory.

Respondents to our survey provided a wide range of instances of their practices which meet these criteria and which can be used to illustrate each specific criterion.

Promoting good *educational* practice which is also antiracist requires meeting educational aims (eg the development of critical thought) using a pluralistic, non-ethnocentric curriculum. It would not be good practice to exclude from the curriculum either minority cultural traditions or material about racism. One history department, for example, reported having developed a syllabus which meets these requirements:

A number of us engage directly with one of the most contentious of all fields of historical study, the history of European Empires. In doing so, we undoubtedly alert students to problems of bias, not least that of ethnocentricity, and to the difficulties of perception and interpretation which follow. Ethnocentric and (much more rarely) overtly racist writings represent only particular (even if acute) forms of a general problem addressed by all professional historians and their pupils. Naturally we may also choose materials for reading and study which will make pupils aware of the diversity of cultures, of the achievements of non-European societies, and of oppressive systems such as apartheid.

As teachers, the approach they take to their material is educationally sound:

As professional historians, all members of this department are engaged in teaching pupils to examine sources and secondary works critically and to be aware of the assumptions built into them.

They suggest that to indoctrinate would be unethical as well as anti-educational:

From our reading and our selection of materials we may hope or assume that students will develop certain kinds of awareness, mental habits, and a sense of the values of tolerance, respect and so on. However, they may not do so, and if they either choose not to do so or simply draw their own different conclusions, that is their right. 'Positive' discrimination and selection to the point of indoctrination, 'positive' antiracist teaching only undermine the integrity of history teaching, however worthy the cause.

Good antiracist practice may be about the general *education for all* students, as with the history teaching described, and it may also include *special provision* of particular interest to specific groups. Thus many extra-mural programmes run by departments of adult and continuing education described courses which might be of particular, though not exclusive, interest to the minority ethnic groups in their region (Leicester and Lovell, 1992). For example, one university organises open courses which mirror the diversity of sociopolitical and cultural experiences of different ethnic groups settled in London (Art from the Indian Sub-Continent, Palestinian Studies, The Jewish Experience, Latin American Studies, Problems of Democracy and Development in Africa, Modern African Music, Third World Cinema.)

Turning from curriculum matters to consider organisational structures, for most respondents promoting a racially just system of education involves making the institution more *accessible to black students*. A number of departments ensure that they publicise their courses in multiracial areas and visit multiracial schools. Some produce information in community languages and ensure that their brochure material incorporates photographs of black students.

At the level of reviewing antiracist practice, only seven departments reported any *monitoring* procedures. These few departments include questions to find out about continuing racial bias in a feedback questionnaire to students at the end of their courses. They incorporate assessment about antiracist progress in their annual review. Two departments have monitoring as part of the role of their equal opportunity committee and one has a special monitoring subgroup, which is composed of members of staff, community representatives and students and monitors everything from staff recruitment to curricula.

Ninety respondents described instances of good practice in connection with *staffing policy and practice*. Some of these are good practices in that they represent fair practice for all candidates, and, thus, simultaneously, tend to counter race and gender discrimination. For example, all candidates are asked the same range of questions in order to ensure that each individual has an equal chance to demonstrate relevant experience and skills. Prior to the interview, these departments had explicitly formulated the qualities and skills required by the post in question. This informs the range of questions to be asked and the subsequent decision about who should be appointed. Clearly this kind of good interviewing goes some way to discourage irrelevant considerations about a candidate's race or gender.

We suggested earlier that in seeking to promote racial justice, antiracist practice, to count as good practice, must also be effective, that is, likely to achieve greater racial equality. The remainder of the staffing practices described to us, while not guaranteeing racial equality in university staffing, certainly increase the chance of black appointments. Thus seven departments quote the department's equal opportunity policy in advertisements for posts. This provides positive signals to potential applicants and thus may increase the number of black applicants. One department makes a practice of specifying the reasons for rejecting all unsuccessful applicants in order to bring to light implicit or indirectly racially discriminatory criteria or assumptions.

Several departments include at least one black person and one woman on all interviewing panels. It is likely to be less daunting for black and female candidates not to have to face all white or all male panels. The small number of departments who reported antiracist staff development had included specific training on antiracist interviewing techniques.

Just one department reported taking 'positive action' in staff selection, and explained that careful attention was given to each application from a black candidate in order to ensure that appropriate skills and qualities have not been overlooked because manifested in 'non-traditional' forms. This *enlightened* 'positive action' was distinguished from 'positive discrimination', though without an example of what such 'positive discrimination' might be – perhaps the waiving of a particular requirement.

Positive discrimination and positive action

As we have indicated, several respondents drew a distinction between positive discrimination, which they regarded as unfair practice, a reverse discrimination in fact, and positive action, which they saw as legitimate. These terms were used in the responses without definition, and it seems important to examine whether they do mark a distinction between fair and unfair initiatives to counter racism. It is not that we are concerned with a terminological quibble. Clearly it matters less what term we use than that we eliminate racism, but it would seem anomalous to seek to counter racism from an ethical commitment to justice, unethically, an issue touched on in Richardson's paper (pp 57–71). On the other hand, if there is no ethical issue here, no ethical or other significant difference, that is to say, between 'positive discrimination' and 'positive action', it would seem sensible to use only 'positive action' which more clearly conveys the intention to act justly, and therefore may cause less concern to those one is seeking to convince.

On reflection, the difference assumed by respondents seems to be this. 'Positive action' is used to refer to those practices adopted to counter existing racial discrimination by eliminating procedures which favour one individual over another for irrelevant reasons connected with race or culture. For example, this would include action to eliminate appointment systems based on patronage, where direct prejudice can influence outcome, and action to eliminate word-of-mouth recruitment practices, which may indirectly discriminate against groups that are not part of the word-of-mouth network. 'Positive discrimination', on the other hand, seems to refer to practices which favour black people over better-qualified whites, as may be required in meeting quotas, for example. Here action is taken to equalise provision between groups (ie to achieve proportionate outcomes) even if this means that an individual may not then have an equal opportunity, uninfluenced by ethnicity, since an individual may be disfavoured because white or a member of one minority group rather than another.

In short, there is indeed a valid distinction between positive action and positive discrimination. The former refers to actions to eliminate unfair discrimination against any individual; actions which do not entail unfairness to any other individual. It seems clear, therefore, that this is action that we ought to take. The latter refers to action to obtain proportionate group outcomes, even when this may be 'unfair' to particular individuals. The difficult question is to what extent this is ethically justified (and therefore not unfair) given levels of existing negative discrimination. Disproportionate racial outcomes are often a sign that unfair discrimination is taking place.

This may be indirect and subtle, but once it has been detected, should positive discrimination to secure proportionate outcomes (say proportionate numbers of minority ethnic group students into the universities) be used? This positive discrimination would consist in taking steps to compensate for these hidden forms of negative discrimination in favour of whites.

The question of whether, and in what circumstances, such positive discrimination is ethically acceptable is difficult, and, unsurprisingly, contentious. In our view, positive discrimination is justified when positive action has failed effectively to counter institutional discrimination and structural inequality. The following discussion of the important issue of access to HE illustrates how positive action can fail to achieve proportionate entry, precisely because of the prevalence of hidden and indirect negative discrimination. At some point, therefore, positive discrimination may be judged to be the only *effective* redress, and justified in that current discrimination favouring whites will be balanced by discrimination in favour of blacks. The apparent unfairness to individual whites is justified because of the degree to which members of the dominant ethnic group have unfairly benefited from their privileged position.

Though the issue of positive discrimination has arisen in relation to access to the universities, it does, of course, have a more general applicability in education because of current levels of racism across the system.

Access and accessibility

There are disproportionately few black students in the universities. Exact proportions are not known. Although the University Central Council for Admissions (UCCA) and the Polytechnics Central Admissions Systems (PCAS) agreed to include an ethnicity question on applications for the 1990 cohort, initially the information was not passed on to the admissions tutors because of concern – particularly by the Committee of Vice-Chancellors and Principals (CVCP) – about positive discrimination. More recently, following a report from the Centre for Research in Ethnic Relations at the University of Warwick (Taylor, 1992), the CVCP have reversed this decision. The CRER report confirms that acceptance rates vary significantly between ethnic groups – even when factors such as their qualifications and social class are taken into account. The applications of ethnic minorities from further and higher education institutions (though not from independent or grammar schools) are less likely to be accepted than those of white students. In addition to the information about ethnicity, in future admissions tutors will receive CVCP guidance seeking to ensure that Afro-Caribbean and Asian applicants are not penalised.

The issue of inclusion and exclusion is a major post-school educational ethical issue, and the access movement has been fuelled by the ideological and ethical commitment of academics, particularly in adult and continuing education, to equal opportunities (Brennan, 1989).

In response to our survey, questions about access proved to elicit most replies. It was encouraging to discover that 89 per cent of departments have recruited students via Access Courses. This testifies to the (albeit small-scale) success of the access movement. (As was mentioned earlier, one in three departments have taken other steps to recruit more black students.)

One department referred to a university-wide admissions scheme, with which it was actively involved. This scheme is designed to encourage people from disadvantaged backgrounds to apply. In some cases the university will require lower 'A' level grades. As part of this scheme, students from minority ethnic groups are encouraged to apply. (This could be seen as an example of positive discrimination.)

However, juxtaposed with this positive response, many of those involved with Access Courses felt that these courses catered predominantly for white, working-class, mature students. All of the departments visited claimed there was some intake of black students through Access Courses. However, all bar one felt that this was fairly limited and that their departments had mainly recruited white, female, mature students.

Thus, in spite of the positive response on access relative to most other questions in our survey, it was clear that access initiatives are themselves recruiting disproportionately few black students.

Open Access Courses tend to attract small numbers of black students unless real efforts are made to reach minority communities. There are issues here about recruitment and admission procedures of the Access Courses themselves. Do they embody antiracist practice? How successfully do antiracist pluralist principles permeate the curriculum, and are some Access tutors themselves from minority communities?

Moreover, predominantly white courses (Access or mainstream HE) may present problems of isolation and even alienation for their few black students:

> On the one hand, such is conventional wisdom and popular stereotype, they are expected to find more difficulties in their studies than other students. On the other hand, their tutors, inexperienced in handling racial and ethnic issues, turn to them for advice and assistance. The combination of low academic expectation and high demand for personal involvement and contribution is a significant burden, but rarely recognised as such (UCACE, 1990, p 8).

A second thrust of the move to facilitate entry by 'non-traditional' students into HE focuses on admission criteria and procedures. The standard admission procedures are both standardised and competitive: even successful 'A' level entrants may have to be interviewed for example. In 1980 the Council for National Academic Awards (CNNA) argued that mature students should be judged on individual merit and pointed out that, provided institutions are satisfied that students have necessary motivation, potential and knowledge to follow a course successfully, then the institutions have discretion to admit them without formal qualifications.

Ironically, although the setting of hurdles like 'A' levels and the assessment of mature students by academics in interview are meant to ensure equity (in that admission is through merit and achievement and not patronage or connection) complex judgements about competing candidates and discretionary judgements about the merits of individual cases are potentially racist. Since academics are mainly white, the current gate-keepers are almost all white. They are as open to the PLU (people like us) factor as anyone else; in other words they may favour people like themselves and are likely to make biased judgements about people from backgrounds different from their own. It is possible that discretionary interviews of mature students, a supposedly facilitating device which may work for other groups of mature applicants (say, middle-class white women) could work against black adults. In order for their procedure *not* to be inherently racist, there would need to be effective awareness training for current admission tutors. Alternatively, a quota system involving positive discrimination could be devised to try to achieve a more proportionate black intake. The justification of current practices, traditional and new, on the basis of equity considerations, in relation to minority ethnic groups is problematic (Leicester, 1992).

The accreditation of prior experiential learning (APEL) is seen as another route to HE for mature students. APEL involves a move to systematise the recognition of knowledge and skills gained through the mature student's reflections on her or his life experiences. In APEL we again have a movement that will benefit some mature students but which may discriminate against minority ethnic groups in two ways. First, as with discretionary interviews, the accreditation will largely be by white (racism unaware) academics. Second, since the experience, and the knowledge gained from reflecting on it, is partly a product of cultural background and tradition, the knowledge and skills of minority ethnic group students may be misassessed against criteria devised solely by the dominant ethnic group.

Our conclusion from these considerations, which were supported by the survey, is that Access Courses and other well-intentioned devices to bring non-traditional students into HE may benefit some oppressed groups while yet leaving black people on the outside.

Positive discrimination as good practice

We took 'good' practice, in relation to antiracist education, to mean ethically acceptable educational practices that counter or are likely to counter racism.

Some of our respondents expressed the view that positive discrimination was not ethically acceptable (it was described as 'unfair') though positive action was taken to be good. Our brief analysis of these terms revealed that there *is* an ethical distinction to be made in that, in furthering group equality through positive discrimination, individuals in the currently favoured groups may be 'unfairly' treated, that is discriminated against. A key question is whether this treatment is ever justified.

In our survey, the questions on access elicited more positive responses than any other, and clearly access to the universities is an important ethical issue. Closer analysis of the data raises questions about how effective the access movement has been for minority ethnic groups. In spite of positive action to increase accessibility to HE for black people, some black groups receive disproportionately few places in the universities.

Positive action ought, indeed, to be taken to promote accessibility to HE for black people. However, because negative discrimination against blacks is so entrenched, and racial discrimination in favour of whites so subtle, this positive action is failing to redress the current inequality. Therefore, in our view, positive discrimination associated with ethnicity and access to the universities *is justified*, and appropriate forms of positive discrimination should count as good practice.

Note

1 In 1991 the History, Politics, Continuing and Adult Education, English, Sociology, Education, Biology and Mathematics departments in all British universities were sent a questionnaire which sought information about antiracist education. Thus departments representing Arts, Sciences, Humanities and Social Studies faculties were included. The questionnaire gained data in two areas; to what extent and in what ways departmental organisation and practices were designed to counter racial discrimination, and to what extent and in what ways their curricula had been developed to counter ethnocentricity.

Responses provided a general picture of antiracist developments in universities. Twenty-one departments which described practices which seemed to the authors might be worth wider dissemination were subsequently engaged in telephone interviews about this work and four of the most interesting were visited. Thus the investigation into good practice was progressively focused.

References

Brandt, G, John, G and Pursani, N (1987) *Black Student and Access to Higher Education: summary of a feasibility study*, FEU, London.

Brennan, J (1989) 'Access courses', in Fulton, O (ed) *Access and Institutional Change*, Open University Press, Milton Keynes.

Great Britain, Parliament, House of Commons (1985) *Education for All*, the report of the Committee of Inquiry into the Education of Children from Ethnic Minority Groups (Swann Report) cmnd 9453, HMSO, London.

Leicester, M (1993) *Race for a Change In Continuing and Higher Education*, Open University Press, Milton Keynes, forthcoming.

Leicester, M and Lovell, T (1992) 'Comment', *Studies in the Education of Adults*, 24, 1.

Taylor, P (1992) *Ethnic Group Data for University Entry*, Centre for Research in Ethnic Relations.

University Council for Adult and Continuing Education (1990) Report of The Working Party On Continuing Education Provision For The Minority Ethnic Communities, UCACE Occasional Paper no 2, UCACE, Leicester.

Williams, J, Cocking, J and Davies, L (1989) *Words or Deeds? A Review of Equal Opportunity Policies in Higher Education*, CRE, London.

Index